VIETNAM
EDITED BY PETER KING

GEORGE ALLEN & UNWIN SYDNEY LONDON BOSTON

© Peter King 1983

This book is copyright under the Berne Convention.
No reproduction without permission. All rights reserved.

First published in 1983 by
George Allen & Unwin Australia Pty Ltd
8 Napier Street, North Sydney, NSW 2060 Australia

George Allen & Unwin (Publishers) Ltd
Park Lane, Hemel Hempstead, Herts HP2 4TE England

Allen & Unwin Inc.
9 Winchester Terrace, Winchester, Mass 01890 USA

National Library of Australia
Cataloguing-in-Publication entry:
King, Peter, 1936-.
   Australia's Vietnam.
   Bibliography
   Includes Index.
   ISBN 0 86861 037 2
   ISBN 0 86861 045 3 (pbk,).
   1. Vietnamese Conflict, 1961-1975—Australia.
   I. Title
959. 704 ' 3394
Library of Congress Catalog Card Number : 82-73045

Set in 10/11 pt Baskerville by Graphic Consultants, Singapore

Printed in Hong Kong

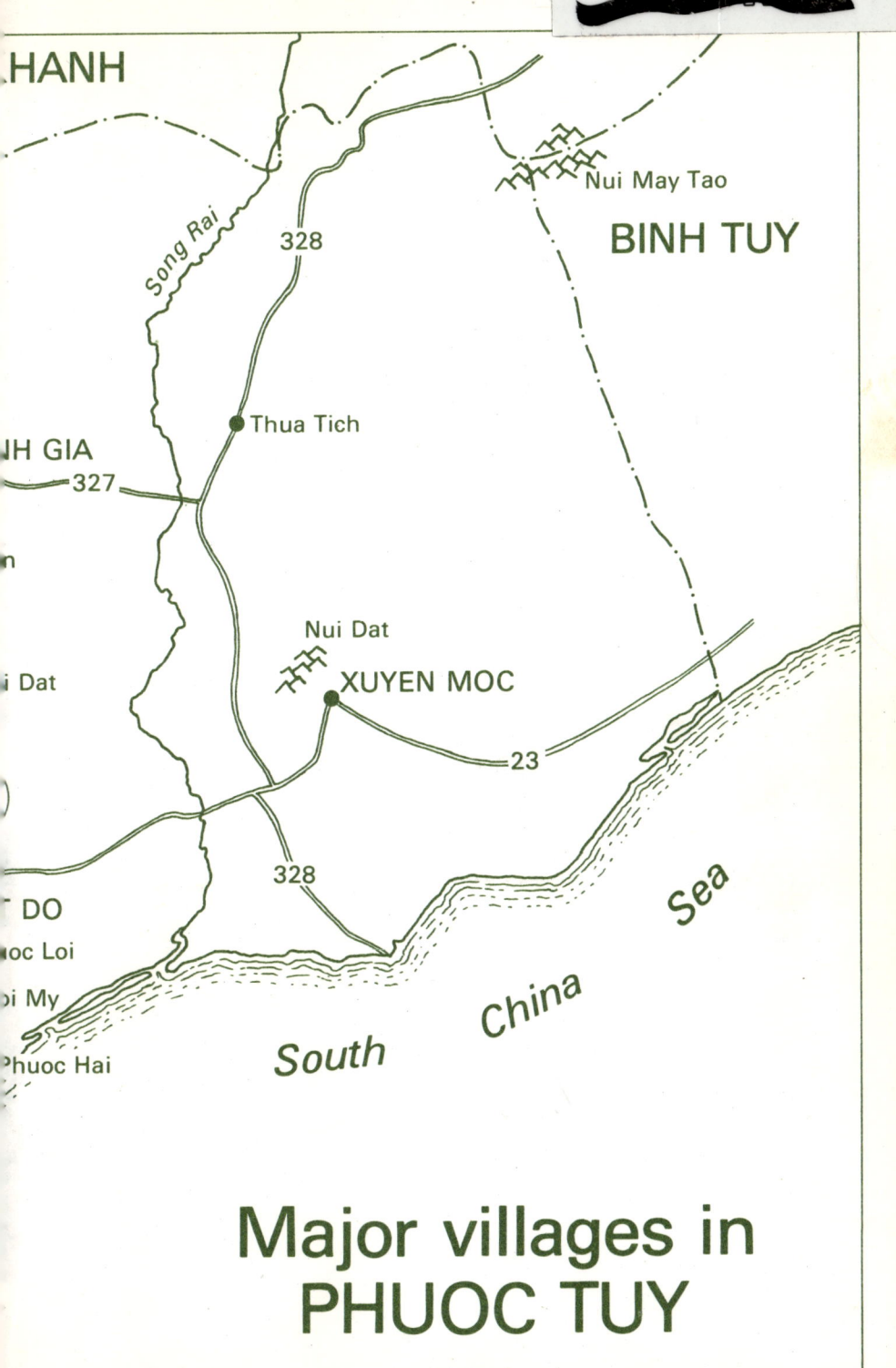

Major villages in PHUOC TUY

Reproduced with the permission of Robert O'Neill

Hist 959.704339 A
Australia's Vietnam
$28.50

DISCARD

AUST

MAIN LIBRARY

Memphis and Shelby County Public Library and Information Center

For the Residents
of
Memphis and Shelby County

AUSTRALIA'S
AUSTRALIA IN THE SECOND
INDO-CHINA WAR

Contents

Contributors   *6*

Preface   *7*

1 Introduction *Peter King*   *9*

2 Vietnam, China and the foreign affairs debate in Australia: a personal account *Gregory Clark*   *18*

3 Federal Labor and the Vietnam commitment *Kim C Beazley*   *36*

4 Australia's war in Vietnam, 1962–1972 *Frank Frost*   *57*

5 Australian soldiers in Vietnam: product and performance *Jane Ross*   *72*

6 The resisters: a history of the anti-conscription movement, 1964–1972 *Michael E Hamel-Green*   *100*

7 Public opinion and the politics of the polls *Murray Goot and Rodney Tiffen*   *129*

8 News coverage of Vietnam *Rodney Tiffen*   *165*

9 Conclusion *Peter King*   *188*

Endnotes   *197*

Index   *219*

Contributors

Kim C Beazley, MHR for Swan, was formerly a lecturer in political science at Murdoch University WA.

Gregory Clark was a member of the Department of External Affairs (1957–65), a journalist in Tokyo, and a consultant to the Department of the Prime Minister and Cabinet (1974–75). He is a professor in the Comparative Culture Department, Sophia University, Tokyo.

Frank Frost PhD has lectured at the University of Sydney and is now a legislative research specialist in the library of the federal Parliament.

Murray Goot lectures in political science at Macquarie University, is the co-author of *Women and Voting Studies* (1975), and has published widely on the political implications of opinion polls.

Michael E Hamel-Green is at present researching the politics of a nuclear-free Pacific region, is co-author of *Conscience and the Law* (1974), and has worked as a journalist in the USA.

Peter King is professor of political studies at the University of Papua New Guinea on secondment from the Department of Government, University of Sydney. He made three field trips to Southern Vietnam during the war years and has published several articles on the politics of the Saigon regimes and Australian foreign policy in the Vietnam period. His other research interests include strategic studies and Soviet politics.

Jane Ross PhD is the author of the *The Myth of the Digger* (forthcoming).

Rodney Tiffen PhD lectures in political science at the University of Sydney and is the author of a number of studies on the politics of the press and public opinion including *The News from Southeast Asia* (1978).

Preface

The idea for this book grew out of the experiences of three field trips to Vietnam during the years of America's war. The Australian role in Vietnam was a highly peculiar one. The United States had four satellites committed in Southern Vietnam after 1965 but two of them—South Korea and the Philippines—played the part of corporate mercenaries. Australia and New Zealand assumed the slightly more distinguished role of non-mercenaries. Australia had earlier taken the part of inciter and goad of its ally yet, while the Australian government wished and plotted for the Vietnam War before its entry, Australia became engaged only marginally in the combat when America's war began in earnest. It seemed to be worth a book to explore the institutional and psychological front lines of Australia's curious commitment; and the authors who volunteered 'to go over the top' have, without much detailed battle planning on my part, compiled impressive complimentary dossiers on Australia's all-round failure over 'Vietnam', and some cogent explanations for the misadventure.

John Iremonger of George Allen & Unwin Australia has been encouraging throughout this book's long march to publication. I would also like to acknowledge helpful critical comments on my own contributions from Frank Frost, Carlyle Thayer and, above all, Warren Osmond the publisher's editor who has left his mark on a number of chapters, and especially my own.

Note: The National Front for the Liberation of Vietnam has been referred to as the NLF throughout the text.

1 Introduction
PETER KING

The Vietnam War, or the Second Indo-China War (1960–75), brought Australian foreign policy since the Second World War to its nadir of ineptitude. It is possible that no permanent damage was inflicted upon Australia's long-term interests but Australian policy contributed to the near-ruin of the three nations of Indo-China, and to the polarisation of international politics in Southeast Asia. American military intervention, and subsequent Sino-American policies in Indo-China, of course, were far more important factors. Nevertheless Australians cannot ignore their own contribution to the problems of contemporary Indo-China.

This book explores Australia's role in the Second Indo-China War, the role of the war in Australian politics, and the responses of Australian institutions and people to the stresses and challenges of 'Vietnam'. An extensive official history of Australia's Vietnam War will no doubt appear in the fullness of time. There already exists a considerable literature, and an impressive array of formerly secret official documents, on the inner politics of Australia's decision to intervene, to 'escalate' its involvement, and then to withdraw.[1] The focus of this book is different: not on the decision-making process itself but on the inputs into decision-making, and on the performance of the institutions and people charged with implementing decisions. It is about the politics of the war in their widest sense.

Much of this book deals with the so-called Vietnam debate, a debate which will continue in one form or another for many years to come. What should be Australia's attitude to communist or revolutionary regimes and movements in Southeast Asia? Is it in Australia's interests to interpose American forces or otherwise intervene in military conflicts in Southeast Asia? Should Australia support the US anti-communist policy towards the region, selective and inconsistent as it sometimes may be? These are perennial questions, and correct answers will differ from time to time, as circumstances alter; they are discussed in a contemporary Southeast Asian context in the conclusion to this book.

The prevailing Canberra strategic perspective during the Vietnam War initially held that China threatened Southeast Asian regimes, and thus

Australia itself, through its influence over a proxy government, the Democratic Republic of Vietnam. After US President Nixon's diplomatic opening to China in 1971-72, the Australian government perforce fell back on the theory of a local communist, Soviet, or Vietnamese threat to Southeast Asia and our strategic environment. The military combat presence of the United States in Indo-China was an unquestioned good. After the Nixon Doctrine of 1969, however, it became clear that US commitment to both Southeast Asia and Australia had been *weakened* by the Vietnam experience in four short years.

After 1969, America commanded her allies and proxies to look first to their own conventional defence preparedness, thereby knocking out the guiding unspoken assumption of the Menzies period that Australia could and would fight in Southeast Asia to the last American.

In the Australian debate on the war, the left aired its objections to American and Australian official thinking with far greater consistency and prescience than the right. The non-communist left argued that the war was a civil war; that Hanoi was the principal, if not exclusive, bearer of Vietnamese nationalism; that the international effects of communist victory could be either contained or even beneficial; and that, after the earlier French experience in the First Indo-China War, further western intervention was doomed to failure. In the centre, critics of US and Australian policy were less confident of the war's outcome but they were inclined to argue that the game was not worth the candle. Some on the right based their support on counting. Better that Vietnamese die during the war than in a 'bloodbath' after victory by the National Liberation Front.

It was clear in 1965 that non-intervention would pave the way to a speedy and comparatively bloodless victory for the forces which had stood against the French between 1946 and 1954, forces which now stood against Saigon with its American military and economic patronage. It was also clear that the people of South (ern) Vietnam would suffer more political repression under the communists, but only a few ideologues came forward to argue that this fact clinched the argument for Western intervention. Simplistic arguments, often tinged with paranoia and messianic visions, carried the day with American planners. Above all, it was believed that America's reputation as anti-communist and counter-revolutionary protector of the world was at stake, and that 'dominoes' would fall unless this role was maintained. This vision of America's role was self-imposed, and largely imaginary.

We can sum up the Vietnam War debate in the west—a debate which racked campuses, and the mass media for years—as a clash between a gratuitous and misplaced will to *realpolitik* on the conservative side, and sensible instincts on the left and (eventually) in much of the centre.

Australia's Vietnam debate echoed American arguments but eventually paid close attention to the regional politics of the war which were likely to affect Australia's interests far more than America's, especially in long run.

With a few honourable exceptions on the left, however, Australians did not concern themselves seriously with the problems and aspirations of the Vietnamese people. This was clear from the near universal usage of one tell-tale phrase: to be 'against Vietnam' in those years was to be against the war which was destroying the country and so many of its people; but the irony of the expression went unnoticed even on the left, while on the right 'Vietnam' was seen as a means to the achievement of Australian ends.

Members of the Australian foreign affairs establishment knew little and wanted to know less about Vietnam, such was their eagerness to involve the Americans there. Reflex anti-communism, misperception of intra-bloc communist politics, and poor reading of the US record in her most recent Asian war (Korea), helped to make Australian policy-makers blind to some important political and geopolitical realities and indifferent to the suffering they were helping to prepare for the Vietnamese people. We also know now that although the United States managed to achieve a kind of indifference to the fate of its anti-communist *protegé* when Saigon finally fell in 1975, the hatchet is far from buried with Hanoi. The major strategic consequence of the Vietnam War has been polarisation between Indo-China on the one hand, and China, the US and the ASEAN states on the other. This polarisation was certainly avoidable but it has now entailed new military conflicts and contains the seeds of future war.

In retrospect, the domino theory has been vindicated to some extent in Vietnam and Indo-China as a whole but for reasons opposite to those cited by President Eisenhower in 1954, reiterated by his successors to President Johnson, and accepted by Australian policy-makers. As I have implied above, three versions of domino theory circulated in the early years of US intervention. In one, Moscow was going to make strategic and, in effect, territorial gains if the Republic of Vietnam were not defended; in the second, Peking would be the beneficiary; and in the third, and later version, Hanoi would extend its power by conquest, support for subversion, and by intimidation.

Whichever theory is accepted, one clear consequence of US intervention was the inevitable 'fall' of Cambodia to some form of communism, especially after the American incursion into that country in April 1970. The Democratic Republic of Vietnam had coexisted with Prince Sihanouk's regime in Phnom Penh from 1954 to 1970. For eight years after the fall of Sihanouk in 1970 Vietnam tolerated the rival communism of Pol Pot's *Khmers Rouges,* who became the government of Democratic Kampuchea in 1975. There had been rich opportunities before 1975 for Hanoi to quietly establish its own hegemony over the Cambodian revolution during the joint struggle with Pol Pot against the Americans and the Lon Nol regime. We must conclude that there was a good chance of survival for Sihanouk's middle way, and thus the Cambodian 'domino', if Hanoi had won victory in southern Vietnam before 1970.

The United States, supported by Australia and other countries, can be reasonably blamed for destroying the Cambodian monarchy. The domino theory was a self-fulfilling prophecy, but that revelation took ten years to become clear.

Australia's Vietnam War began with America's: both countries despatched combat troops to Vietnam in 1965. But the Australian commitment was small and almost half-hearted. In 1968 Prime Minister Gorton placed a ceiling of three battalions on Australian involvement, thus alerting Washington of the limits of Australian support. By 1971 the McMahon government had withdrawn even these troops in step with Nixon's (appallingly named) policy of 'Vietnamisation'.

Less than ten years after the despatch of the Australian Army Training Team to Vietnam, the new ALP government finally broke with the policy of intervention, cancelled conscription, and withdrew the training team which had preceded and survived the Task Force. Ten years of conservative policy were thereby repudiated, and rightly so. What the contributors to this book demonstrate is that Australian institutions and elites, and the great public itself, largely failed the test of Vietnam in the years to 1972, and that the sources of this failure deserve close study.

Gregory Clark's chapter, based on his first-hand experience as a diplomat, shows how much wilful misperception existed during the Vietnam years in the foreign affairs establishment, among both ministers and senior officials. Policy emerged from an ideologically stark world-view in which China became the epitome of the forces of darkness in the years following the Korean War while the United States remained, as it had been since 1941, the best and probably the only hope for Australia's security. The paradox of Australian policy was that, while independently formulated and not subjected to undue external pressure, it scarcely allowed for the possibility of independent diplomatic action; all the while avoiding any serious military commitment to the chosen ally.

Thus, although conscription was reintroduced in anticipation of the combat commitment to Vietnam, and although a prime minister as late as 1967 was arguing that the fall of South Vietnam posed as security threat to Australia, conscription remained highly selective. It barely filled the three rotated battalions which were eventually sent to Vietnam. Combat commitment remained token and symbolic until withdrawal commenced. The magnanimous policy assumption that Australians would fight to the last American lived on beyond the Menzies period. It was not an inspiring posture.

Australian fears were ill-grounded. Peking was not aggressive, as Clark demonstrated at the time.[2] Hanoi was not Peking's puppet. The communist bloc was in disarray. The revolution in Southern Vietnam *was* under orders from Hanoi but, as Frank Frost points out in his chapter, it was grounded in nationalist groups and forces which had carried through the liberation from France between 1946 and 1954. Clark's final judgement is that Australian foreign policy was 'childish and inconsistent' in the

INTRODUCTION

Vietnam years before 1972, when Labor came to power.

Certainly, Australian policy's tendency to stereotyping, its wilful ignorance of Vietnamese cultural and social patterns, and its short-sighted effort to engage the Americans anywhere, anytime, anyhow in Southeast Asia, could all be called 'childish'. And in their swings of obsessive fear from Moscow to Peking to Hanoi and (since 1975) back to Moscow, Australia's conservative foreign policy makers have certainly displayed a bewildering inconsistency. Why have largely groundless fears been such an important impulse? Clark scatters a few substantial hints through his chapter, and I have speculated on the reasons myself in another place.[3] It is ironic that the only serious threat to Australian security—that posed by Soviet nuclear attack on American strategic facilities here—was created by the same leaders who shaped the Vietnam commitment. The strategic bases were also first conceded in the early 1960s and followed the Vietnam pattern of deliberate, undue and largely ignorant entanglement of Australian with American interests. Getting to the bottom of groundless conservative security fears is a major task for future research, but the materials from the Vietnam War period will be crucial.

Kim Beazley's chapter brings out an often overlooked aspect of Australian Labor Party policy on Vietnam: that in retrospect it seems much better than it really was at the time because the 1964 conscription legislation made Labor opposition to troop commitments inevitable. It is sobering to recall with Beazley that in February 1965 the federal parliamentary Labor Party's Foreign Affairs Committee supported 'Operation Rolling Thunder', the first systematic US bombing campaign against the Democractic Republic of Vietnam. The left-right division in the ALP—the division between Cairns and (for the most part) Calwell, on the one hand, and Whitlam and Barnard on the other—took shape in 1963 when the party as a whole failed to take a stand against the US strategic communications base at North West Cape.

The fear of an electoral stampede, should the Americans be firmly disowned over the Vietnam War, left the ALP's policy in a rather pusillanimous or contradictory state until 1969 when left-wing counsels began to prevail. Until 1969 Whitlam (leader from 1967 onwards) persistently argued that the solution to South Vietnam's problems should be political, economic and social rather than military but he further contended that a stabilising US military presence was required before aid could be effective and reforms commenced. The Labor Party eventually rescued Australian honour in Vietnam, recognised the Democratic Republic and acknowledged the claims of the National Liberation Front in the year 1972. It had taken too many years, however, to clearly sound the retreat.

Frank Frost's painstaking evaluation of the military performance of the Australian Army Task Force in Vietnam brings out two serious failures of Australian policy. First, there was a lack of overall political or strategic guidance given to the Task Force command. Should it engage in battles with the main-force units of the guerrilla enemy, or undertake 'pacification' in the villages of Phuoc Tuy province? The Task Force was not properly equipped for either role and, perhaps fortunately, it performed badly in both.

Secondly, the government failed to inform itself and the army about the political and social realities of the Vietnamese countryside, including the real roles of the counter-revolutionary ally and the revolutionary enemy. Some of the soldiers learnt the surprising history of Phuoc Tuy's anti-French resistance tradition from the local citizenry; some never understood why villagers very close to the Task Force base never accepted the Australian presence. The army's ignorance of Vietnamese society and the Vietnamese revolution had severe practical results, for example in the minefield fiasco described in Frost's chapter.

Still, the policy of ignorance enjoyed success of a kind: few Australians, soldiers or civilians, ever asked themselves by what right the Australian army was hounding the heroes of the Vietnamese resistance, and their sons and daughters, to death.

If the army had been capable of learning, Phuoc Tuy provided an excellent case-study, for despite the decimation of local and main-force NLF units in the aftermath of the Tet uprising of February 1968, the realities of the political situation at village level changed little. As Frost's chapter shows, the guerillas were weak, but the cadres—the party and front— remained very strong; the corruption of officials, the poor motivation of Saigon's soldiers, and many other deep problems of the Republic of Vietnam, remained unchanged despite a military victory. In this sense, Vietnam was a political war fought under grave handicaps on the Saigon side, and one such handicap was the active presence of resented foreign troops. There is little evidence that Australia's conservative policy-makers, including the present Prime Minister, and then Army Minister, Malcolm Fraser, have taken these lessons to heart. Influential diehards have asserted, despite everything, that the prime lesson of the Vietnam conflict is the failure of *American* persistence and will.[4]

Jane Ross has composed a sociologist's and social psychologist's portrait of the combat soldier who went to Vietnam, and especially the conscripts who the army was so anxious to socialise. 'Only soldiers here', in the words of the Task Force Commander she quotes. She brings out the sordidness of the war on the allied side, especially at the level of inter-allied human relationships. How could the war be won when racism tainted relations with our putative allies in Vietnam, and when only a grudging respect which never quite transcended racism was accorded our declared 'enemy' in that country? I myself observed the murderous attitudes of ordinary Australian soldiery towards their guerilla enemy. Many practitioners of war, from the lowest to the highest ranks, were obsessed with the objectively measurable 'kills'; the mess conversation often smoked with blood.

INTRODUCTION 15

At the level of operational psychology, the 'other war' scarcely existed for the Task Force. Civic action was limbo, as Jane Ross points out, and the techniques for giving aid to villagers were so crude that a handout from the back of an army truck which I witnessed in 1970 degenerated into a sort of riot which only reinforced racist sentiments amongst the soldiers. As Ross concludes, the Australians came to regard the enemy as less than human, an attitude which even extended to the Vietnamese ally. But Ross shows that the Australian Task Force cohered while many American units disintegrated and became worthless in combat after 1968. This cohesiveness was some sort of achievement; and the Australians also seem to have resorted far less to atrocity.

Australia's largest offence lay in what it 'endorsed', and in its very presence. The Americans had initiated 'relocation' of several former Vietminh villages in Phuoc Tuy before the arrival of the Australians in 1965. Many cadres were thus in the 'Task Force village', Hoa Long, the bane of the Australians and the scene of many Australian ambushes. No Australian bombing occurred in Phuoc Tuy, RAAF Canberra Bombers being based at Phan Rang in central Vietnam; Australians performed no defoliation; and they probably caused fewer civilian casualties than any other combat force of similar size in South Vietnam. Yet, as Ross indicates in her chapter, echoing the journalist Ian MacKay, many conscripts returned home appalled at what they had done, or been forced to do, in Australia's name.

Jane Ross's last theme is 'bringing the war back home—the psychological and medical problems of the returned soldiers. It is to be hoped that when the Agent Orange issue, the long-term physiological effects of American defoliants, is finally resolved in the American courts and in Australian repatriation policies, some thought will be given to the prime victims of American chemical warfare in South Vietnam, namely, the peasants who have borne the effects of this ecological and medical disaster without compensation or significant relief. Bearing this in mind, the Australian soldiers who were poisoned in Vietnam deserve better treatment from the Australian government.

Murray Goot and Rodney Tiffen render a double service in their chapter on Vietnam and opinion polls. With scrupulous documentation and argument they sustain the serious charge of 'manufacture of opinion' on the Vietnam issue. In another careful argument with their academic predecessors, they produce a definitive profile of the evolution of public opinion on the war and related 'period' issues such as threat perception, partisan voting trends, the US alliance, and Indo-Chinese refugees in Australia.

The fact that biassed and ignorant survey items largely escaped criticism, and that surveys repeatedly failed to ask questions which might challenge pro-Americanism reflect badly upon the state of the Australian public opinion industry itself at that time. Thanks to polls which were launched in the early 1970s, Goot and Tiffen are able to show that on defence issues, on attitudes to Southeast Asia and the US alliance, Australian opinion was little influenced by the Vietnam War experience and its aftermath.

There was one momentous change in Australian opinion, of course, namely, the steady development between 1967 to 1969 of a majority opposed to the war. Goot and Tiffen show that 1969 was a watershed year in electoral terms. The Vietnam issue had hindered Labor in 1966, but it began to help Labor in 1969, and may even have been decisive in the 1972 election. But the voters caught in public opinion polls continued to show great hostility towards conscientious objectors, draft resisters, and after 1970 to the moratorium marchers. We may speculate that the public were influenced by anti-war militancy despite themselves.

Did the 'swinging' poll respondents subliminally conclude that the only way to reduce the divisiveness engendered by the unholy combination of the Vietnam War and conscription was to abandon one or the other? Or, as the Labor Party eventually decided, both? Labor's decision left several fundamental issues in Australian foreign policy, especially the nature of the American alliance, unresolved. But there was little evidence, as Goot and Tiffen indicate, of any popular desire to resolve them. The conclusion to this book explores the possibilities for fundamental reform in Australian foreign policy, given the constraints of public opinion as lucidly presented by Goot and Tiffen.

Rodney Tiffen's pioneering comparative study of the performance of the Australian and American press yields a summary of press coverage over time and also important insights into the performance of individual newspapers and journalists. Tiffen's account is hardly flattering. Making the necessary allowances, he finds the Australian press 'deplorably inferior' to its American counterpart.

Tiffen indicts the western press as a whole for falling in with the confidence trick executed by Lyndon Johnson after the Tonkin Gulf crisis in 1964, a 'crisis' which legitimised US escalation. Tiffen also deplores the morally numbing and largely falsified corpse counting which comprised the staple of daily reporting of the war. He has no special cheers for the Australian press whatever; no Australian journalism compared with the reporting which led to David Halberstam's *The Making of a Quagmire*, the book which did so much to alert the receptive American public. A handful of Australian journalists wrote useful books more or less against the war, and the press response to Tet in 1968 helped to make the war more unpalatable at home. But as Tiffen shows, 'the other war'—the political and social struggle for the villages and the souls of Vietnamese people—was neglected or, at best, vulgarised. The Australian public remained ill-informed on crucial issues in the Vietnamese revolution from first to last.

Michael Hamel-Green's chapter on the Vietnam draft resisters can be read as a heartening case study of the politics of conscience and imagination, countervailing the politics of myopic conservatism and presumption. The Australian government in 1964 wished to strengthen its own ability, symbolically at least, to support an American combat role in Vietnam. The method adopted, a highly selective form of conscription, was a folly the chief victims of which were the 20 year-olds 'balloted in' as conscripts. This was a presumption, in that an American policy involving a remote injustice (to the Vietnamese revolution) was supported by an injustice at home.

The young men concerned were spiritually and intellectually sustained by such historical (and, it turned out, ironic) absurdities as Prime Minister Menzies's claim that the struggle of the National Liberation Front represented a strategic thrust by China between the Indian and Pacific Oceans. (China later became a firm friend of conservative Australian governments under Malcolm Fraser). I myself went to court during those years—in vain—for a young conscript who was spurred to read the background of the Vietnam War by the imminent prospect of his transfer to Phuoc Tuy province. He did not like what he read about the allied cause but was sent anyway.

One can only admire Michael Hamel-Green's potential conscripts who uttered a determined 'no' to the government and then devised resistance tactics of the utmost originality and subtlety to press home their long and ultimately victorious legal and extra-legal campaigns. There was an exquisite irony in the many situations which arose; for example, when the government was gingerly arresting a tiny proportion of the resisters in the interests of credibility, the resisters were busy forcing the government to prosecute more of their own ranks. The crowning irony was the government's rather desperate remedy for unwelcome potential martyrs: forcible exemption!

All this resistance—including the professors and hundreds of others who supported illegal resisters and rendered legislation unworkable, and the moratorium marchers in 1970 and after—was regarded with some distaste by the great *petit bourgeois* public, as Goot and Tiffen show in their chapter. But, as I have suggested above, the conscription resisters and moratorium marchers almost certainly helped to swing Australian opinion around and paved the way for the Labor government which ended Australia's Vietnam War.

2 Vietnam, China, and the foreign affairs debate in Australia
A personal account
GREGORY CLARK

There is no doubt that .... part of this (the insurgency in South Vietnam) is the determination of Communist China to establish hegemony throughout Southeast Asia, working in the first place through the agency of her North Vietnamese puppets (Australian Minister for External Affairs, Paul Hasluck, in Foreign Policy statement to House of Representatives, June 1964).

I have argued elsewhere that a major factor behind Canberra's Vietnam policies was an obsessive fear of China.[1] The following incident might give some idea of just how obsessive that fear was.

In October 1964 messages began to arrive at the Australian Embassy in Moscow (where I happened to be posted at the time) asking us to arrange the itinerary for an urgent visit by the then Minister for External Affairs, Paul Hasluck. The visit was to include, if possible, talks with Foreign Minister Gromyko, and Premier Kosygin. We were told Hasluck had a most important message to convey to the Soviets about Vietnam.

Soviet officials were rather surprised by this sudden approach. Canberra had already staged quite a few confrontations with Moscow in the UN over New Guinea and Southeast Asian policy. And Hasluck was well-known in Moscow for his rigid, almost theological anti-communism. But we were told politely that, while no official invitation would be forthcoming, he was quite free to come privately and talk to whomsoever might be available.

And so Hasluck arrived. He was obviously nervous, and during the two or three days he was kept waiting for appointments he began to give out hints of the important message he carried and how it could change the course of world affairs. Then in typical Soviet fashion we were told abruptly that we would probably soon be able to see an important Soviet leader. The next day we were suddenly summoned to the Kremlin complex and ushered into a large conference room with the usual long green baize table. On the other side were Kosygin, Gromyko and a row of MID (Foreign Ministry) officials.

Kosygin made a few remarks designed to make Hasluck and Australia seem more important in Soviet eyes than they really were, and then asked what it was that had brought the minister so far and so suddenly. Hasluck immediately launched into a complex discourse on the nature of world affairs. There were, he said, in any society or community of nations certain bad elements that abused the norms of civilised behaviour. And in saying this he was not passing ideological judgement. There were norms that applied regardless of ideology. And if one nation set out deliberately to break them, then all others regardless of ideology, should be concerned. This, he said, was his first point.

Point two was what to do about such international renegades. In an ideal world it would be possible to get together and solve such problems with moral persuasion *via* international bodies such as the United Nations. But in the real world this was not possible. Power was the only way these bandits could be restrained. And the number of nations with real power was limited—the US, the Soviet Union .... It was beholden on those with power to use it, with responsibility of course, to maintain some stability in world affairs.

At this point Kosygin interrupted quite strongly to say that power in the sense of force (the Russian word for power, *sila* has both meanings) should never be used as a means of settling international disputes. We hastened to explain that Hasluck was of course using power in the milder sense of the Russian word. Kosygin then suggested that it would be simpler for all if the discussion could move from philosophy to practical details. Hasluck obliged. There was, he said, not a single nation in the world that could remain unconcerned by the dangerous behaviour of the Peking government. Even the Soviet Union had felt the need to denounce the extremism of its former ally. And if the Soviets were so concerned, how much more concerned were we in Australia lying directly to the south of China and protected only by a ring of weak, unstable Southeast Asian nations? Already that ring was being breached by China's expansionism in Indo-China.

Of course, Hasluck continued, Australia realised that the Soviet Union shared the same basic communist ideology as Peking. And to some extent it might feel bound for ideological reasons to offer support to the Hanoi regime. But what was happening in Vietnam went far beyond communist versus anti-communist. It was yet another step in the pattern of Peking's deliberate territorial expansionism, something that had to concern the whole world regardless of ideology. And this territorial greed was not just directed southwards. Even the Soviet Union had been threatened. Australia had noted how Peking was laying claim to the Soviet territory of Sinkiang [*sic*]. And the Chinese were long on record as seeking to take over territory in the Far East of the Soviet Union. These efforts to grab Soviet territory were of great concern to others. Would it be too much to ask the Soviet Union to share our concern about China's expansionist designs southwards? More specifically, could Moscow use whatever influence it had in Hanoi to prevent the North Vietnamese from being used as an instrument of Chinese expansionism?

Kosygin was clearly taken aback by all this, but said nothing. Eventually Gromyko intervened. Sinkiang, he noted dryly, had belonged to the Chinese for a long time. Why would the Chinese want to claim something that was already their own? As for the Far East (*Dalyniyi Vostok*), he was not sure just what the Chinese were supposed to be claiming. China itself was after all a large part of the Far East (the interpreter had Hasluck as saying Far East rather than *Soviet* Far East). There were some small areas of disputed border territory between China and the Soviet Union, but that was a purely bilateral matter to be settled by the two countries. It did not involve Australia. The same applied to the ideological dispute. As for Vietnam, the Soviet government and people would of course continue to honour their commitments to a fraternal socialist people subject to imperialist aggression. Even the Chinese, he noted even more dryly, had felt obliged to offer some support to Hanoi.

By now Hasluck was beginning to realise that his *démarche* was coming unstuck. But he persisted bravely for another few minutes, until Kosygin suggested that it would be more fruitful to talk about questions of bilateral Soviet/Australian interest. There was, as I recall, a desultory discussion about expanding scientific exchanges and some problems of exit visas for Soviet citizens wanting to join relatives in Australia. Kosygin made it clear that time was up, and we disbanded.

Despite this failure, Hasluck still felt he could and should try to swing the Soviets to his side. In a March 1965 foreign policy statement he went out of his way to relate events in South Vietnam to China's allegedly extreme position in the Sino-Soviet dispute. In an April 1966 statement to the House of Representatives he repeated his 1964 signal to the Soviets: 'The security of the whole world would be damaged grievously .... by hostilities against any of China's neighbours, including the Soviet Union'.

Nor was it just Hasluck. James Plimsoll, the then External Affairs Secretary, went to quite unusual lengths as a bureaucrat to lend his name to the anti-Peking/pro-Moscow cause. In a September 1965 address to Sydney University students he came up with one of the more original arguments for keeping China out of the United Nations: 'Peking would set out to introduce resolutions which followed the orthodox lines of pure Marxism and would put the Soviet Union on the spot'. Two months later in New York he told the US General Assembly First Committee how China had made armed attacks on India *and the Soviet Union.*

This was not merely some temporary and rhetorical exaggeration brought on by the excitement of the Vietnam intervention. It had begun with a much earlier and carefully prepared 1963 New Zealand address in which the then External Affairs Minister, Garfield Barwick, said: 'There is not a country in the whole Asian region which .... is not preoccupied with the problem of Communist China. This applies even to the Soviet Union. The Chinese have reminded Moscow of *two almost forgotten treaties* [italics added ....] by which Russia obtained from China extensive areas of Siberia. This is typical of the anxiety which all of us who are in any sense a neighbour of China must face'.

Our best diplomatic brains had clearly decided well before formal intervention in Vietnam that the Sino/Soviet dispute should be used to Australian diplomatic advantage. They had accepted the conventional wisdom that the Soviets were the moderates in the dispute, trying anxiously to counter the extremist Chinese. By supporting Moscow both ideologically and territorially, Canberra hoped to open a 'western front' to restrain China's alleged expansionism in Asia.

Today, of course, Canberra sees things very differently. In 1964 Paul Hasluck travelled all the way to Moscow to warn the Soviets about alleged Chinese designs against Sinkiang. In 1976 Malcolm Fraser went all the way to Sinkiang to help the Chinese resist alleged Soviet designs against Sinkiang!

How and why did Canberra develop such erratic and inconsistent policies? One factor was simple ignorance of what was supposed to be happening in Asia at the time. The location and ownership of Sinkiang was one example. There were many others. Throughout the entire period of Australia's intervention in Vietnam the Department of External Affairs (EA) did not have a separate North Vietnam desk; desk-level study of Hanoi's policies was handled by a junior officer, 80 per cent of whose time was devoted to other matters. Unlike the British and the Canadians, no attempt was made to talk to Hanoi, even on routine trade or consular matters. Nor were EA's efforts to assess what was going on in South Vietnam much better: for most of the war it did not have a single Vietnamese speaker, let alone specialist. The usual approach seemed to be to take the most optimistic of the various US assessments available, and put this forward as the official view. On this basis Canberra ended up as an enthusiastic believer in the wretched strategic hamlets solution, the alleged popularity of the Diem regime and the claimed strength of the pro-Saigon forces. On this basis too it could state with open-eyed conviction until as late as 1966 that Hanoi was a Peking puppet.

I was more involved with Sino/Soviet affairs in those days, but my one direct involvement with Indochina was revealing enough. In late 1964 Wilfred Burchett arrived back in Moscow from a long visit to NLF-controlled areas in South Vietnam. He was quite happy to talk about this experience to Australian diplomats in Moscow and I obtained permission to meet him. His account suggested the NLF had much stronger control over South Vietnam that most realised at the time. And we did not have to rely simply on his word for this. He had a mass of photographs of NLF units and jungle factories. These convincingly disproved the popular theory that the NLF was just a terrorist rabble totally dependent on Hanoi, and ultimately on Peking. I sent much of this material back to Canberra, thinking that it would at least be welcomed as an addition to the raw intelligence available on the area. The only reaction I got was a sharp rebuke for seeming to endorse a pro-communist like Burchett.

(I heard later that the material had been passed to Washington for comment. The American reply had ignored the photos and concentrated on Burchett's claim to have travelled all the way to an NLF-controlled village on the outskirts of Saigon. There, he had said, he had been able to watch the planes landing at Ton San Nhut airport. The Americans said this was clearly false. They said it was impossible for any villages near the airport to be under NLF control. Some time later rockets fired from surrounding villages under NLF control started landing on the airport!)

With China the EA personnel situation was somewhat better; in theory, at least, Canberra was not so completely dependent on the US for assessments. A full-time desk officer in the East Asian section covered mainland China and Taiwan. The section, branch and division heads above him were also expected to spend much of their time on China. A small office in Hong Kong—a middle-ranking EA officer, assisted after 1960 by one Chinese-language trainee (myself from 1960–62)—was supposed to concentrate on reporting mainland developments. And both London and Washington were assigned Australian officers whose duties included seeking out and analysing whatever information they could get from Foreign Office and State Department specialists on China.

But none of this seemed to help Canberra to reach an accurate view of what was happening in China. The London and Washington material often seemed designed to encourage us to go along with UK or US policies. (The UK, despite, its official recognition of China, was actively and covertly involved in various anti-Peking exercises, many at the dirty tricks level. Some of the longer background reports prepared by the better US or UK experts were interesting, but few in Canberra ever got round to studying them objectively. In particular the so-called Tibetan documents—a vast amount of Chinese intelligence briefing material captured or stolen from the Chinese along the Sino-Indian border in 1962—provided a fascinating insight to the defensive nature of Chinese defense and foreign policies. They alone were enough to end the myth of an expansionist China. But I could never get anyone in EA to read them, let alone appraise them in this light.

The Hong Kong operation was a particular disappointment. Most EA men sent there spent their time trying to win tidbits from their US and UK colleagues; their occasional forays into independent research were usually quite ludicrous. I recall how one of them suddenly discovered that Peking often referred to 'more than ninety per cent of the population' as being pro-Mao. He sent a formal memo to remind Canberra that even Peking admitted it had 60 million potential enemies in its midst. (He was later promoted to EA Secretary.) Only a few had any serious background or interest in China. Fewer made any real effort to go out and talk to the large number of educated Chinese in Hong Kong with mainland China experience, many of them refugees. These were the people who could make you realise that for all the dissatisfaction in China, the idea of a pro-KMT uprising there—then still the lingering hope in US and Canberra policies—was laughable.

The Chang Shih-chao incident typified Canberra's anti-Peking isolationism at the time. Chang was an elderly intellectual who had been Mao's library teacher in Peking back in the twenties, later joined the progressive wing of the KMT, but stayed in China after 1949. The Peking regime trusted him, and he was allowed to spend the winters in Hong Kong where, among other things, he acted as a channel for communications. He was reportedly very close to Chou En-lai.

I heard about Chang from some UK government contacts and suggested that I be allowed to try to meet him. At the time EA had a strict policy banning all contact with Peking people. I was given a reluctant approval, however, since I was only a Chinese language trainee and the diplomatic import of my dealing with the 'enemy' was negligible. Chang turned out to be frank and friendly. He gave a good account of the Chou's foreign policy at the time and even had a few prepared words to say about Australia. I passed all this on, together with a suggestion that we try to maintain contact with Chang. The response was quite negative although the British used him a lot.

Back in Canberra shortly after, and working on the China desk in the East Asia section, I was to learn a lot more about the depth of Canberra's anti-Peking suspicions. The overall attitude seemed to be that one should never in any situation attribute any reasonable or even neutral quality to what emerged from Peking. At the same time Chou En-lai was making very genuine efforts to open a dialogue with the west *via* his intermediate zone theory embracing Japan, Australia and Western Europe. Peking was also offering to patch up differences with Taiwan and to settle border disputes with its neighbours. But for the China experts in Canberra, none of this could be taken at face value. At best it proved Peking was getting desperate. At worst it concealed a Chinese plot. In the meantime we should maintain our defences and cooperate with US anti-China initiatives in the UN and elsewhere.

The major achievement of the East Asia section in those days was to get the term 'hegemony' into general circulation as the official tag for China's alleged aims in Asia (as in the Hasluck quotation that heads this chapter). Here, they felt, was a word which aptly described the subtle blend of power and intimidation with which Peking planned to dominate the Asian nations and draw them into its fold. I tried to suggest some debate on all this, and was quickly put down. If Peking was not hegemonistic, I was told, why did it show such hostility to the pro-west governments in Asia? No one seemed to realise the basic principle of cause and effect in foreign affairs: that if A is hostile to B then it is highly likely that B will respond by being hostile to A. Our foreign policy experts had put it all into reverse: the fact that B had reacted with hostility proved that it was right for A to be hostile in the first place.

This was the situation in the East Asia section. Elsewhere it was much worse: hegemony was seen as much too mild a word for Peking's plots. In the Southeast Asian branch it was taken for granted that all left-wing movements in Asia were financed by Peking, that one could at all times and places talk indiscriminately about Chinese 'subversion' and 'infiltration'. Sarawak, and to some extent Singapore, were major areas of concern at the time, even though Peking had done almost nothing to assist materially the far from illegitimate grievances of left-wing Chinese in both places. (No one was very interested in my suggestion at the time that China's reluctance to get more involved in both places deserved some analysis. Among the Australian military and intelligence bureaucracies the anti-Peking hysteria was beyond control. Even my conservative superiors in the East Asia section were sometimes upset by the primitive anti-communist and anti-China crudities that appeared regularly in the assessments and briefs produced by these people. But no one tried to oppose or correct them.

The Sino-Indian dispute provided a good example of how easily hardliners could dominate foreign policy. As desk officer in EA, I had been following the evolution of the dispute through 1962. It was obvious that Peking wanted to compromise, and that it was the Indians who were taking the extreme position. Of course, if the Indian boundary claim line had the strong legal backing claimed for it, then the Indians would have been entitled to some extremism. In fact their backing was quite weak and included some falsified material which did not take much effort to discover. But as usual my superiors were not very interested in this sort of detailed research, particularly if it seemed to cast a less than totally hostile light on the nature of Chinese policies.

When the fighting broke out in October 1962, however, they had to show more interest. And to anyone who simply bothered to look at a map it was clear that the fighting had started on the Chinese side of even the most ambitious Indian claim line. In other words, India *must* have launched the first attack. I sent cables to London and Washington asking for a check to see whether this was in fact the case. When the reluctant confirmations came in a day or so later I felt the time had come to move, particularly since Canberra had already made sweeping denunciations of 'unbridled Peking aggression' and was actively considering military aid to the Indians.

In those days EA had a quite democratic 'submission' system, not unlike the much-studied *ringi* system (or bottom-up discussion and decision-making process) in Japan. Desk officers could at any time draw up a submission to any superior, even the minister, on any subject within their brief which they considered important, setting out facts and making recommendations. The submission would then pass up through immediate superiors who might add their comments or rewrite it, but in general tried to avoid killing it unless there was good reason to do so. This was a valuable means of encouraging initiative among junior officers and keeping open the information arteries.

So I prepared my submission, explaining in some detail why the Indian case might not be quite as strong as some might have assumed. I suggested that prolonged hostilities would favour China rather than India, and recommended that any offer of military aid to India should be tied to an attempt to get the Indians to negotiate seriously with Peking. I never expected the submission to reach the minister. It was nevertheless important, I felt, to get the facts of the dispute to the upper EA levels since they were already carrying on as if Peking's guilt was beyond all doubt.

It is to the credit of my rather conservative East Asia section and branch heads at the time that they accepted the submission without too much argument. It got no further however. The South Asian branch head at the time, a hawk who later became our Ambassador in Saigon, also had to give his stamp of approval. He wrote into the margin: 'I fail to see that it is not in the Australian interest to have the Chinese and the Indians at each other throats.' No one of equal or greater seniority felt inclined to argue with this particular piece of wisdom. So the submission was killed, and with it one chance to get the facts of the dispute into circulation. It was not until 1970 that the gospel of Chinese aggression against India came under any serious intellectual challenge in Canberra. By then the damage done to any hope of serious debate on China was enormous. In briefings, ministerial statements, university seminar rooms and the media, it was taken for granted that China had a proven track record of open and unprovoked aggression. It was, as I have suggested, a classic example of how easily ideological bias can be reinforced by the suppression or denial of information.

This was the situation in 1962. When I returned to Canberra in May 1965 after two years in Moscow, it was far worse. My suggestions—that Hanoi might be closer to Moscow than Peking, that to realise this one need only look at the numbers of Vietnamese trainees in Moscow, not to mention the position Hanoi was taking in the Sino-Soviet dispute—were ignored. The idea that we should take a closer look at just what the Chinese were saying in their ideological and frontier disputes with Moscow, to see whether they really were as extreme as Canberra assumed, was dismissed as much too academic.

In 1962 one could, at least within the safety of EA walls, seek to put forward submissions which contradicted the beliefs of conservative politicians or the military/intelligence community. By 1965 this freedom was no longer available. Australian foreign policy had frozen into a rigid orthodoxy that ruled out any study or suggestion which questioned the official line. Peking was the enemy; Hanoi was its puppet; the NLF was the creature of Hanoi; and that was that.

Some have since argued that it was irrelevant to debate the bases of Australia's policies at the time because Canberra had no choice but to go along with the US anyway, and the US was determined to go into Vietnam. But as I wrote at the time,[2] and has since been confirmed, there were large areas of independence in the Canberra/Washington relationship. On China/Vietnam, Australia actually stood to the right of the US. We skillfully lobbied the US right-wing to encourage the greatest and firmest commitment possible in Vietnam. Australia was terrified that the US might one day go soft on China and Asian left-wing movements, particularly in Indonesia. Its position was rather similar to that of the harder-line east European regimes vis-a-vis Moscow: because they were smaller and more exposed to the corrosive domino effect of a strong hostile ideology, they were often more anxious than Moscow to see intervention against the bearers of that ideology.

Others have argued that some at least of Canberra's anti-Peking progpaganda during the 1960s needs to be taken with large quantities of salt, that it was part of an attempt by the LCP to divide and discredit the left-wing in Australia. But that was not my impression: if anything, the policymakers were more alarmist about Peking in private than they were in public. They really believed that in China they faced an enemy whose evil and malevolence matched that of Hitler in the thirties (and this was the moderate pre-Cultural Revolution China of Liu Shao-chi, Chou En-lai and Deng Xiaoping!). They assumed, and some such as Gorton and Hasluck even said as much, that history would see them as brave men who refused to make Munich-style compromises with an aggressive enemy. (Someone should rewrite Santayana to read: 'Those who obsess themselves with the mistakes of the past are destined to repeat them.')

One of the more embarrassing of Canberra's initiatives at the time (April 1965, as I recall) was a classified round-robin directive to all our west European posts, emphasising Australia's concern at the failure of the Europeans to realise the sinister nature of events in Vietnam and China's 'aggressive' intentions in the area. Our diplomats were instructed to convey this concern to the foreign ministries of the respective countries to which they were posted. They were told to tell the Europeans that we Australians, by virtue of our closer association with Asia, were better able to make an objective analysis of what was happening in Indo-China. I doubt if any government would impose such embarrassment on its diplomats unless it was firmly convinced of what it was saying.

A 1971 incident was fairly convincing proof, for me at least, that Canberra's anti-China fears were both genuinely felt and far to the right of anything found in the US. I was then working as a correspondent in Tokyo and involved myself in a one-man attempt to persuade a group of Australian table-tennis players that they should accept an invitation to visit China. At first they denied having received an invitation from the Chinese at the Nagoya World Table Tennis Championships in April that year.

Later they said they had got an invitation, but had rejected it on the advice of the Department of External Affairs, which, together with the Nationalist Chinese Embassy in Canberra, had arranged an alternative visit to Taiwan. The Nagoya invitation was of course part of Pekings now historic opening to the West—the pingpong diplomacy. Even the Americans had realised its importance and had gone out of their way to encourage their own team, and others, to accept. But Canberra in its anti-Chinese wisdom had decided otherwise. Ironically, it was a photo of the US team being received in Peking by Chou En-lai that finally allowed me to persuade the Australian team to ignore Canberra's pressure and head for China.

How could so many quite intelligent and well-educated people (EA had over 200 diplomatic officers) have been so blind and conservative over issues of such importance to Australia? For all its hawkishness, the US State Department produced quite a respectable handul of public dissidents on both China and Vietnam policy. By 1971 it was working actively to open contacts with Peking. And for at least a period of the mid-seventies there was open revulsion against the mistakes made in Vietnam. In Canberra, however, even after relations with Peking had been opened and the folly of Vietnam because obvious, there was little sign of remorse. I myself know of only one or two EA people in any position of seniority who have since admitted to any dismay over previous policies. At the time those policies were being implemented there were none.

There are, of course, those who believe that EA was and remains infected with a deep right-wing bias, the result of deliberate recruitment policies, but I doubt it. In nine years with the department I never met anyone who openly admitted to DLP sympathies, for example. Few would even admit to being strongly pro-LCP. If anything, a mild progressive bias existed, certainly in domestic affairs, and to some extent in foreign affairs. The department I entered in 1957 was still somewhat influenced by the left-wing nationalism of the Evatt years. Many middle-level officers were products of the strongly progressive atmosphere of the universities immediately after the war. True, these influences were partly over-ridden by a conservative streak at the top—the older generation who had been in at the creation, so to speak. The Evatt period recruits were later undercut by the more anti-communist generation of the fifties (of which I myself was a typical example, until subjected to the obvious folly of Australian policy on China). True, the Petrov affair had caused some corrosion of will; many were reluctant to seem soft on any issue involving communism. And the Stalin revelations of the mid-fifties also did much damage; the Australian left seemed to have staked a lot on the Soviet model, and when that model collapsed it had little else to turn to, unlike in most other western countries where the left usually had a stronger intellectual base for its position.

But even allowing for all this, the progressive bias within EA still remained quite strong. Throughout the late fifties and even into the early sixties there was an identifiable group of mid-level moderates, the 'Young

Turks' as they were called, who regularly and willingly proposed alternative views on questions such as Suez, West Irian, or decolonisation. Sometimes they directed influenced policy, but when it came to China and Vietnam in the 1960's, they were quite silent.[3] Many of them actually supported the government line.

When I told EA in 1965 that I wished to leave over Vietnam and China policy, Plimsoll suggested I should just take a few years' leave of absence to think about things and possibly return when 'the Vietnam thing' was over. It was a generous offer, and I decided to accept it, provided I could feel that if and when I returned, there would at least be a basis for rational policy-making on China and Vietnam. I soon realised, however, that this was a futile hope.

Nor was the situation much better outside official circles. When I left EA in September 1965 I had not intended to become involved in the anti-Vietnam War debates. I still felt loyal to the department and wished to return to it if the government ever changed hands. But some personally insensitive behaviour by EA soon after quickly convinced me I should abandon this emotional link. In November of that year I wrote an article for the *Australian* pointing out the military and ideological weakness of the western position in Vietnam. The editors titled it 'Australia and the Lost War'. By running it prominently, they launched me, willy-nilly, into the ranks of the 'anti-war' camp.

True, there were some people who tried seriously and intelligently to counter the government's position, especially the University Study Group[4] and the Quakers, the magazine *Dissent,* and other academics. But in Canberra, in particular, apathy prevailed amongst academics.

In time I became involved with the ALP. I joined the Canberra branch in 1966, and found it split between a majority of pro-war right-wingers and a minority of anti-war leftists. Accepting this situation, which was common at the time, I sought to influence the right-wingers. But in 1968, after seeing some of the tactics used by the NSW Executive (of which Whitlam was a member) in a pre-selection struggle involving an anti-war member, I allowed my ALP membership to lapse.

Whitlam's position at the time was very curious. I first met him in 1966, when some aides brought together Whitlam, Stephen Fitzgerald and myself. We spent the whole lunch listening to him talk about his friend Lee Kwan Yew. We never discussed China or Vietnam policy, despite the fact that both Fitzgerald and I had resigned from EA on these matters. Whitlam did not give us the opportunity to pass on our knowledge of government foreign policy blundering.

Later in 1966 I became involved in an attempt to devise a compromise policy on Vietnam. It was then obvious that the Calwell policy of simply denouncing the 'filthy and unwinnable' war in Vietnam was inadequate. Shortly before the election and the visit to Australia of American President Lyndon B Johnson, I proposed to the ALP the 'enclave solution': that the war should be seen as a civil war; that outside help to Saigon should be kept at the same level as outside help to Hanoi; and that if Saigon could not prevail, then Australia would assist the US to secure a coastal enclave—a little Taiwan—for South Vietnamese anti-communists. If the US should reject this solution, then Australia would withdraw its forces.

To his credit, Dr J F Cairns accepted this rather right-wing alternative, despite criticism from the Victorian ALP Executive. All that we then needed was Whitlam's agreement, and the new policy could then be presented to Calwell in time for his meeting with LBJ in Canberra. But Whitlam refused even to consider the proposal, and Calwell went on repeating his unfruitful line of attack. The ALP, as is well-known, went to a crashing defeat in the 1966 election.

In 1967 Whitlam visited Vietnam, returning with one of the more original arguments against the government's policies. He said on television and in the press that the war had already been won by the Americans and by Saigon, and that what was required was not military aid but civil aid to reconstruct the countryside. (This detail has been conveniently forgotten by uncritical Whitlam admirers.) I later discovered that before leaving Saigon, Whitlam said even more effusive things to American officials about their so-called victory. One of his aides had been forced to take action to prevent these remarks being published in the Australian press. The only record we now have, therefore, is the reports in the Saigon press at the time. Clearly, Whitlam had been snowed.

I spent some time attempting to discover the basis of Whitlam's position. Obviously a man of intellect and some principle, he became an active reformer when he finally realised the atrocity in Vietnam and the stupidity of Canberra's China policy. But why was this realisation so belated? I have some evidence that, like many others, he was influenced by the then popular version of the Sino-Indian dispute: if even socialist India was the victim of Peking's aggression, then clearly the Asian version of communism was more virulent than the Moscow version. And as his flirtations with the *Quadrant*-Cultural Freedom push in Sydney showed, he was not particularly pro-Moscow either.

On several occasions I found that Whitlam did not read the material essential for his foreign affairs brief. He particularly feared any course of action which might strengthen the positions of his ALP rivals. Had Cairns not dominated intellectual left-wing opposition to the Vietnam War, Whitlam might have moved to a more progressive position more quickly.

Really, Whitlam's position was similar to that of many progressive intellectuals and academics in Sydney and Melbourne. He wished to take a 'progressive' position, but was intensely embarrassed by the prospect of being labelled as pro-Hanoi, pro-Peking or 'extremist'. Like many others, therefore, he concentrated on trimmings such as revamping the relationship with America, criticising SEATO, and drawing up new alliances with Asia,[5] In turn, this approach later provided the intellectual context for his wretched deal with the Indonesian generals over Timor.

Whitlam's 1964–68 position on Vietnam also enabled Canberra to evade the real problems in policy-making. The progressive tradition of the fifties may have been weakened in EA, but there was still a feeling that the department should seek out a centrist position on major foreign policy issues. Jim Cairns and John Wheeldon could easily be rejected as 'extremists', but if Whitlam had evolved a well-reasoned anti-war position, he would have created a mild crisis of conscience in the department.

Could the anti-war movement have handled its case better? I sometimes felt it wasted too much time trying to argue the situation on the ground in South Vietnam. Details about obscure sects and Vietnamese opposition leaders for the most part simply added to the sinister 'Oriental' nature of it all. Attempts to point out NLF legitimacy and independence were equally hopeless, although in retrospect this was the strongest argument. Most now realise that if the NLF had not been so thoroughly destroyed by US gunships, it would now be working to moderate the extent of Hanoi's current control over the south. But at the time the NLF, as jungle guerillas, had an even more sinister image than Hanoi.

My own efforts in this and other directions were largely futile. The argument that Canberra was dangerously to the right of Washington made little impact on the anti-war leftists who were determined to paint Canberra as an American lackey. I also tried to point out the parallel between Soviet efforts to stop 'dominoes' from falling in Eastern Europe, and the American use of the domino argument in Asia.[6] The very idea that the forces of good could be faced with the same pragmatic problems as the forces of evil was too shocking for most to contemplate. Even today, after Afghanistan, most remain blind to the parallels between Soviet and US behaviour towards their 'unreliable' client governments.

Attempts to carry the argument back into the EA camp were even more hopeless. As late as 18 August 1966, Paul Hasluck was still talking in Parliament about 'Chinese aggression' against Vietnam. When most reasonable observers had realised that Hanoi was not Peking's puppet, EA simply switched its line to heavy denunciation of Hanoi's 'aggression' against the South. I once suggested to Bill Hayden MHR that he place a question on notice to discover whether the government would protest as 'aggression' the clandestine raids Taiwan was then making against mainland China. EA blandly replied, on the official record, that it possessed no evidence of such raids. I also arranged for Hayden to ask why, if our Asian allies were so keen on the Vietnam War, was a conservative Japanese politician, Masayoshi Ohira, comparing the war to the Japanese mistakes in China thirty years' before? EA replied, again on the record, that Mr Ohira was not a very important politician.

The problem with EA—and the Vietnam War period highlighted this—was its blend of immaturity and arrogance, its belief that it was the repository of all foreign affairs truth. But this characteristic later survived three years of Labor government in the seventies.

Its origins are complex: the department's elitist selection procedures; its isolation from the community (partly inevitable, given the location of Canberra and then the frequency of overseas postings); and the excessive size and bureaucratisation of the department since the latter half of the sixties.

If I had to choose one single factor, however, I would emphasise the lack of professionalism, especially the failure to learn Asian languages and undertake specialist studies of Asian societies. EA had done almost nothing to train Asian language speakers during the fifties. China was then being ignored; Japan was defeated; and the rest of Asia was supposed to be beholden to the white man. Matters improved slightly in the sixties, when a handful of recruits were sent to learn Chinese and Indonesian. But today the overall situation remains totally inadequate.

In Tokyo, for example, the Australian Embassy has never had more than one or two fluent Japanese speakers, and most of them are far from fluent. Worse, the few sent to learn languages quickly learn that they face a 70–80 per cent risk of being shunted aside as 'specialists'. In Hong Kong in 1961 I sought EA approval for an extra year of training in Chinese (necessary to gain fluency). The then EA representative took me aside, saying in a fatherly manner: 'What the department wants is generalists ... Tag yourself as a narrow specialist and you are finished'. He was quite right. He had once been sent off to learn Arabic, but learned to spread his talents widely and thinly, avoided contact with Arab affairs, and ended up as departmental head.

It can be imagined that languages like Vietnamese, Cambodian or Lao were not regarded seriously in the department. In 1967 I decided to raise the language question in the context of the anti-war debate. I obtained and publicised the official figures on the number of EA personnel qualified in the various languages of Asia. 'Our Diplomats Ignorant', said one headline. Whitlam then went into action, sensing that he had an issue on which he could safely attack the government. He asked a question on notice in Parliament, but EA quickly evaded the issue. The department produced other figures based on an old list, whereby anyone who knew a few words of any Asian language was allowed to rate himself a linguist.

How can this negligence, structured ignorance, and anti-Asian prejudice be explained?

I would begin with the strange particularism in EA attitudes to Asia. I use particularism in its sociological sense—the propensity to judge the world exclusively on the basis of one's personal or particular situation, experience and relationships, as opposed to the more universalistic approach which tries to see issues in more abstract terms and judge them on their intellectual and moral merits. Most EA men seemed to me to have a quite childish and emotional view of Asia. On the one side were the pro-west Asians whom they met with often and knew well. They were our 'friends'.

Why? Because we knew them well and met with them often. On the other side were our enemies—the Asians who for some reason had taken an anti-west position and were outside the range of daily contact. If they were pro-west it did not matter if our 'friends' were corrupt and inefficient, because that was their only means of holding or seeking power. The fact that they were on our side was enough. It did not matter if the anti-western Asians had quite legitimate reasons for their position. They were opposed to our 'friends'. So that made them the 'enemy'.

In this sense EA's anti-communism was quite different from the more intellectually rounded, ideological anti-communism of, say, the US State Department or even perhaps a Menzies. As already suggested, in domestic affairs the average EA man was fairly tolerant and non-ideological; the right of Australian communists to seek support and propagate their cause was quite acceptable. Many EA men could vaguely appreciate the right of suppressed left-wing movements in Europe, Latin America or even Africa to resort to arms when denied political freedom. And most appreciated the genuinely civil war nature of the 1936 conflict in Spain but for some reason none of this liberalism applied to Asia, Sinitic Asia in particular. EA saw it as quite natural if anti-communist Asians—our friends—set out to imprison and kill their pro-communist opponents—our enemies. When the pro-communists retaliated this was seen as quite sinister. Terms like guerilla and insurgency took on a new and quite frightening meaning in the Asian context. Civil war never entered Canberra's vocabulary.

Vietnam provided innumerable examples of this highly exaggerated particularism in action. No one that I came across in EA at the time showed any sign of wanting to realise that the 1954 Geneva denial of the 17th parallel as an international boundary, Canberra's recognition of Saigon as the government of 'Vietnam', or Saigon's repeated threats to attack North Vietnam, undermined the 'aggression from the North' thesis. Angry references to Hanoi's 'unprovoked attacks' and Vietcong 'atrocities' were prominent in serious EA analysis and briefing material, unlike the US or UK diplomatic material which focussed much more on national or ideological interest considerations. Clearly the aggression and atrocity issues were factors that weighed heavily and genuinely in the minds of the Canberra policy makers. And, to the extent that they were underlain by a humanitarian concern for the pro-Saigon Vietnamese, their position was not unattractive.

But at no stage did I ever find any mention of Saigon's much earlier and much larger atrocities against pro-communists in South Vietnam. No one seemed to realise that they were looking at the typical civil situation not unlike that of Spain a generation earlier. No one ever seemed able to grasp how a man who has had to spend all his mature life fighting in the jungle for a cause which even the US at one stage admitted was valid, who has seen hundreds of colleagues killed barbarously in the process, might feel when he finally comes face to face with his opponents. As far as Canberra was concerned, this man was a vicious enemy, to be destroyed at all cost.

If Vietnam was the climax, then perhaps Korea was the formative stage of this particularism. A generation of EA men served in the Korea area during the early fifties. Most of them seemed to come away from the experience with a strong anti-communist antipathy. The best example was (Sir) James Plimsoll, a man of quite humane and progressive inclinations, who emerged in the mid-sixties as one of the most rigid and influential of the anti-China hawks. Several elements may have contributed to Plimsoll's views, but I have reason to believe that Korea was an important one. Like most others he seemed to have been deeply upset by the sufferings of the anti-communist Koreans, and saw China with its sinister Asian communist ideology as largely responsible. Few gave any sign of seeing the war for what it was—a civil war in which both sides were equally guilty of provocation and atrocity, and where the Soviet Union bore much more of the initial responsibility than China.

Singapore remains, however, the most clear-cut example of this particularist folly in action. I have written about it elsewhere[7] and return to it only because nobody else seems willing to take up the question. Its facts are a total indictment of Western post-war diplomacy in Asia, a perfect example of how foreign policy experts, especially the intelligence community, have worked to guarantee pro-communist support throughout the area.

In 1959 our foreign affairs experts managed to convince themselves that Lee Kwan Yew was a potential communist agent whose election had to be opposed at all costs. Of course, it all seems quite ludicrous now; Lee is one of the west's most reliably anti-communist friends in Asia. But at the time the experts had decided otherwise. Large funds were covertly chanelled by our intelligence agencies to help the election of Lee's weak and unsuccessful opponent, Lim Yew Hock. (Lee later got his revenge by sending Lim as High Commissioner to Canberra, a job that proved to be well beyond his competence.

Why did our experts oppose Lee? Well, he was an unknown to the colonial establishment to begin with. Worse, he angrily criticised British rule and spoke about organising a party of the masses dedicated to social reform—all things that communists liked to do. No one ever bothered to try to make contact with him, to find out whether he really was the sinister Chinese revoluntionary they assumed. Indeed, he was officially boycotted by the large Australian intelligence and diplomatic community in Singapore. But we talked to Lim Yew Hock. He was pro-western (as he had to be, since he had no other basis of support), which fact automatically made him our friend. Even after Lee was elected, the no-talk policy continued. Eventually it reached such a ridiculous stage that Lee had to seek the removal of our official representative there in order to get some basis of a working relationship with Australia. (The new representative was later put in charge of China policy.) To this day, Lee makes no secret that his attitude to Australia is still coloured by the 1959 events, a fact that our diplomatic historians seem conveniently to have overlooked.

The other side of the particularistic coin was the strong pro-US bias. A whole generation of EA men had grown up in the days when the US was all-mighty and apparently all-wise. Almost all had been seduced to a greater or lesser extent by the sense of power and ideological confidence that exuded from their American colleagues in those days.[8] From there it was but a short step to conclude that what was good for the US was good for Australia. A man like Dean Rusk, with his authority and deep hatred for the Peking regime, had an enormous (and still largely unrecognised) personal influence on Australian foreign policy makers, particularly on Plimsoll who remained as EA Secretary through the vital years of 1965–70. The idea of American omnipotence and omniscience was of course a totally naive assumption for which, sadly, the Vietnamese would pay heavily.

But the ultimate proof of the particularism was the flip-flop in China policy. At first Peking was the enemy. We did not know or have contact with the mainland Chinese. Therefore they must be the enemy, and their enemies in Moscow or Taipei must be our friends. Then, thanks to the Whitlam initiatives of the early seventies, having discovered that the Chinese were human beings just like the rest of us and quite intelligent human beings, that they gave us nice dinner parties and made a fuss of us, the whole direction of Australian foreign policy was thrown into reverse. From Hasluck in Moscow seeking a holy alliance against Peking we have Fraser in Sinkiang seeking a holy alliance against Moscow. From a ban on contacts with Peking we moved to a ban on contacts with Taiwan.

To repeat, how does a nation like Australia come to be afflicted with such a childish and inconsistent foreign policy? Obviously the foreign policy bureaucrats and conservative politicians bear some responsibility, but equally clearly they do not bear all the blame. The problem is much deeper, and concerns the very nature of Australian society. In most of the media, the universities and the intelligentsia generally one found the same immature attitudes to China and Vietnam, the same particularistic reasoning, the same toleration of intelligence agency abuse[8], and the same refusal to stand and debate on principle that one found in Canberra. The ALP was no exception, with a large sector tacitly accepting government policies to Vietnam and China during the sixties.

Then in the seventies we saw the same flip-flop, accompanied this time by the same lack of moral responsibility for previous attitudes or policies. Those who in the sixties had quite happily used (and abused) their establishment power to discredit critics of China/Vietnam policies, retained that power and in many cases used it equally happily to promote exactly opposite policies in the seventies. In the same ANU seminar rooms where, in the sixties, academic careers were destroyed for daring to suggest that Chinese policies might not be without their logic, one could in the seventies listen to pro-Cultural Revolution fanatics denounce Deng Xiaoping as a 'capitalist roader'. In the US those in the media and universities who had cooperated with the intelligence agencies in the sixties faced embarrassing exposure or worse in the seventies. In Australia there was nothing like this, despite three years of left-wing government. Indeed the intelligence agencies not only survived the Whitlam years intact, they were even able to influence ALP policy execution. (Whitlam's stalling over the NARA Treaty with Japan was one result.) Something in the Australian ethos seems to work to prevent sensible and responsible handling of affairs which involve foreigners, even if the same ethos operates quite effectively in domestic affairs.

Some blame it all on isolation and the small size of our population. But New Zealand is even smaller and more isolated, and does not display the same symptoms; its Vietnam debate was conducted with some sense of intellectual responsibility. Its intelligence agencies were kept under some control. When the Vietnam intervention failed there was some sense of guilt, some attempt at postmortem. We saw little or none of this in Australia, though here guilt (in terms of actively encouraging and working to prolong the US intervention) was far greater.

The only parallel I can find is Japan. It too operates on a highly particularistic ethic. The result in domestic affairs is an attractive pragmatism, a sensitivity to human relations, strong group loyalties, a healthy disrespect for legalism and a freedom from disruptive ideological debate all not dissimilar to what one finds in Australia. But in foreign affairs the same ethic has disastrous results. Quite apart from the emotionalist slapdashery, there is the ugly refusal to accept moral guilt or responsibility for past mistakes. The people responsible for those mistakes are still respected as having somehow tried to seek the best interests of the nation. The people who opposed them are still distrusted as 'trouble-makers' (yes, they use the same term as Australians do), while the society as a whole flip-flops quite easily from one foreign policy to its opposite as the mood or the need of the moment dictates, without any sense of the intellectual inconsistency involved.

3 Federal Labor and the Vietnam commitment
KIM C BEAZLEY

The decision by the Australian Liberal-Country Party government in April 1965 to commit a battalion of troops in support of the American effort in the war in Vietnam (and subsequent additions to that force in August 1965, March 1966, December 1966 and October 1967) dominated foreign policy debate in Australia for the rest of the decade. The commitment supported intense diplomatic activity by the Australian government to involve the United States in the Southeast Asian region and to avoid any political settlement in Indo-China which might involve an American withdrawal from the region's affairs.

The Vietnam commitment, and a prior government decision to support its forward defence strategy in Southeast Asia with selective compulsory military service, were important issues in the 1966 House of Representatives election. In the 1967 Senate and 1969 House elections these issues remained important, though lacking the intensity of the 1966 election.

In all the campaigns the Australian Labor Party (ALP) was popularly identified as opposed to the government's commitment to the war. It suited the government's electoral strategy in 1966 and 1967 to maximise the impression of clear-out division between the parties. The reality was more complicated. There was near unanimity on opposition to the original commitment of forces, and to subsequent increases, within the ALP. There was little agreement in the party until 1968, however, on the process or even the desirability of withdrawing the Australian Forces committed. Further, the federal leadership of the ALP was attempting to convey its opposition to the Vietnam commitment within the context of continuing broad support for the American alliance.

The government sought to portray the Vietnam War debate as a clash between alternative strategies for the defence of Australia—between its reliance on a tried and true friend and the opposition's experimentation with neutralist or isolationist doctrines, possibly motivated by a secret adherence to alien ideologies. Labor's leadership always portrayed party differences on the issue as tactical—as if only a cynical grab for electoral advantage prevented the government from accepting bipartisanship in

Australia's foreign policy posture.

Within the ALP there was considerable disagreement, however, over the detail of the policy and its presentation. This was a period of intense factional dispute in the party, reflected in disputes in policy areas such as state aid for private schools and reform of the party's extra-parliamentary structure. The trend in the latter was toward a (strongly contested) reassertion of the Federal Parliamentary Labor Party's (FPLP) authority in policy formulation.

Policy on Vietnam was thus inevitably incorporated in broader factional disputation which had both personal and ideological aspects. To simplify a complex set of opinions; those on the ALP 'right' combined a commitment to enhancing the influence of the Parliamentary party, sensitivity to perceived electoral opinion, support for EG Whitlam's leadership, and a concern to minimise the impact of opposition to the Vietnam commitment on support for the American alliance; those on the ALP 'left' tended to assert an educative role for the party where preferred policies clashed with public opinion, they opposed Whitlam's leadership and structural change in the party, and they were not convinced that the American alliance represented a solution to Australia's foreign policy problems.

General trends in ALP foreign policy 1961-65

The ALP's response to American and Australian efforts to bolster the failing South Vietnamese regime was formulated against a background of a determined effort by the party's parliamentary leadership, notably AA Calwell and Whitlam, to channel foreign policy in directions which did not preclude support for American involvement in the Southeast Asian region. While the changes in party policy emphasised retention of Australia's capacity for independent initiatives and stressed priority for home defence, they removed prohibitions on support for aspects of the government's forward defence strategy and encouraged cooperation with the United States in the Indo-Pacific region.

Alterations to party policy occurred at two crucial federal conferences in 1963, one a Special Conference to deal with the establishment of the American naval communications installation at North West Cape in March, and the other the regular biennial conference in July. The two conferences reversed the party's post-1955 flirtation with non-aligned policies and opposition to the forward basing of Australian troops. The latter had been implicit in the party's opposition to assistance given the British during the Malayan emergency.

The ground for this change of emphasis was prepared by the right-wing majority on the party's Foreign Affairs and Defence Committee in their report to the Special Federal Conference. In the section of its report on ANZUS the committee drew attention to the fact that the alliance provided for collective defence by the signatories: 'Labor believes that such a defensive alliance with the United States of America and New Zealand is essential and must continue'.[1] The left at the conference attempted to prevent passage of this resolution, recognising it would place them at a disadvantage when substantive issues such as the naval communications installation and the forward basing of troops were discussed. Their efforts were unsuccessful.[2]

Having lost the initiative at the outset of the Special Conference, left-wing delegates found themselves confined to making minor amendments to the general thrust of new policy which left open the question of Labor support for a forward defence strategy. An example of this process was provided when C T Oliver, the Foreign Affairs Committee chairman, moved a section of his report which read:

> (iii) Cooperation with the United States in the area of the South Pacific and Indian Ocean is of crucial importance and must be maintained and extended in accordance with the spirit of this declaration;
> (iv) Within its alliances Australia must remain free to order its policies in accordance with the principles of the UN Charter and Universal Declaration of Human Rights ...

F E Chamberlain, the left-wing secretary of the WA Branch, successfully moved an amendment combining the two paragraphs to read:

> Cooperation with the United States in the area of the South Pacific and Indian Ocean is of crucial importance and must be maintained, subject to the understanding that Australia must remain free to order its policies in accordance with the principles of the UN Charter and Universal Declaration of Human Rights.[3]

Having secured a basic reorientation of the party's foreign policy, the right was cautious in dealing with the 1955 policy of opposition to the presence of Australian troops in Malaya. The government had made clear shortly before the conference that the troops would be retained to assist the new government of Malaysia after the creation of the federation in September of that year.[4] Opposition to the Malayan commitment had been central to the ALP left's stand on avoiding Cold War entanglements and the remnants of imperial involvements. Malaysia's move to independence, and support of Singapore's socialist Prime Minister Lee Kuan Yew for the new federation, appeared to alter circumstances. After failing at the Special Conference the Foreign Affairs Committee finally secured at the July conference a resolution which would permit a Labor government to station forces in Malaysia, provided such commitment was associated with a treaty arrangement. It read:

> Labor does not believe that forces should be committed overseas except subject to a clear and public treaty which accords with the principles of the declaration which gives Australia an effective voice in the common decision of the Treaty Powers.[5]

The reorientation of ALP foreign policy was a product of changes in Australia's international environment as perceived by key policy-makers, and a more general concern within the party over the state of domestic public opinion. The significant international perception, shared with the government, was that Australia's region was becoming dangerously unstable. From 1961 onwards a growing number of ALP policy-makers believed that Indonesia constituted an expansionist and powerful regime. Furthermore, in South and Southeast Asia the interests of Australia and nations friendly to Australia were threatened by an aggressive China. The support Indonesia received from China augmented the perception of a growing threat.

During the West Irian crisis in 1961–62 Calwell asked:

> If Indonesia moved into West New Guinea in a blatant act of aggression ... can we be satisfied that it has no aggressive intentions. If Indonesia seizes West New Guinea ... why should it not look greedily first perhaps at Timor then at Papua New Guinea and finally ... at Northern Australia.[6]

One increasingly prominent foreign policy spokesman on the ALP right, K E Beazley, linked Indonesian irredentism and China in a 1963 speech:

> Indonesia's purpose appears to be to eliminate Western influence in Southeast Asia. Indonesia's illusion is that if Western influence is eliminated it will be replaced by Indonesian influence. It will not. It will be replaced by Chinese influence ... .[7]

On the ALP left distinctions were drawn between Soviet and Chinese policies, thus placing China in an unfavourable light. C R Cameron, a South Australian MP argued:

> [China] believes that certain territories ought to be absorbed by her ... She believes that until she can reabsorb Formosa, and perhaps other parts of Asia which she claims to be Chinese her task will not be completed. Soviet Russia, of course, has too much to lose by war ... .[8]

American policy in Vietnam was seen as part of an effort to contain China. Speaking in a debate prior to the commitment of Australian troops, Whitlam suggested that the 'United States of America is clearly the greatest counter weight to China in this part of the world, just as she has been to Russia in Europe. But she realises she cannot conquer China'. In Vietnam, Whitlam asserted, the US was demonstrating to China that the United States could not be defeated.[9]

The belief in Australia's increasingly dangerous environment did not necessarily mean that party policy-makers agreed with the government's portrayal or its policy for dealing with it. Both Whitlam and Calwell were critical of the agreements under which troops were sent to Malaysia, believing that a treaty was necessary to ensure mutuality of defence obligations and the capacity to shift Australian troops from Malaysia to elsewhere in Asia.[10] The ALP continued to disparage SEATO as an inappropriate vehicle for collective defence in Southeast Asia. On the Indonesian question some spokesmen argued for a mutual non-aggression pact. In a lecture delivered in July 1963 Whitlam advocated 'a pact of friendship, trade and non-aggression with Indonesia'.[11]

The basic thrust of party defence policy, on which all factions agreed, was the need to bolster Australia's home defence. J F Cairns, the left's principal foreign policy spokesman, asserted in October 1962 that ALP defence policy should be based on a concept of continental defence.[12] In his 1963 election speech Calwell emphasised that Australian forces ought to be self sufficient and capable of dealing with local threats independently of Australia's allies.[13] Nevertheless the party leadership sought policies that would keep open support for American initiatives in the region.

From 1961 the FPLP leadership responded positively to the apparent willingness of the Kennedy administration to involve itself in Southeast Asian affairs. The Thanat Khoman/Rusk agreement of March 1962, which asserted that SEATO members had the right to respond individually as well as collectively to threats in the treaty area, provided a framework for American initiatives. During visits to the United States, Whitlam and Calwell gained an understanding of the new direction of American policy, and their responses were favourable. Indeed, following briefings with the Secretary of State Rusk, Calwell and Whitlam determined to find a formula that would permit Party support for the North West Cape installation.[14] Returning from a trip to the United States in August 1964 Whitlam argued:

> The United States alliance is important for America, but it is essential for Australia. The ALP supports it, as the British Labour Party and all socialist parties in Western Europe support NATO. We can but help our allies by letting it be known throughout South Asia that we are cooperating with them not merely because we have a treaty with them or because we want to earn their help in case we need it ourselves—but because we must help neighbours who are attacked or subverted, and because we are willing to spare our skills and resources:[15]

In the same year Whitlam sharply rejected ALP flirtations with nonalignment, saying that such views, 'have always been in a minority and since the Chinese invasion of India a small minority indeed'.[16]

To this redirection of party foreign policy the ALP left provided little effective opposition. In part this was a product of electoral calculations, but to a considerable extent the left accepted the notion of a more threatening environment. L C Haylen, then chairman of the FPLP's Foreign Affairs Committee and the drafter of the left's statement of opposition to North West Cape at the Special Conference, reported in August 1963 on return from Southeast Asia that he had found genuine concern with the Chinese threat and could find few who wanted a withdrawal of Australian troops.[17]

In addition the left was confused as to how to respond to the Kennedy and Johnson administrations, which appeared more reasonable than Republican alternatives. They seemed willing to adopt radical domestic policies and less ready to threaten global conflagration in foreign policy. Even when opposing the first major American bombing raids in Vietnam, W H Hartley, the Victorian Branch Secretary argued that:

> Unlike the sycophantic Sir Robert Menzies, President Johnson is a sincere man. No one can doubt the integrity of his remarks when he speaks out against the crippling legacy of bigotry and injustice in the South of the United States. But it is up to him to extend the cause of domestic justice abroad.[18]

Though opposing the American position in Vietnam even Dr Cairns in 1965 did not advocate the removal of the United States from Southeast Asian affairs.[19]

Overshadowing all the party's deliberations, at least until the intense leadership dispute between Whitlam and Calwell in 1965/66, was the fear that the electorate would accept no alternative to the American alliance. While Cairns wondered in 1965 whether, 'the practice of more or less agreeing with the Government about the threat of commuism and then adopting a policy which is inconsistent with it' had damaged the party's electoral chances[20], the party as a whole was not prepared to confront the electorate directly, because many in the leadership believed the government's perception of the threat was only mildly exaggerated. In the run-up to the 1963 and 1964 elections the party leadership sought to exclude the left (as far as possible) from policy pronouncements. Calwell, for example, used his authority to determine the order of speakers in parliamentary debates to exclude supporters of left positions.[21] Losses in 1963 and 1964 merely confirmed the convictions among the ALP right that policy-making authority should shift to the FPLP and that support for the American alliance should be unequivocal.

The initial response to the Vietnam War

The initial response of the ALP to the developing crisis in Vietnam was heavily influenced by the trends outlined above. In 1962 and early 1963 when Australian military advisors were first sent to South Vietnam, only E J Ward spoke out consistently on the matter. He presciently warned in April 1962 that 'The real danger of Australia's becoming involved in a war is not as many people believe in West New Guinea ... but in South Vietnam'.[22] Despite the worsening situation in Vietnam no suggestion emanated from the ALP that the advisors should be withdrawn. Whitlam merely asked that the treaty arrangements under which they were present should be clarified.[23] Party speakers confined themselves to criticism of corruption and undemocratic behaviour in the Diem regime in South Vietnam. Diem's overthrow for a time diminished criticism.

Throughout 1964 it became clear that South Vietnam posed bigger problems than Malaysia. Calwell took advantage of the mid-year ALP state conferences in Victoria and New South Wales to support the Johnson administration, and warned against the election of Senator Barry Goldwater as President.[24]

He told the New South Wales Conference that Johnson could be trusted not to expand the conflict in Indo-China. He was mildly critical of a government decision to increase the number of advisors but his main complaint was the government's failure to explain that action to the people.[25]

In August 1964 the Federal Executive of the ALP produced the first authoritative statement of party policy. The tenor of the statement, strongly influenced by left opinion, was more critical than the FPLP leadership of the government's position. On the issue of the presence of Australian military advisors, however, the executive (like the FPLP) implied its support. It merely 'deplored the lack of any formal agreement to cover the presence of the Australian contingent in South Vietnam'. The same resolution requested the FPLP to advocate a reconvened Geneva Conference to 'resubscribe and honour the agreements' made at the 1954 Conference partitioning Vietnam and neutralising Laos and Cambodia.[26]

Calwell was increasingly in a quandary. Averse to any escalation in Australian involvement, he was concerned at the introduction of compulsory military service and the possibility that conscripts could serve overseas in Southeast Asia. At the same time he feared the electoral consequences of such views. The Senate election approached. His solution was to affirm his devotion to the American alliance and to reject neutralism or pacificism. Sacrifices for the defence of Vietnam, he believed, should be in the form of increased economic aid and expenditure on Australia's *national* defence.[27] Later he stated that an ALP government would not withdraw from commitments already undertaken in Vietnam.[28]

> Whitlam was equally emphatic in his support for American military involvement in Vietnam. He praised the prompt reaction by the Administration and Congress to the alleged attack by the North Vietnamese on American naval units in the Gulf of Tonkin.[29] He advocated a negotiated solution to the conflict and he wanted the United States to negotiate from a position of strength. He indicated in August 1964 that this would require a more secure military position than the US and its South Vietnamese allies currently enjoyed.[30]

This support reached its high point in February 1965 when the FPLP Executive endorsed a statement from the FPLP Foreign Affairs Committee supporting Johnson's decision to launch large-scale bombing raids against North Vietnam. They accepted the American explanation that bombing raids were aimed at securing the conditions for peaceful settlement and preventing an alteration in the situation by North Vietnamese 'terror and violence'.

The FPLP Executive said:

> This statement of American purposes is unexceptionable, and the case for the American action of recent days, as based on the aim of shortening the war and achieving a negotiated settlement, which would establish and maintain the rights of the South Vietnamese people, deserves sympathetic Australian understanding.
>
> The demand of the Soviet Government for the immediate departure of all American and other foreign forces from South Vietnam would be in the interests of neither the people of South Vietnam nor the people of Australia. Its immediate consequence must be a Communist take-over of South Vietnam, snuffing out the hope of freedom and democratic independence in that country and extending the area of Communist control closer to this country.

This support for American intervention was only qualified by the terms the Johnson administration imposed on itself: a 'holding' operation for 'temporary purposes' as indicated by the 'American Government in its message to the security council'.[31] The only area of disagreement with either the American or the Australian government concerned the quality of the South Vietnamese regime. The resolution called for the withdrawal of support for military governments in South Vietnam and the installation of a reformist civilian government capable of securing popular support.

This strong endorsement was drafted by A D Fraser, the committee's chairman, and Dr Cairns, each of whom had been critical of American policy. Cairns had been unimpressed by the Gulf of Tonkin incident. In no way, he said, had the alleged actions of the North Vietnamese torpedo boats threatened the security of the United States.[32] In October Cairns told Parliament that the US and Australia were confronted with two types of war in Southeast Asia: the 'national', to which a Korean type response was appropriate, and the other 'revolutionary', as in Indo-China, which was a product of social and economic causes indigenous to a particular country. He rejected the theory that the success of a social revolution in one country would necessarily spread civil conflict to others and lead to communist domination of the whole region. He did not believe that intervention in such a conflict was either justified or likely to be successful. Democratic institutions could not be imposed. Whatever emerged would be a dictatorship.[33]

Further explanation of the personal views of Fraser and Cairns is required. In Fraser's case, while sceptical of America's reliability as an ally, he did not wish to discourage its involvement in Southeast Asia. Cairns was convinced that the United States was sincere in its efforts for a negotiated settlement, and even that the strategy might secure it. When Johnson's action appeared to have produced no response from the North Vietnamese, Cairns' role in the executive's statement was increasingly criticised by his left-wing colleagues.¹⁴

The event provoked the first serious debate in Caucus on Vietnam policy. It was evident from this debate that the leadership's dominance of foreign policy debate would now be contested, at least on Vietnam. W G Hayden argued that the use by the United States of napalm, phosphorous bombs and nauseous gas had created a new situation. In the light of these morally objectionable weapons, the support given the United States by the FPLP should be retracted, and he chastised the executive for failing to consult the FPLP.³⁵

The FPLP Executive then had constitutional authority to make decisions on behalf of the FPLP during Parliamentary recesses. The objection by left-wing members reflected less a concern for constitutional niceties than an objection to executive policy. After lengthy debate, two right-wing Caucus members F R Stewart and D R Willesee successfully moved endorsement of the executive's action.³⁶ In the Parliamentary debate which followed in March and early April the extent of division on the issue became evident.

Some members were difficult to distinguish from government spokesmen. P Galvin, chairman of the FPLP Defence Committee, defended the American use of gas as humane—more humane than the reported use by Viet Cong of women and children as shields. He fulsomely praised Johnson.³⁷

Left-wing spokesmen such as Cairns, Hayden and Cameron evaded mention of the FPLP statement. They vigorously criticised, however, American conduct of the war and the nature of the South Vietnamese regime. Whitlam and Calwell, although they supported the American position, began to set out in more detail their views on a political settlement for the war and in this they were closer to left-wing speakers. Whitlam stated, for example:

> I want Vietnam to be neutralised in the sense that it will be internationalised ... The best position we can achieve in regard to Vietnam is that position which obtains in Finland or Yugoslavia. International peace-keeping forces would be established there as they are in Berlin.³⁸

There was an air of detachment about this whole debate, which took place less than a month before the commitment of Australian combat forces. The FPLP was unaware of the well-laid plans for the commitment of Australian forces when desired by the United States. Among the FPLP leadership there was a tacit understanding with the Australian government not to discuss in detail the role of Australian military advisors. The announcement of the commitment of a battalion of troops came as a surprise.³⁹ It was made without notice to the FPLP, and in the absence from Parliament of Calwell and Whitlam.⁴⁰ It was an action which confirmed Caucus fears that the government disdained genuinely bipartisan foreign policy.

On 4 May 1965 a special meeting of the FPLP passed a resolution authorising Calwell to *oppose* the despatch of troops to Vietnam. The resolution was placed directly before Caucus, evading the normal route *via* the Foreign Affairs Committee and Executive, bodies on which the right-wing was then strong. After discussion, partly concerned with this procedural tactic, the resolution was unanimously adopted.[41]

This unanimity requires explanation. The attitudes of the ALP right and the February 1965 FPLP statement appeared to indicate that some support for an increased commitment would be forthcoming. On the other hand the party had assumed that the American action was sufficient to secure a negotiated settlement. At the same time, opposition to an initial commitment of Australian forces did not necessarily mean support for their immediate withdrawal. Around this point much intra-party debate subsequently revolved. The decision made difficult the type of support given to increasing American involvement by some members of the ALP right. It was difficult to appear convinced of the need for an increasing American military effort at the same time as opposing an increased Australian commitment.

The parliamentary debate which followed was unlike any other in the previous decade. For the first time the FPLP subjected the government's picture of Australia's external environment to systematic attack, contradicting in the process much of its own art work. The shift was symbolised by Calwell's decision that Cairns should follow him in the debate, which effectively brought the left 'in from the cold'. At the same time Calwell and Whitlam continued to be cautious in their condemnation of American policy, anxious to demonstrate that the alliance would not be effected by a future ALP government.

In particular ALP spokesmen retracted any previous implications that what was involved in Vietnam was anything other than a civil war without implications for Australian security. Calwell argued that it was a civil war 'aided and abetted by the North Vietnamese Government, but neither created nor principally maintained by it'.[42] Beazley disputed the government's belief that China exercised a controlling influence on North Vietnamese policy.[43] While Calwell, Whitlam and Beazley emphasised the local nature of the conflict, Cairns went further to argue that the war in Vietnam was an aspect of a major historical change in Asia. Almost satirically, Cairns pointed out to the government that those involved in revolutionary changes do not sit up at night thinking of Australia and how they might come to this country for all the good things that are here.[44]

The main divergence in the arguments of the left and right lay in the significance attached to the American alliance. Left-wing spokesmen like G Bryant stated that Australian involvement in an unwinnable war demonstrated the foolishness of an uncritical adherence to the American alliance. As an alternative Australia should give serious consideration to lowering its dependence on the alliance by building strong forces for its self-defence.[45]

Calwell and Whitlam were more circumspect. They argued that United

States required a candid friend. Calwell warned that American involvement in an unwinnable war would advance Chinese power and damage America's reputation.[46] Whitlam considered that Australia had limited its ability to act in a mediatory role.[47] More importantly, Whitlam and Calwell considered it important to demonstrate that no alliance obligations were involved in Vietnam and that Australia was meeting all reasonable obligations. Whitlam argued that Australia was not officially involved under SEATO and that most SEATO members were not participants.[48] Calwell argued that with obligations in Malaysia, Australia was overcommitted—'The only country committed on two fronts in Southeast Asia'.[49] Whitlam expected that the United States would understand Australia's different position. American involvement in Asia was not necessarily permanent, but Asian opinion could be offended by Australian imprudence.[50]

As it emerged in 1965, the Vietnam issue was an important test of the validity of the reorientation of Labor's foreign policy under Whitlam and Calwell. The policy adopted in 1963 anticipated support for American initiatives, military as well as diplomatic, in Southeast Asia. The problem for the ALP was that it had no clear understanding of what this entailed. The precedents for likely American initiatives in Vietnam were very different from the policy which emerged. From 1961 to 1964 it appeared unlikely that the United States would commit its power and prestige in a major way. Kennedy seemed to understand the sensitivities of the nonaligned nations in his support for India during the Sino-Indian border conflict, offering 'no strings attached' military aid. He had also accepted a neutralised Laos after exercising a small degree of military pressure. The overthrow of Diem suggested, on the surface, American awareness of the importance of the political aspect of the war in Vietnam.

Concealed from the ALP leadership was the systematic planning in Washington and Canberra for a major deployment of American power in Vietnam and an increased Australian involvement. The support for 'operation rolling thunder' by the FPLP can be seen as a response based on calculations which had to undergo dramatic revision once the scale of American involvement became obvious. The problem for the ALP leadership was how to reconcile a response to this apparently ill-advised change in American policy with firm support for the American alliance.

Factionalism in the ALP and Vietnam policy 1965-66

Debate in the ALP in 1965-66 was conducted against the background of the conflict between Whitlam and Calwell for leadership of the party, and also between Whitlam's supporters and the left over the parliamentary party's role in policy-making. Calwell was increasingly forced to rely on backing from the FPLP left, the left-wing Victorian Branch and the federal organisation. Whitlam directed his attack at the attitudes of the Victorian Branch, in particular, and by implication attacked Calwell. After two election losses Calwell was highly vulnerable. The struggles meant that no clear line emerged from the Party. Only a generalised view of opposition to government policy was conveyed to the public.

From the outset Calwell's presentation of foreign policy was a central element of Whitlam's attack. In March 1965 Whitlam attacked the Victorian Branch, accusing them of damaging anti-Americanism. He was critical of Calwell's handling of the FPLP Executive which met, he alleged, only when the United States made a foreign policy error.[51]

Whitlam's attack provided an opportunity for the Federal Executive to support Calwell. Calwell complained of Whitlam's behaviour to the executive. He requested the Federal Secretary, Cyril Wyndham, to investigate Whitlam's statements.[52] In May, the Federal Executive took advantage of a variety of post-election comments by State branches expressing confidence in Calwell to endorse his position as leader.[53] Calwell's reliance on the Victorians was cemented by his decision to stand for a position on the Victorian delegation to Federal Conference. His move was perceived by the right as a defence of the Victorian leadership, then under attack for permitting 'unity tickets' with communists in union elections and for undemocratic internal rules.[54] At the Federal Conference Whitlam scathingly attacked the Victorian Branch whilst Calwell devoted one-third of his speech to its defence.[55]

As a Victorian delegate, Calwell was bound to support all Victorian resolutions, including those which most emphatically rejected the government's Vietnam policy. At the 1965 Federal Conference it was obvious that Calwell had moved closer to the left. He supported an unsuccessful amendment by fellow Victorian delegate S H Cohen to place greater restrictions on the ALP's policy concerning the deployment of Australian forces overseas.[56]

But the conference was ultimately circumspect on the Vietnam question. Bearing in mind the common anti-Labor allegation that the FPLP was dominated by its machine, conference phrased its policy as an endorsement of the FPLP's stand on the commitment of troops, condemned conscription, and supported Calwell's call for UN involvement in Vietnam. An ALP government would assist in the maintenance of a UN peace-keeping force.[57] The resolution left unresolved the question of the withdrawal of Australian troops and also left the determination of future policy in the hands of the federal Caucus.

Between February and April 1966 the leadership struggle reached its zenith. In February the Federal Executive purged a number of its committees, including the Foreign Affairs Committee, of right-wing members.[58] Whitlam scathingly attacked the executive, particularly its exclusion of Fraser (Chairman of the Foreign Affairs Committee) shortly before he was due to meet American Vice-President H H Humphrey.[59] Motions highly critical of the Executive were tabled at the next FPLP meeting. These were withdrawn only when Calwell promised to raise the matter with the

Federal Executive. The executive retreated and for the first time permitted the election of FPLP representatives to the executive's committees.

Calwell defeated a direct challenge to his leadership in April by 49 votes to 24.[60] Despite this comfortable margin, his leadership was subjected to constant harassment. He found himself constantly caught between his previous concern for the American alliance and his dwindling but increasingly left-oriented power base.

In the midst of these troubles the FPLP endorsed a further statement on Vietnam from its Foreign Affairs committee which formed the basis of policy for the 1966 election. This reiterated opposition to the commitment of Australian combat forces, but it went further to state that conscripts would be withdrawn without delay by a Labor government. 'Full regard to the safety and security of the Australian forces' would be given in such a withdrawal. On the question of regular forces, an ALP government would 'have regard to the situation in Vietnam as it exists at the time and to the importance of maintaining future cooperation with the United States'. Nothing would be done without American cooperation, but an ALP government would insist on the return of Australian forces as soon as possible.

The policy also advocated a programme for ending the conflict in Vietnam: the American administration should cease bombing North Vietnam and transform the war in the South into a 'holding operation'; Australia should take the initiative to secure a ceasefire and peace negotiations; and Australia also should support the 1954 Geneva accords for the withdrawal of all foreign forces and non-intervention by external powers in the affairs of the area. An ALP government would be prepared to commit Australian troops to any UN peace-keeping operations in South Vietnam.[61]

Despite his increasing reliance on the ALP left Calwell remained embarrassed by policy critical of American conduct of the war and war objectives. He refused to support calls from the left to demonstrate against the visit by President Johnson to Australia, a visit widely interpreted as a government election ploy. He praised Johnson's efforts to obtain peace in Vietnam and called on the North Vietnamese to respond.[62] Earlier, when Vice-President Hubert Humphrey visited Australia, Calwell was anxious to point out that the ALP did not demand the unilateral withdrawal of American troops.[63]

Beazley captured some of his leader's dilemmas in an article for *Australian Outlook* in 1966:

> In most countries a government is on trial at elections. At least from the time of Evatt's assumption to leadership (except for 1961) it has been a special feature of Australia that the Government is never on trial: the Opposition is a party which is always resolving and is always explaining. 'Qui s'excuse, s'accuse' seems to apply, for the Australian electorate dislikes intellectual explanations and suspects them. How do you explain a strong defence policy while abolishing National Service? How do you explain respect for an alliance while withdrawing troops

from the side of your allies? These are genuinely difficult concepts for the electorate.[64]

Calwell's resolution of the problem was to concentrate on the simple conscription issue. Opposition to conscription was a consistent feature of his long political career: 'We have always been an anti-conscriptionist party and we are proud of it. When we cease to be that, we cease to be an Australian Labor Party'.[65] When criticism of the stridency of his campaign mounted in the party, he argued that anti-conscriptionism enjoyed some public support. On one occasion he read Caucus a letter from journalist Don Whitington about a survey showing 70 per cent of the electorate opposed to conscription.[66]

During the campaign Calwell's preoccupation with conscription outweighed much of his restraint on other aspects of the Vietnam issue. At one rally he told a heckler: 'You are beyond military age. I will not allow you or Holt or Menzies or anyone to plunge your arthritic hands wrist deep in the blood of Australian youth'.[67] In the process he dropped his previous concern with making ALP policy appear consistent with the alliance. He resisted efforts by the FPLP right to modify the policy statement of May 1966.

In August a number of Caucus members who had visited Vietnam returned to read speculative reports that they would recommend reversal of the commitment to withdraw Australian forces. One of them, Len Reynolds, in a cautious article for the New South Wales *ALP News*, suggested that the United States was winning the war.[68] Whitlam identified himself with the views of the returning members. One of his supporters in Caucus, C K Jones, not unreasonably moved that the recent visitors to Vietnam report their findings to the Foreign Affairs Committee.[69]

Under Fraser's chairmanship the Foreign Affairs Committee had been highly critical of government Vietnam policy, but it was also sensitive to the impact of the issue on the American alliance. Nevertheless Jones accepted an amendment from Senator P Kennelly that the members report directly to *Caucus*. An amendment by Uren to request the members to circulate their reports in writing, with no specified time for Caucus discussion, was defeated.[70]

The members duly reported. During the discussions Caucus witnessed a direct clash between Whitlam and Calwell on the status of previous party policy. Calwell ruled that all policy statements including that of 12 May were binding on party members. Whitlam countered that while the Federal Conference resolution of 1965 was indeed binding, Caucus was at liberty to vary its own statements since that date, provided the variations did not contradict the 1965 resolution.[71] Whitlam's interpretation of party rules was undoubtedly correct but Caucus was unprepared to challenge Calwell. In such an atmosphere, the reports were received without comment.

The ALP left became increasingly impatient with the efforts of the right to modify policy for electoral purposes. Cairns criticised Beazley's article in *Australian Outlook* for its implication that the ALP was damaged by its association with vigorous anti-war demonstrations. Left-wing radicalism, Cairns believed, had its 'back to the wall'. Association with extremists who supported aspects of the ALP policy was unavoidable. 'The question in Australian political life today', he stated, 'is whether there is to be any place for left-wing radicalism'.[72] Calwell too, abandoned his previous caution. Commenting on one demonstration directed against the prime minister, he stated that it was 'no use for Mr Holt moaning over his experience because he helped to provoke the action by the brutal manner in which he caused the young conscript William White to be taken into custody'.[73]

Hostility between Whitlam and Calwell came to a head in the middle of the election campaign. Whitlam sought to rebut government criticism that the proposal to withdraw conscripts from Vietnam would endanger regulars and cause dissension with allies. In the *Daily Mirror* he said conscripts would be withdrawn 'as soon as possible'. No further conscripts would be sent to Vietnam, but if 'after consultation with the American and Vietnamese governments, or after the reconvening of the Geneva conference, or after a resolution by the United Nations, the Labor Government judges that there should still be Australian troops in Vietnam, it would send regular troops'.[74]

The implication of Whitlam's phrase 'as soon as possible' was that the question of withdrawal of conscripts was negotiable. The statement of 12 May indicated that Australian troops would operate only under the auspices of an international agency, otherwise all troops would be withdrawn after consultation with allies. Whitlam interpreted this to mean that if consultation with allies revealed a continuing necessity for Australian troops, regulars might remain.

Next day, Calwell indicated a more unconditional different line. Referring to all Australian troops he stated: 'I didn't say that after consultation we would withdraw them. We will not be taking part in a dialogue with the Americans as to whether we should or should not withdraw'.[75]

When Whitlam repeated his remarks Calwell directly repudiated him. In doing so he slightly altered his own position. *Conscripts* were to be withdrawn immediately and the rest were to be withdrawn after consultation with allies.[76] Calwell's view appeared to be that consultation was to be on the process of Australian withdrawal not on the principle of it. Whitlam's interpretation encompassed a possible retention of Australia's forces in Vietnam.

Whitlam shortly afterwards charged that Calwell had 'debauched' the debate on Vietnam.[77] By this he meant that the emotional issues Calwell concentrated on detracted from serious discussion of Australia's interests in the conflict and the American role in the region. Whitlam's central concern, however, appeared to be that Party policy gave little room for a Labor government to manoeuvre. He believed that Australia's interests lay in critical support for an American military and economic role in the Southeast Asian region. He was not convinced that the Americans would lose the war; he believed that at least a compromise settlement could be achieved, and worried that insufficient pressure was being placed on the Americans for a negotiated settlement. He did not believe that a Labor government could place that pressure on the Americans if it remained committed to an immediate withdrawal of Australian troops.

Vietnam and Whitlam's leadership

Calwell's defeat in the 1966 election suggested to Whitlam's supporters that their views on foreign policy issues had been thoroughly vindicated. From his replacement of Calwell as Leader in February 1967, Whitlam placed a high priority on securing direction of foreign policy in order to neutralise it as a factor in Australian domestic politics. Since he was largely successful, his means deserve worth brief examination here.

In the first place Caucus appeared prepared to give him considerable latitude on foreign policy. At its first meeting after the 1966 election it elected an Executive which balanced the factions. Whitlam secured as Deputy Leader Lance Barnard, a supporter, although an ally (Willesee) lost the Senate leadership to L K Murphy, and another figure identified with the left, S H Cohen, was elected Senate Deputy.[78] Nevertheless, at a later ballot for the newly amalgamated Foreign Affairs and Defence Committee, Whitlam supporters secured seven of the nine places and the Chairmanship was given to Beazley.[79] Caucus also reversed the prohibition against joining the all-party Parliamentary committee on foreign affairs—a move the left feared might lead to bipartisanship in foreign policy. Caucus further indicated unwillingness to restrict Whitlam by rejecting a motion from Senator J M Wheeldom which read that 'The FPLP Executive be requested to bring back to the next Caucus meeting a recommendation clarifying party policy on the retention of Australian troops in Vietnam'.[80]

As Leader, Whitlam was also able to appoint himself and Barnard respectively as official spokesmen for Foreign Affairs and Defence. As the 'shadow cabinet' system gained acceptance with the mass media, pronouncements of Whitlam and Barnard were accorded more significance than those of other party members like Cairns. With most of the means by which Caucus formulated and articulated foreign policy firmly under Whitlam's control, the left lost interest in the Caucus forum for foreign policy debate. This trend was enhanced by the influx of Whitlam supporters after the 1969 election. My careful reading of Caucus minutes for the period 1969–72 reveals only two relatively minor foreign policy matters placed before Caucus. Left spokesmen were increasingly attracted by extra-parliamentary forums, especially the Vietnam moratorium campaign. While not repudiating his colleagues, Whitlam refused to participate in demonstrations. He preferred to express policy views in Parliament or the more traditional forums of media interviews and party meetings.[81]

To establish 'acceptable' policy Whitlam sought to combine an attitude of support for the American alliance with Evattesque attitudes to international justice, social democracy, and support for national independence. In a pamphlet written for the Victorian Fabian Society, *Beyond Vietnam*, he argued that a correct socialist position was internationalist and identified opposition to the American alliance as isolationist. Within this framework, he argued, lay the possibility for independent Australian initiatives on social, economic and security matters in the Asian region.[82]

The centre of opposition to Whitlam's foreign policy shifted out of Caucus to the extra-parliamentary machine. Here it became entangled with his efforts to increase parliamentary influence in the organisation. The West Australian State Secretary vigorously attacked statements made by Lance Barnard during a visit to Vietnam, where he suggested that the Americans were winning the war and that policy should be reviewed in light of 'current realities'.[83]

F E Chamberlain's language, endorsed by the WA State Executive, was reminiscent of Arthur Calwell: 'Even if we have no feelings whatsoever for the suffering of the Vietnamese people, surely we should spare a thought for the young Australian and American boys who are facing death ... in what has been justly described as an unjust, filthy and unwinnable war ... '[84] Chamberlain also suggested that Barnard had not talked with representatives of Hanoi in either North or South Vietnam.

Whitlam responded that Chamberlain's conduct 'establishes how essential it is that in matters concerning federal Parliament, the ALP should be based on the rank and file and not on state bureaucrats'.[85]

Whitlam had secured reforms of the party structure which ensured the representation of State and federal Parliamentary leaders at Federal Conference and in the case of FPLP leaders, the Executive as well. He also obtained considerable influence on the Executive's Foreign Affairs Committee, being its chairman for most of the period of his leadership. While the committee and conference virtually gave him the foreign policy he wanted, policy on Vietnam was the notable exception. At the 1967 Federal Conference Whitlam finally secured a committee *recommendation* which was sufficiently vague to cover all attitudes to the withdrawal of Australian forces from Vietnam, leaving Whitlam free to pursue his own policy.[86]

But the conference would not give him this latitude. Rather, it carried a resolution moved by N C Batt (Tasmania) which stated that Australia had no treaty obligation to involve itself in Vietnam, and proposed a threefold process to revise Australia's policy: an ALP government should first request its allies to cease bombing North Vietnam; secondly, recognise the NLF as a negotiating party; and thirdly transform operations in Vietnam into holding operations. Should the allies fail to meet these conditions, then a Labor government would 'consider that it had no alternative but to withdraw forces'. A more restrictive amendment moved by Chamberlain which baldly stated, in part, 'that all Australian troops will be withdrawn from Vietnam', was defeated.[87]

Whitlam was embarrassed by the new policy and particularly upset by the implication that, if the United States did not agree with all conditions, Australian troops would be withdrawn.[88] In an interview in early 1968 he stated that troops would be withdrawn only if 'no notice' was taken of Australian proposals. He left the phrase 'no notice' undefined.[89] Barnard was more convinced of the new ALP policy. While he argued for the policy in detail, Whitlam tended either to ignore aspects of it, talking generally about the problems of regional security, or to advocate it through statements of support for such views made by leaders of allied nations.[90]

Despite their differences of emphasis, Whitlam and Barnard agreed that action which would seriously embarrass the US was undesirable. Whitlam's main concern was his belief that America ought to play a continuing and important role in security arrangements in the Southeast Asian region. He did not believe that these arrangements need depend entirely on the United States, only that their success required the 'military, economic and political involvement' of the United States.[91]

The Viet Cong's Tet offensive in early 1968, consequential changes in American policy, and Prime Minister Gorton's decision in March to place a ceiling on the commitment of combat forces, all transformed the debate on Vietnam within the ALP. For Whitlam the offensive had particular importance. Shortly before, he had visited Vietnam and conferred with a number of figures who disagreed with confident American and South Vietnamese pronouncements of imminent political and military successes. By the time his visit ended, he was more convinced than before that allied policy in Vietnam would fail. Further, he began to believe that even the more limited objectives suggested by the ALP might be difficult to achieve.[92]

In the Parliamentary debate which followed the Tet offensive, speakers on the ALP right like Beazley and Barnard stressed their disillusion with misinformation on the conduct of the war objectives. American prestige had become the motivation for continuing the war but this was not longer sufficient rationale. The left considered that events vindicated its stand and also saw that its views were now close to the right. Cairns even praised Whitlam's speech.[93]

All sections perceived that the Vietnam War issue no longer won the government electoral support. The government's foreign policy dilemmas increased when the Nixon doctrine appeared to imply for Australia the type of regional role and association with the United States that the ALP right had long advocated. This difficulty was enhanced when coincidentally both Whitlam and Nixon visited the People's Republic. The timing of the withdrawal of Australian forces, a matter which had long exercised the Party, no longer seemed so significant because *American* troops were gradually withdrawing.

In the 1969 election Whitlam subjected the government's Vietnam policy to unqualified criticism. The government, he said, 'lied and lied and lied just to keep that war going, while thousands have died and died and died, with no other result than that the war has just been kept going'. He stated his intention to visit Washington, immediately, should a Labor government be elected, to make arrangements for the withdrawal of Australian troops.[94]

As a postscript to the debate, it should be noted that Whitlam and Barnard uninhibitedly criticised President Nixon's strategy for withdrawal from Vietnam. The Labor leaders were disturbed by the bombing of Laos and Cambodia and the consequent destabilising of neutralist regimes. Both had hoped that a neutralist Laos and Cambodia and, if possible, a neutralist South Vietnam would emerge from the struggle. Nixon's policy, they believed, precluded that possibility.[95]

Conclusion

An analysis of ALP Vietnam policy does not reveal a party with a strong sense of direction except until the failure of its opponent's policies was evident to the general public. There was general recognition in the party that the Liberal/Country Party policies were inappropriate but no unanimity on the alternatives. It must be doubted, however, that even if a coherent criticism of the government's policy had been developed it would have more than marginally affected the 1966 election result.

At the root of the party's problem was the reorientation in policy which occurred between 1961 and 1965. Differences existed in the government's view of a threatening environment and the ALP leadership's views, and there were also differences on the degree to which the American relationship permitted independent action. Those differences, however, were seen by the leadership as marginal. Furthermore, the ALP was not in a position accurately to calculate what costs might be imposed by the American relationship.

Southeast Asia had formerly been seen as a British sphere of influence and political parties had been accustomed to measuring British capabilities and intentions. The ALP had been careful in its revision of policy in Southeast Asia but the content of American post-war involvement in Southeast Asia was unclear to its American exponents and to their allies.

All sections of ALP looked with favour on the tone of Kennedy and Johnson Administration foreign policy. In the absence of independent Australian information on the situation in South Vietnam, there was a preparedness, including important spokesmen on the ALP left, to extend to Democratic Administrations the benefit of the doubt. The extent to which the ALP considered that American policy would require no more than token support was evident in the uncritical attitude to Johnson's 'rolling thunder' operation only weeks before the commitment of Australian combat forces.

As soon as combat forces were committed the costs appeared unacceptable. At that point, however, the ALP leadership found itself trapped by the logic of its previous position—advocating American-Australian co-operation while refusing it when it was requested. The leadership could argue that there had always been in alliance policies a degree of independent initiative, but this could readily be portrayed by opponents as an exercise in nitpicking.

It was largely the question of the importance attached to the relationship with the United States which divided left and right on the timing of withdrawal of Australian troops. For much of the period Whitlam envisaged no limit, seeing the troops as a type of bargaining counter (along with the American bases) which enabled Australia to influence the direction of American policy.

There were significant differences between Whitlam's position and that of the government. If the government used the troops as a bargaining counter it was to press the Americans to increase their involvement. It was Whitlam's good fortune that the policy he advocated appeared to dovetail with American administration after 1968, while the Liberal/Country Party government dithered.

The Vietnam war coincided with a period in which the ALP's policy-making procedures were under internal challenge. The Federal Conference and Executive were reluctant to impose policy on the Federal Parliamentary Labor Party. The FPLP was given considerable freedom to determine policy between 1964 and 1967. At the same time the FPLP's leader was increasingly criticised and was unable to impose a line on the Party. His difficulties were compounded by his own uncertainty as to the correct policy. He recognised that his right-wing colleagues adopted positions he had supported, whilst those on the left offered support for his leadership and argued a policy on Vietnam which conformed to his intuitive judgements.

Whitlam imposed his authority on the party in most areas of foreign policy but he was compelled to make compromises on Vietnam. It was not a situation in which he felt comfortable. In the circumstances it is perhaps surprising that the public perception of Labor policy on Vietnam was one of unqualified opposition to Australian involvement. It is indeed possible that this perception owed more to the presentations of Labor's opponents than to those of Labor itself.

South Vietnam: GVN Province and Military Regions

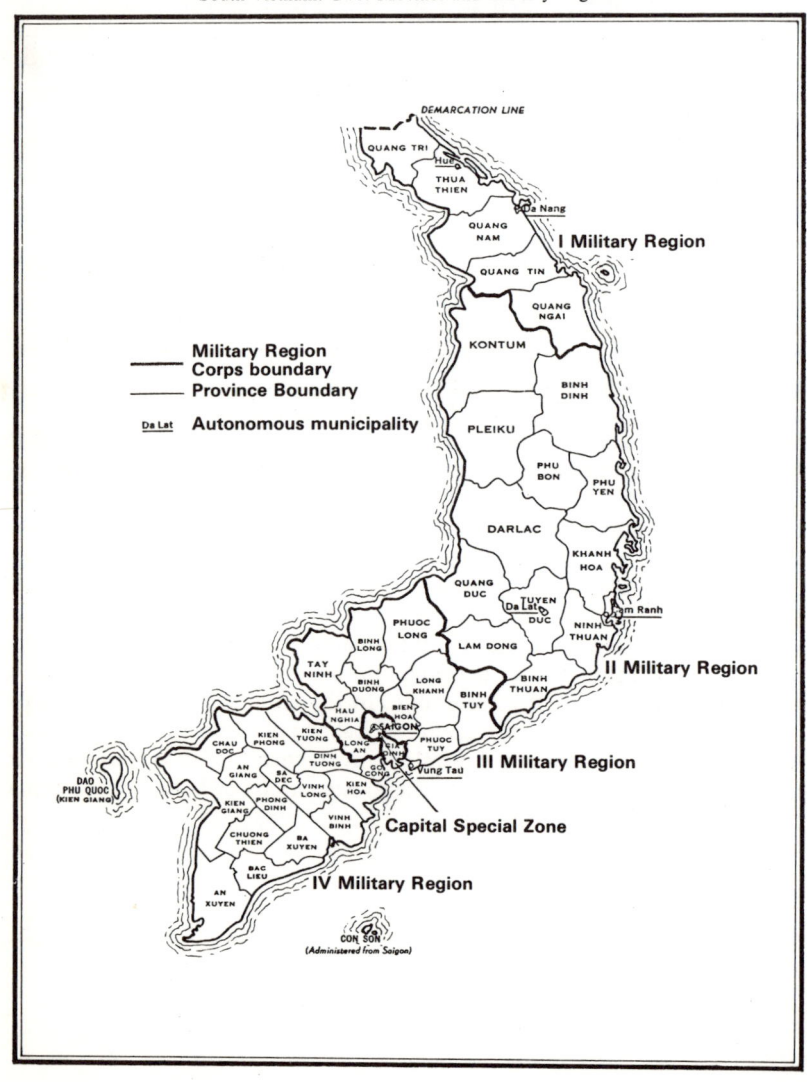

4 Australia's war in Vietnam 1962-1972

FRANK FROST*

The Australian government's approach to the Vietnam conflict, and its implications for regional security and Australia's foreign policy interests, produced the most significant commitment of Australian military forces overseas since World War II. The Australian force at its peak strength amounted to 8300 men and was two-thirds larger than that committed to the Korean War. A total of 46,852 Australian military personnel served in Vietnam, including 17,424 national servicemen, and Australian casualties in the conflict totalled 494 killed and 2398 wounded.[1] The direct financial cost to Australia was at least $A218.4 million (according to official estimates) and possibly as much as $A500 million.[2]

Though this commitment was obviously substantial by Australian standards, the military forces and their activities were seldom the major focus of attention in the Australian debate on the war. In the overall context of the war, the Australian involvement was a small part of a total 'allied' force of over one million. The Australian force itself could thus at no stage be seen as having decisive military importance in the war. During the period of the involvement, most public discussion in Australia of the government's policies in relation to Vietnam accordingly focussed on the broad issues of the nature of the conflict in southern Vietnam, on the validity of US policy towards the conflict, on the importance and desirability of the US alliance for Australia, and on the significance of the military commitment in strengthening that alliance, rather than on the specific policies and problems of the Australian military force itself.[3] Since the end of the military involvement, much attention has been focussed on the issue of the effects on Australian servicemen of chemicals used in defoliation programs,[4] but there has been little discussion of the policies and experience of the military forces in Vietnam. Australia's involvement in Vietnam, however, was a major undertaking for the Australian military which revealed both inadequacies in the Australian government's understanding of

---

* The views expressed in this chapter are those of the author, and are not to be attributed to the Department of the Parliamentary Library.

the Vietnam conflict and the problems which could arise for a small Australian allied force in a situation of revolutionary war in Southeast Asia.

A wide variety of Australian units from all three services operated in Vietnam, including an Army training team, Naval destroyers and a diving team, and Air Force transport, helicopter and bomber units. The centrepiece of the Australian commitment, however, was the Australian Task Force which was based in Phuoc Tuy Province for five and a half years from May 1966 to November 1971. It was the Task Force which confronted most sharply the dilemmas resulting from the decision of the Australian government to support the US involvement in the revolutionary war in southern Vietnam. To provide an assessment of the Task Force's experiences, this chapter will discuss the origins of the commitment of the Task Force, the physical and political environment it encountered in Phuoc Tuy, the nature of the role it was assigned by the Australian government and the extensive problems it experienced in operating as an ally of both the US and the government of the Republic of Vietnam.

Origins of the military involvement 1962-65

The Australian military commitment to Vietnam originated from the desire of the Australian government to support and encourage US involvement in Vietnam. In the words of an official assessment of the military commitment issued in 1975,

> The provision of military aid by Australia was decided upon for political reasons and was in support of the fundamental aim of Australian policy towards South Vietnam, which was to ensure the long-term defence interests of Australia. These were seen in terms of the ANZUS and SEATO Treaties and the theory of forward defence against the victory of communism in Southeast Asia, an area seen as vital to Australia's future. This was a policy developed in Australia independently of any outside pressure. The cornerstone of this policy was seen as a compelling necessity to commit the power of the United States to the Asian area and then to commit her to a tactical guarantee of active support to Australia through the ANZUS and SEATO Treaties.[5]

While Australian governments in the early 1960s were anxious about the developing war in South Vietnam, they were also concerned by developments elsewhere in the region (notably Indonesia's 'confrontation' of Malaysia). Moreover, a series of very low defence budgets in the 1950s meant that Australia by the early 1960s had a very small Army (of only four battalions) and little capacity to respond to any perceived security threat. Australia's initial military commitment to the Vietnam conflict was thus very minor. At a meeting between Department of External Affairs and armed services officials in November 1961 which considered possible involvement, 'the Services were unwilling, for manpower reasons, to make more than a token commitment to the Republic of Vietnam'.[6]

On 24 May 1962, the first Australian military commitment was announced and 30 instructors left for Vietnam in July. This commitment marked the advent of the Australian Army Training Team, Vietnam (AATTV). Described in 1967 by (then) Minister for the Army, Malcolm Fraser, as 'the unsung heroes of the Vietnam war'[7], the AATTV, which had grown to 100 men by 1965, trained regular units of the Republic of Vietnam (RVN) Army, Special Forces, covert forces designed to fight communist cadres, and RVN local force troops.[8] The Team was composed of experienced veterans of previous Australian campaigns (including the Malayan 'emergency' and 'confrontation' in Borneo) who were highly regarded for their tactical military skills: a 1971 news report described them as 'certainly responsible for Australia's high military reputation in Vietnam'.[9] A number of Team members later served in Phuoc Tuy as advisers, but as will be pointed out, their ability to assist and train troops who were essentially under-motivated was inevitably limited.

As the situation in South Vietnam deteriorated in 1963 and 1964, official Australian concern that the US should maintain and expand its involvement mounted. In January 1965 the Australian Ambassador in Washington was informed that Australia would give its full diplomatic support if the US expanded its war effort by launching airstrikes against the infiltration system from northern Vietnam. On 29 April 1965, after further consultation with the US and a hastily arranged formal request from the RVN, Prime Minister Menzies announced that Australia would despatch a battalion of troops to Vietnam.[10]

The First Battalion, Royal Australian Regiment (IRAR), served for a year from May 1965 with the US Army's 173rd Air Cavalry Division. The US unit was assigned to protect the large air base at Bien Hoa (northeast of Saigon) and to operate against NLF forces in the nearby and long-established base area 'War Zone D'. The experience of operating as a part of a US unit seems to have produced considerable problems for the Australian troops and concern among Australian officials. Among the troops of IRAR there was dissatisfaction at US tactics which were felt to involve excessive aerial resupply and a willingness to sustain higher casualties than were acceptable to the Australian force.[11] Official concern was reflected in a statement by the Secretary of the Department of the Army, Bruce White, in a speech in Canberra in November 1966. Mr White was reported to have said that the Americans (with whom IRAR operated) 'took risks one could not afford to take'[12] and in a subsequent official statement he said that ' ... command, communication and logistics proved difficult ... ' and that ' ... because of this we did welcome the opportunity to take over a sector such as Phuoc Tuy Province and operate within it under our own direct field commander'.[13]

The Australian Task Force and Phuoc Tuy Province

The expansion of the army through conscription (introduced in 1964) enabled the government to increase the Australian commitment and field a somewhat more independent military force. In March 1966, the government announced an increase in the Vietnam force to 4500 men, who would, for the first time, include national servicemen. It was decided to deploy the augmented Australian force into an operational area where the army would have more tactical independence and would constitute a more distinctly Australian 'presence' in Vietnam. An Australian Army group led by the Chief of the General Staff, Lt-Gen Wilton, decided that Phuoc Tuy Province provided the most favourable location. The province, southeast of Saigon and to the north of the major port of Vung Tau, was a relatively significant area to the RVN because it contained a major road (Route 15) between the capital and the port. By 1966 most of the province was out of RVN control. The location of the province close to Vung Tau, it was felt, would enable an Australian force to establish its own logistic system and the absence from the province of any major US or RVN units would enable the Australian force to pursue its own operational styles. A further advantage of the province was that the close proximity of Vung Tau would enable the Australian force to withdraw using its own resources if a deteriorating military situation in South Vietnam necessitated this.[14]

With its location determined, the Australian units (organised as the First Australian Task Force (IATF) comprising two infantry battalions, with artillery and other support units) entered the province in May-June 1966 and established a base in the centre of the Province at Nui Dat. The province proved a most difficult environment for the Australian force for two major reasons: geographically it was very well suited to the support of sustained guerilla warfare and politically it was the scene of a well established revolutionary force with extensive local links and a 20 year experience of guerilla fighting.

As an Australian observer pointed out in 1970, Phuoc Tuy Province provided 'an almost classic environment' for guerilla warfare.

> It has a rich farm area dotted with villages and hamlets, a long coastline, a complex delta area of mangrove swamps and numerous canals and channels, isolated ranges of very rugged mountains and a large area of virtually uninhabited jungle containing all the most loathsome combinations of thorny bamboos, poisonous snakes, insects, malaria, dense underbrush, swamps and rugged ground conditions that the most dedicated guerilla warfare expert could ask for. It is also ... within less than forty miles of the national capital and within easy reach of the Parrot's Beak feature which juts out from Cambodia towards Saigon.[15]

The major villages were concentrated in the south of the province. The peoples' major occupation was rice growing, but there was also a French-owned rubber plantation to the north of the area selected as the Task Force base, and several fishing villages on the coast. Most of the population were long-term residents who were descendants of earlier Vietnamese settlers in the seventeenth and eighteenth centuries, but there were two large and prosperous villages settled by Catholics from northern Vietnam who migrated south in 1955. As well as the large mangrove swamps in the southwest (the *Rung Sat*—'Jungle of Death'), there were three groups of hills situated to the north, the northwest and the south which were close to the populated areas and which provided excellent bases for guerillas. All three groups of hills had caves which could be used as camps and shelters, and they were highly resistant to either ground or air attack.[16] By 1966, the National Front for the Liberation of South Vietnam (NLF) had made good use of this favourable environment.

The Australian government's interpretation of the origins of the NLF and of the Second Indo-China War assumed that the conflict derived from an attempt by the Democratic Republic of Vietnam (DRV) to conquer the south through an externally-inspired and directed campaign of terrorism and guerilla warfare. The NLF was seen as a creation of the DRV which obtained compliance through terrorist coercion of the southern population.[17] The war was, in the words of External Affairs Minister Hasluck on 23 March 1965, a ' ... new form of international aggression'.[18] The reality in Phuoc Tuy, as in much of southern Vietnam, was very different. By the mid 1960s, Phuoc Tuy had a twenty-year tradition of communist-led guerilla activity which had originated in the period of resistance to the French presence from 1947 to 1954.

Phuoc Tuy provided strong resistance to the incoming French colonial forces from as early as 1859 and while opposition to the French presence subsided until the early 1940s (as it did generally in southern Vietnam), the area became a strong centre of opposition during the First Indochina War. The limited historical evidence available specifically on Phuoc Tuy during the late 1940s and early 1950s indicates that while the French were able to maintain a presence in the province capital of Baria, the Viet Minh resistance was able to prevent all but large French forces from moving east of Long Dien from 1947. As well as gaining strong support among the population, the Viet Minh forces established several major bases in the groups of hills suitable for guerilla bases. The 'Hat Dich' base area stretched from the Province's northern border down to Route 15, while the 'Minh Dam Secret Zone' encompassed the Long Hai hills and the area of Long Dien and Dat Do.[19] Control of these base areas meant that the Viet Minh dominated almost the entire province, with the exception of Baria. It was notable that 20 years later, villagers in Phuoc Tuy recalled with pride their role in the anti-French war in discussions with members of the Australian Task Force.[20] It was also notable that when the NLF re-established bases in the same areas that had been used in the anti-French war, the Viet Minh names for the bases continued to be used.

Phuoc Tuy, along with the rest of southern Vietnam, experienced only a few years of peace after 1954 before mass guerilla warfare again emerged. When widespread armed opposition to the Diem regime developed in 1959, the NLF forces rapidly gained strength in the Province. As Dr Robert O'Neill has written, the NLF forces began the process of political organising in the Province in 1959–60, 'holding meetings, recruiting members for the Party, propagandising against the Diem regime and organising their own administrative system for the Province'.[21] By early 1966, the NLF had available forces of up to 5000 troops for operation in the Phuoc Tuy area, including a 'main force' unit (the Fifth Division, comprising 274 and 275 Regiments), a locally recruited and based provincial battalion called D445 and hundreds of village guerillas. Route 15 was cut and the RVN controlled only the province capital and a few outposts.[22]

The Australian Task Force faced a formidable political and military force when it arrived in Phuoc Tuy in mid-1966. At the village level, the NLF cadres worked to mobilise political support among the population and to provide intelligence information, manpower and supplies for the NLF armed units. Above the villages the NLF had district and provincial organisations which coordinated village activities and organised NLF political and military activity in the areas they covered.

The district and provincial organisations based themselves in the hills adjacent to the villages. Each level of the organisation maintained armed forces under strict Communist Party control to promote and protect NLF political interests. Village organisations had local guerilla groups, the districts had forces of company size while the provincial structure organised local battalions.[23]

The most notable such local unit in Phuoc Tuy was the 'D445 Provincial Mobile Battalion', the first armed unit to be formed by the NLF in the province in the early 1960s. D445 was locally recruited and most of its members came from the area of Dat Do in the east of the province. It had a number of bases in the province, strong links with the local population particularly in Dat Do, and it proved particularly adept at maintaining its existence and organisation in the face of much Task Force pressure between 1966 and 1971. Some of the Australian battalions' unit historians readily acknowledged D445's strength. The 6RAR's history of its tour of duty in 1969–70 noted that 'D445 battalion could well be considered 'Phuoc Tuy's own' as it was raised, reinforced and succoured by local inhabitants of the Province ... and had intimate knowledge of the ground over which it operated'.[24] Another battalion history stated that D445 was 'most dangerous force in the Province' and had 'proved itself to be highly trained, highly motivated and aggressive'.[25] In addition to and above these local force units, the NLF could call on larger, more extensively equipped 'main force' regiments containing both southern and northern personnel to support the provincial NLF structure.

The force which controlled most of Phuoc Tuy in mid-1966 was thus a sophisticated political-military organisation with extensive local political structures and several levels of armed forces. The NLF in Phuoc Tuy was clearly part of a national movement which, as a number of writers have shown, was at all times led and directed from the DRV.[26] The NLF in Phuoc Tuy, however, had also clearly been able to attract thousands of recruits and both its political and military organisation had strong local links with much of the population and were heirs to a popular tradition of anti-colonial resistance against the French—an experience which would have been fresh in the minds of most adults in the province in the mid-1960s.

The Task Force operational role

Given the political and military strength of the NLF in Phuoc Tuy in 1966, the Task Force was obviously entering a difficult and dangerous environment. Its problems were compounded by the fact that the Australian government appears to have assigned the Task Force to the Phuoc Tuy area without giving sufficient consideration to the exact operational role which it would fulfil and with insufficient attention to the question of how close and effective cooperation would be achieved with its allies, particularly the RVN authorities.

The Task Force was placed under the direction of the Commander, Australian Force Vietnam (COMAFV, based in Saigon) and under the 'operational control' of a US unit (II Field Force Vietnam.) The Task Force had to coordinate closely with its American allies because it depended on them for much military support, including transport by heavy-lift helicopters. The Task Force also had to cooperate with the RVN Provincial civilian and military administration which controlled the province's 'local force' troops. These forces were locally recruited and based soldiers assigned to combat the NLF by operating in and near the villages: they were organised as Popular Force (PF) platoons and Regional Force (RF) companies. The Task Force was assigned to assist its US and RVN allies by weakening NLF influence in the province. In Phuoc Tuy the Task Force faced both the NLF's local and main force military units and the political structure supporting them in the villages. It has been argued, however, that its exact role in countering these forces was never adequately defined.

In the recent article on the Vietnam commitment, an army research officer (Major Ian G McNeill) commented that Task Force commanders found ' ... a certain ambiguity in the role of the force'.[27] One former Task Force commander interviewed by this writer argued that the Australian government's failure to develop a detailed concept for a specific function for the Task Force was indeed a major problem.[28] He stated that it had been a major problem for the army that 'we weren't given a task, an aim ... its the first war we've gone into without a political aim that's expressed as an aim'. In considering the tasks which the Task Force might have been specifically directed by the government to perform, he argued that there was a conflict between the possible aim of fighting the NLF and Peoples Army of Vietnam (PAVN) main force units[29] and the aim of contributing more directly to the security of Phuoc Tuy. As he saw the question of the potential roles of the Task Force, the government had three choices in 1965: to provide military forces to participate in battles against main force units; to provide military forces to participate in 'pacification' and 'counter-guerilla' operations (by which he meant operations to inhibit the influence of the NLF in the villages, and operations against the NLF's local guerila units); or to provide forces to do both. If the force was to participate only in operations against main force units, it would have had only slight contact with the RVN and the Vietnamese population, and there would have been no need for the elaborate facilities necessary for the achievement of close coordination with the RVN. Such a force, he felt, would have required more fire support and mobility (for example tracked vehicles and helicopters) than the Task Force in fact had, and a base in the middle of the province, like Nui Dat, would not have been needed because the Task Force was located at Nui Dat to enable it to contribute to the security of the populated areas of Phuoc Tuy.

If, on the other hand, the aim of the force had been to participate in 'pacification' and 'counter-guerilla' operations, then the ties between the civilian administration and the Australian force should have been as close as possible. Such a force, he argued, would have needed a complete advisory system similar to that provided in Phuoc Tuy by the US CORDS organisation.[30] Australian civilian experts would have been needed to advise the RVN in fields such as agriculture, economics, propaganda and police and this would have been expensive. To combine the requirements of both tasks would have required a force much larger than the Task Force, which would have been capable of splitting into two groups to perform each of the tasks. He regarded the fact that the government had apparently not carefully considered these options and not committed the resources to enable one of them to be carried out effectively as creating serious dilemmas for the force.

The Task Force between 1966 and 1971 was in fact given the responsibility of both operating against main force NLF and PAVN units and of attempting to counter the influence of the NLF at the village level. In its anti-main force role, it experienced problems of shortages of personnel, equipment and supplies particularly in the period before the arrival of the third battalion in late 1967.[31] In its 'pacification' role in Phuoc Tuy, the Task Force faced the problem that at no point was it given full responsibility for the security of the populated areas of the province. The populated areas where naturally primarily the responsibility of the RVN provincial administration. However, the responsibility for advising and assisting the local administration in civil and military matters rested not with the

Australian Task Force, but with the US CORDS organisation. The result of this arrangement was that while the Task Force did maintain liaison with the RVN administration, day to day contacts and the potential to develop intimate knowledge of political and administrative problems in Phuoc Tuy was the province of US advisers.

The fact that the Australian government did not attempt to assume the full advisory role in Phuoc Tuy is one of the most controversial aspects of the Australian presence. Denis Warner wrote in 1971 that the US government in fact offered the full advisory role but that 'Canberra politely refused'. He continued:

> Acceptance of the offer would have made Phuoc Tuy Province an area of genuine Australian responsibility. An Australian would have taken over as chief province adviser and other Australians would have moved into the district headquarters and in other provincial roles to ensure maximum co-ordination of the Australian-Vietnamese effort at all levels ... (C)o-ordination between the province officials and the Australian Task Force would inevitably be much closer if Australians and not Americans were sitting in all the key advisory posts.[32]

There are likely to have been considerable problems in an Australian assumption of the advisory function. The Australian officials in Phuoc Tuy would have had to coordinate with the US organisation which ran the advisory programs in the RVN overall, and it would probably have been difficult for such an Australian group to pursue policies very different to those being advanced by the US authorities. An Australian assumption of the advisory role, however, would have increased the amount of information available to the Task Force about the specific character and problems of the province. While it could not have solved all the problems which the Australian Army faced in its relations with the RVN authorities, it might have helped avoid costly mistakes based on inadequate information on local conditions—of which the laying of an extensive minefield was the most serious example.

The Task Force: political and military problems

Against this background of an imprecisely defined role, the Task Force operated for five and a half years until late 1971. While most of its activity was directed towards Phuoc Tuy, its operations varied according to the level and type of NLF/PAVN activity in Phuoc Tuy and in the RVN generally, and according to the overall strategies being pursued by the US and the RVN. The Task Force's operations can be seen as falling into three major time periods: May 1966—December 1967; January 1968—May 1969; May 1969—November 1971. In the first time period, the under-equipped two battalion Task Force operated solely within Phuoc Tuy. It fought a number of major engagements with NLF/PAVN main force units (including the 'battle of Long Tan' when an Australian company fought an NLF regiment near Nui Dat in August 1966) and also attempted to combat the NLF's political structure through a series of 'cordon and search' operations in the villages. In the second phase, which was dominated by the NLF's Tet offensive (February 1968) and its aftermath, the force (now expanded to three battalions) frequently operated outside Phuoc Tuy in battles against NLF/PAVN main force units. There was correspondingly less emphasis on Phuoc Tuy. In the final phase of Task Force involvement, attention was again focussed by the Australian force on the province. The NLF/PAVN forces were now considerably weaker in the aftermath of the massive losses sustained in the year of the Tet offensive and the RVN's security position seemed correspondingly somewhat stronger. The Task Force directed much of its efforts against the NLF village forces and for the first time made a major effort to train and assist the RVN's locally recruited and based forces. The Task Force also expanded its program of 'Civic Action' which provided direct assistance to the local people and the province administration in fields including construction, health and education.

While the Australian force conducted many tactically proficient operations in these years, its presence in Phuoc Tuy was marked by continuing major problems in trying to cooperate with and assist the RVN and in attempting to weaken the NLF in the province. These problems included a lack of adequate knowledge about the Phuoc Tuy environment (especially in the first phase of operations), the persistent weakness and unwillingness to fight of the Task Force's RVN allied forces, and the continued ability of the NLF to maintain both its village level political networks and its guerilla bases. The significance of these problems can be illustrated by examining the issues of the Dat Do—Phuoc Hai minefield constructed by the Task Force, the NLF bases in the Long Hai hills, and the NLF's continued strength in villages such as Hoa Long and Dat Do.

Much of the Task Force's operational activity in Phuoc Tuy was directed towards attempts to separate the local NLF guerila units and political cadres from their popular bases in the villages. The most important single attempt at such operations in the first phase of Task Force involvement was the laying of a twelve-mile long minefield in early 1967 from the village of Dat Do in central Phuoc Tuy to the coast at Phuoc Hai. As Dr Robert O'Neill has explained in his account of 5 RAR's operations in 1966 and 1967, the minefield was designed to prevent NLF traffic between the eastern unpopulated areas of the province and the central and southern villages.

> A barrier fence and minefield would present a formidable obstacle, provided that it was patrolled daily to check for breaches or attempted breaches. The patrolling commitment required for the maintenance of the fence and minefield would be far less than the activity needed to close the area off entirely by a moving fence of men ... [33]

The security of the minefield clearly depended on adequate patrolling. According to a statement in Parliament by the Minister for the Army (Mr Peacock) in August 1969, it was envisaged at the time of the laying of the minefield that it would be protected by a company of Australian troops, by an RVN battalion and by a number of companies and platoons of RVN local force troops. The minister claimed that the protective measures were carried out satisfactorily, but he also stated that,

> It must be recognised however that no system of protection of a minefield could guarantee complete day and night protection for an extensive minefield in varied terrain against a fanatical enemy prepared to accept the risks involved in removing mines. Small VC minelifting parties did in fact gain access to the minefield but information from enemy sources indicates that the VC sustained at least thirty fatal casualties in removing mines from the Dat Do minefield.[34]

The laying of a minefield to which the NLF were able to gain access proved a costly error for the Task Force because many mines were removed intact and subsequently used to protect local NLF bases in the Long Hai hills and in offensive operations against Australian patrols in the area.[35] It ultimately became necessary for the army to remove the entire minefield, but this process was not completed until May 1970.[36] It seems clear that it was an error for the Task Force to have relied on the inefficient local RVN forces to carry out an extensive protective role. It seems likely that had the Force had more extensive contacts with and knowledge of the local RVN administration in 1966-67, it would not have pursued a plan that relied on cooperation from local RVN forces which was unlikely to be provided.

With the failure of the minefield to block NLF movement across the province, the NLF was able to continue to make use of its valuable bases in the Long Hai hills on the southern coast of Phuoc Tuy. The Long Hais are a good example of the favourable geographic environment which Phuoc Tuy provided for guerilla warfare. They served as a base area for the Viet Minh in the 1940s and early 1950s and for the NLF throughout the period of the Australian presence. The hills were attacked at least three times by the Task Force (in early 1967, early 1968 and early 1970) and base areas were dislocated and equipment was destroyed or captured on each occasion.[37] The army, however, did not have the capacity to occupy the hills or continually cordon them off, and so these operations were followed inevitably by a return of the former occupants.

While continued access to base areas in the hills was important to the NLF, it would have been meaningless unless continued support could be obtained from the populated areas. In the third phase of Task Force involvement from mid-1969, many operations were directed at the NLF's access to its popular bases. In this period Task Force units launched programs of ambushes around many villages in the province, continued to operate against the local force NLF units and launched liaison and training programs (using a number of AATTV members) to attempt to assist the RVN local force platoons and companies which theoretically were to prevent NLF access to villages. With its tactical skills and superior material support, the Army killed a large number of NLF members and supporters in ambushes; in one such operation alone, in August 1970, nineteen members of an NLF local force company were killed and five captured while on a resupply mission to Hoa Long, a village adjacent to the Australian base at Nui Dat.[38] The emphasis of army operations on the village-based NLF forces in Phuoc Tuy from 1969, however, focussed increased attention of the problems of cooperating with the local RVN administration and with the local RVN force troops.

In his account of the Australian military involvement, Major Ian McNeill commented on the problems experienced in attempting coordination with the RVN administration.

> When IATF operations were well clear of populated areas, commanders found it was possible to scrape by with a fairly low level of cooperation, and the Sector (the military arm of the Province) and IATF could plan their operations more or less independently. With the switch to pacification support and the upgrading of the Regional and Popular Forces a much greater IATF presence became necessary in and near the populated areas, and with it, a greater need for cooperation and control. What commanders felt was necessary was the formation of an Area War Executive Committee (AWEC) along the lines of the Malayan situation. This was found not to be possible in Phuoc Tuy. As the Vietnamese controlled all civil and military functions in the Province other than IATF, any initiative towards an AWEC would have had to come from them. The Province Chief held official authority, but this was undermined by dissent, cross-currents of loyalties, distrust and competing ambitions in the Vietnamese camp. Even had an AWEC been formed, it would have been unlikely to work. Alternative measures were therefore instituted ... All for varying reasons were only of limited success. One major result of this absence of a central coordinating authority was that while the Task Force was carrying out its operations in depth, the enemy was consolidating in the population.[39]

In its final phase of involvement the army was able to establish effective liaison with many RVN local force units by introducing Mobile Advisory Training teams from April 1970. The team members provided training to the Vietnamese soldiers and encouraged them to patrol more actively. Combined operations were also mounted between Task Force elements and local force units. The local Vietnamese forces however, did not share the Australian enthusiasm for pursuing the war against the NLF in the province. McNeill commented that,

> There were indeed many attempts to upgrade the ARVN and Regional

Forces by retraining schemes and the leavening of Territorial units with Australian troops ... It was found however, that such measures produced no lasting improvements or were only effective while Australians remained in the units. The basic reason appeared to be a lack of motivation by the personnel of Territorial Force units.[40]

He added, in reference to the forces' lack of motivation:

> The reason for this may be more easily understood when it is realised that the Territorial Forces had been under the same Viet Cong pressures as the remainder of the population in Phuoc Tuy before the Task Force arrived, had witnessed and been victims of the same government ineptitude, and very often came from divided families where brothers and sisters may be on opposite sides (but nevertheless met amicably under the family roof). The Territorial forces seemed to have some accommodation with the Vietcong.[41]

With a weak and divided administration it is hardly surprising that there was little organised challenge to the political structure of the NLF. Cadres were certainly at risk from military operations of the Task Force and it is likely that many were killed or injured particularly in the last two years of the force's presence. However, there was little coordinated activity by the variety of RVN intelligence-gathering agencies involved and the US advisory organisation was unable to materially affect this situation. The province chief confirmed in an interview in March 1972 (after the Task Force had departed) that while the NLF local force units were relatively weak, its cadres were still a strong force in the villages.[42] A year earlier, a 'senior Task Force officer' was reported to have made a similar assessment to the *Australian*, when he said that

> all the villages have a (Vietcong) chapter and party organisation. The strongest element in the province has always been, and still is, the Vietcong infrastructure which is very difficult to come to grips with.[43]

The Task Force withdrew from Phuoc Tuy in late 1971 in accordance with the prevailing US policy of 'phased withdrawal' of forces from Vietnam. By this time, the aftermath of six years of US operations and the losses sustained by the southern revolutionary forces of the NLF had left it much weaker in southern Vietnam than it had been in the mid-1960s and much more dependent on military forces from the DRV.[44] These developments were reflected in the situation in Phuoc Tuy: both the NLF local forces and the NLF/PAVN main forces were considerably weaker and the scale of the conflict had dropped markedly from that of the mid-sixties. It was equally clear, however, that the NLF continued to maintain the capacity to operate in Phuoc Tuy from most of its traditional base areas, that it continued to be able to draw on support from popular bases and that its political structure, while weakened, was still operational.[45] The Task Force's period in Phuoc Tuy had not seen the development of policies of effective cooperation between Australian and RVN forces which were likely to have any decisive impact.

By 1972, the Australian involvement had reverted to the type of force first committed: a small military advisory group remained to provide training assistance, until it was withdrawn by the incoming Labor government in December 1972. McNeill noted that

> When the Task Force withdrew, the Training Team remained in Phuoc Tuy. Its members observed the gradual return of Viet Cong influence, and the erosion of Government control. This process was continuing when the Training Team too, departed from Vietnam.[46]

The experience of the Australian military forces in Vietnam highlighted the problems inherent in a limited Australian involvement in a revolutionary war as a junior ally of a major power and of a Southeast Asian regime.

The Australian government sent forces to Vietnam primarily to extend diplomatic and political support to the US and to the RVN. The forces were expected to make a useful military contribution because of their tactical skill, training and experience in counter-guerilla operations in Southeast Asia, but they could not in themselves be regarded as being of decisive military importance in the conflict overall. When the government despatched combat troops to Vietnam they initially operated directly under a US unit, but this proved unsatisfactory. It was then decided to deploy a larger force to a particular province, which could operate more independently as a more distinctively Australian commitment to the conflict. The government, however, does not appear to have considered just how extensively the military forces in Phuoc Tuy should have become involved in operations at the local level in association with the RVN. The Task Force did spend much of its time in local operations in the province and this necessarily brought it into the position of having to try to cooperate closely with the local RVN administration. The Task Force, however, was not adequately equipped for this role and it did not have the full operational responsibility for advising and assisting the RVN administration in the military and political struggle in Phuoc Tuy.

In Phuoc Tuy itself, the Task Force was committed against a well established and organised political and military organisation with extensive local links and a very favourable geographic environment in which to operate. The RVN administration, by contrast, was ineffective and internally uncoordinated and many of its local forces clearly did not support fully the national government which the provincial administration represented. In this situation the Task Force operated against local NLF units, political activists and supporters in a variety of ways, but while it was carrying out this operational role, the strongly entrenched NLF was still able to both mobilise support for its struggle in the villages and continue to maintain (albeit with great difficulty) its armed forces and their traditional base areas. Task Force attempts to cooperate closely with the local administration revealed acute problems of both disorganisation and lack of commitment, especially among the locally recruited RVN soldiers who had the responsibility of 'securing' the villages. In this situation, the Task Force's tactical proficiency and experience in jungle warfare could not prevent its involvement in the conflict in Phuoc Tuy from being ultimately futile.

Given the acute problems faced by Australian forces in Phuoc Tuy it is doubtful if a more extensive advisory role *vis-a-vis* the RVN would have affected greatly the outcome of the involvement. It is possible, however, that much closer and better organised contacts between the Task Force and the RVN administration might have given the army and the Australian government a better opportunity to closely study the nature of the conflict and to gain accurate assessments of the exact capacities and problems of the local government organisation. Such contacts might at least have enabled the error of the Dat Do-Phuoc Hai minefield to be avoided. They would undoubtedly have also brought into sharp focus the political premises on which the whole involvement was based.

5 Australian soldiers in Vietnam
Product and performance
JANE ROSS

The size and composition of the force

The initial commitment of Australian soldiers to Vietnam (nominally in a non-combat role) was the 30 man Australian Army Training Team Vietnam (AATTV) in mid-1962. The first intentionally combat troops came with the arrival in 1965 of IRAR, a wholly regular battalion of 778 men attached to the US 173rd Airborne Brigade at Bien Hoa. It was soon joined by other units such as artillery, engineers, air reconnaisance, etc., bringing the total Australian commitment to 1477 in September 1965. At this early stage, even more so than later, AFV (Australian Forces Vietnam) was able to take advantage of extensive US logistic support, and this accounts for the very high fighter:support ratio in the Australian component.

Taking the Bien Hoa Battalion Group (1096) as a proportion of the total force (1477), 74.2 per cent were in a combat role, and at least a further 100 (the AATTV) were not engaged in a support role. This figure can be compared to the US Army in 1969, where 26 per cent of enlisted men were described as 'ground combat' (and this figure was declining)[1], while in the Australian Army in 1970 some 24 per cent were infantry, 6.2 per cent artillery, 3.4 per cent armoured corps and 9.5 per cent engineers—a total of 43.1 per cent fighting arms.[2] The AFV was subsequently increased, both in the army component and by the addition of navy and airforce units. The Battalion Group at Bien Hoa became a Task Force centred on two and later three battalions located at Nui Dat, with the headquarters of AFV remaining in Saigon and the support group Australian Logistic Support Group (or lALSG) at the popular beach resort of Vung Tau. At its largest from 1968 until withdrawals commenced in 1971, there were some 8300 Australians in the AFV. The fighting component of the army commitment still remained high. The battalions plus the SAS (Special Air Service) Squadron made up 49 per cent of the Task Force, and 36 per cent of the whole AFV, in June 1968. The strengths were located as follows:[3]

IATF (Nui Dat)		HQAFV (Saigon)		1 ALSG (Vung Tau)	
4808	72%	455	6.8%	1420	21.2%

Total 6683 army component AFV.

Source: *1971 CGS Exercise*. See Vol. 2 'Exercise Papers'

The addition of artillery, engineer and armoured corps units brought the total fighting arms proportion to 3647 : 6683 or 55 per cent.

National Service

Despite denials of its intentions, the Liberal Country Party government introduced a selective national service (NS) scheme in 1965 which seemed obviously designed to boost army strengths during and because of the Vietnam commitment. The First NS intake was in mid-1965; the first 'nasho' entered a regular army unit in November 1965; the first 'nasho' casualty in Vietnam occurred in May 1966 shortly after the arrival there of the first units containing NS men.

It is interesting to compare the cost of the National Service scheme ('the amounts which would have been saved by the army had national service not been introduced') with the cost of Australian involvement in Vietnam ('the excess over normal costs in Australia for each of the three services').[4]

Table 5.1 Cost of NS scheme and Australian involvement in Vietnam

Year to 30th June	Cost of NS Scheme $m	Cost of Australian involvement in VN $m
1965	3.278	1.112
1966	31.175	3.876
1967	60.922	28.994
1968	79.665	42.225
1969	82.845	43.652
1970	90.595	43.113

Note: These figures are from the Defence Department.

While part of the cost went into capital improvements, the extraordinarily high cost of the scheme compared to the cost of maintaining the AFV makes one wonder at its logic. Although conscripts provided a substantial boost to the size of the army and its fighting component, they imposed a strain on training facilities and personnel.

There were four NS intakes of 20 year olds per year, each of approximately 2150, giving an annual intake of 8500. Length of service was only two years (in the later years reduced to 18 months), so that at any one time there would have been over 15,000 conscripts in the army—a very significant proportion of the total strength. A high proportion, around 44 per cent of those 'balloted in', failed to meet the physical, educational and psychological standards of the army.

Table 5.2 Strength of army 1966-71

Strengths—army as at 30 June	Permanent	NS	Total	% NS
1966	24 583	8 119	32 702	24.8
1967	25 721	15 743	41 464	38.0
1968	27 152	15 792	42 944	36.8
1969	28 044	16 007	44 051	36.3
1970	28 325	16 208	44 533	36.4
1971	28 107	15 662	43 769	35.8

Source: *Army Manning Review (AMR)*, 1966-72.

However, the availability of conscripts for effective service was not as high as these figures indicate, since they were involved in training for a significant proportion of their 24 months service.[5]

The NS recruit spent ten weeks learning drill, basic fieldcraft and the army way of doing things at one of three recruit training battalions (RTBs) at Kapooka NSW, Singleton NSW or Puckapunyal, Victoria. He was then allocated to a corps, received a further 2-3 months training and was posted to an operational unit. Those selected for officer training were sent from the RTB to do six months at OTU (Officer Training School) Scheyville, although only some 50 per cent graduated as second lieutenants. NS men with professional medical or dental qualifications were commissioned to the rank of captain, following only six weeks of basic training.

Corps distribution

In contrast to the American draft system, where involuntary soldiers were made more unwilling by being placed in the least desirable corps, in the Australian system national servicemen were wisely distributed fairly evenly through the corps. The corps in which they were under-represented—for example, Survey, Aviation and Intelligence—contained a disproportionate number of officers and highly-trained personnel. The short-term NS man was restricted to corps for which he could be trained and still give at least some effective service.

In early 1971 I visited Vietnam and extensively interviewed Australian soldiers, mostly NS men; and in the years 1969-71 I gave pre-tested questionnaires to some 558 NS recruits and 250 NS discharges. These covered social background, attitude to call-up, and various measures of response to army life. Unless otherwise stated it is to these surveys that I refer in this chapter.

Most NS men reported being happy with the corps to which they had been allocated. In the sample dischargees, a total of 72 per cent replied 'yes' to the question, 'Was this the corps which you most wanted to be in?'; 11 per cent failed to answer the question. Of the rest, 5.6 per cent (14) had wanted to be in engineers, 2.4 per cent[6] in service corp, and 1.6 per cent (4) each in armoured, infantry, and electrical-mechanical engineers.

AUSTRALIAN SOLDIERS IN VIETNAM

The table below shows that the proportion of NS men in each corps did vary considerably overall, but was fairly similar in the large corps to which most NS men were allocated. Infantry contained the highest proportion of conscripts, but was closely followed by the Service Corps. It was not true that the army used conscripts simply as 'cannon fodder'.

Table 5.3   National Servicemen by corps—30 June 1970

		NS %	Numbers
Staff Corps		—	—
RAAC	armoured	38.42	586
RAA	artillery	37.98	1 074
RAE	engineers	38.34	1 615
RA Svy	survey	8.57	52
RA Sigs	signals	33.30	1 068
RA Inf	infantry	40.45	4 259
AA Avn Corps	aviation	6.18	10
Aust Int Corps	intelligence	9.27	24
RAA Ch D	chaplains	—	—
RAASC	service	39.01	1 741
RAASC-AACS	canteen	29.93	41
RAAMC	medical	33.19	516
RAADC	dental	36.50	77
RAAOC	ordnance	29.52	763
RAEME	elec/mech engineers	24.89	997
RAAEC	education	30.83	70
RAAEC-PR	education - PR	33.3	9
AACC	catering	39.93	747
RAAPC	pay	—	—
AALC	legal	23.52	4
RAA-Pro	provosts	31.05	136
AA Psyc Corps	psychology	37.37	37
AABC	band	14.47	54
Non Corps	trainees, etc	63.22	2 328
Total		36.66	16 208

Source: Army Manning Review (AMR) 1969-70.

However, since infantry is by far the largest corps in the Australian Army, this was where a high proportion (25 per cent) of NS men found themselves. The second largest number of NS men at any one time (14.3 per cent) was undergoing training prior to corps allocation.

Rank and activity

Apart from the functional differentiation of corps, the hierarchical aspect of rank was perhaps the main feature of the conscript's experience in the army. Most remained as they began, as privates, but an appreciable number did become corporals. While the proportion of NS men (10.1 per cent) who gained non-commissioned rank was not large, these corporals and sergeants provided a sizeable proportion of the army's junior NCOs (non-commissioned officers). For instance, one-third of lance-corporals were NS men. Similarly although only 2.15 per cent of NS men were commissioned, 38.31 per cent of second lieutenants in 1970 were NS men.

Not always related to the two variables of rank and corps was the sort of work which soldiers reported spending their time doing. The question was asked, 'During your time in the army, what sort of actual work did you mostly do?' Most answers were difficult to codify, but eventually seven categories were selected.

Table 5.4 Categories of work

Task	N	%
Unconstructive	15	6.72
Rifleman	28	12.55
Dangerous — technical	19	8.51
Technical	53	23.76
Administration	28	12.55
General	38	17.03
Driving	42	18.83
Total	223	100

The 'unconstructive' workers were those who reported doing 'nothing', 'sitting around', 'walking', or 'sleeping'. 'Riflemen' had specified themselves as such, while the 'dangerous technical' people were those who performed some skilled but also possibly dangerous task such as the disabling of mines. 'Technicals' were mostly in RAEME corps (electrical and mechanical engineers). 'Administrators' were clerks, or people who said they 'ran things'. 'General' workers were storemen, stewards, or self-described as 'just soldiering'. A surprising number described themselves as doing 'driving', but it is not possible to tell if they were drivers or merely passengers.

The table reveals some interesting self-identities; only 19 per cent of the sample described themselves in fighting terms, as riflemen or involved in dangerous technical jobs. By far the greatest number were employed at tasks which were not seen as specifically military. Unfortunately it is not possible to tabulate the tasks performed specifically by NS men in Vietnam, but we can infer that a larger proportion there would have identified themselves as riflemen or used other combat related descriptions.

Surprisingly, the task which a soldier reported performing was not significantly related to his corps. It was, however, related to his rank and to his education. For example, a soldier with tertiary education would tend to be an officer or NCO who reported doing 'administration'.

National servicemen and Vietnam

The policy of the army was that NS men were to constitute no more than 50 per cent of each unit in Vietnam, and they served only one 12 month tour. (Regulars who served in Vietnam were required to have a minimum gap of two years between tours). NS men generally constituted about 40 per cent of army strength in AFV.

Once allocated to their unit, NS men were treated in the same way as regular soldiers; and official army policy was that no-one knew who in their unit were regular soldiers, who were conscripts. While this official ideology was patently false,[7] and everyone was very well aware of the recruitment status of fellow-soldiers, the 'one army' concept did appear to be relatively successful.[8] The fixed proportions of NS and regulars in each unit provided a leavening of experienced and committed soldiers among the short-term, possibly more reluctant conscripts.

Training for service in Vietnam

All units and individuals were required[9] to have completed a course at the Jungle Training Centre (JTC) Canungra, as well as training in small arms, physical efficiency, field defences and section and platoon training. The JTC course for units occupied four weeks for infantry, three weeks for other corps. Shorter courses were available for individual replacements or reinforcements. But of course this four weeks at the JTC was only meant to be the icing on the cake. A battalion, for instance, could spend months if not years in training orientated towards a Vietnam tour.

The unit history of 7RAR summarises its activities from the time the battalion was raised in September 1965 until the departure for its second tour of Vietnam in February 1970.[10] After initial training, the diarist describes 7RAR as 'prepared for war' in June 1966. Units then proceeded to JTC and were engaged on various exercises until embarkation for Vietnam in April 1967. After their return in April 1968 and the subsequent loss of almost all members (including all officers) due to discharges, transfers and repostings, the battalion did not attempt another full-scale exercise until April 1969. Then, 'the tempo of training was to continue almost without interruption through the year ahead', until JTC in September-October and then embarkation for Vietnam once more in February 1970. After arrival at Nui Dat, a further in-theatre training program was completed.

So the men of 7RAR gave an 'effective' Vietnam service of 12 months for each (approximately) 22 months of training. Lest this be construed as a criticism of the battalion or of the training standards of the Australian Army, it should be noted that commentators attributed many of the problems of the US Army in Vietnam, including incidents such as the My Lai massacre, partly to inadequate training in unit formations, as well as to its rotation and reinforcement policies.[11]

Attitude formation?

It is a frequent allegation that military institutions are not only concerned with military training, but also either deliberately or coincidentally are responsible for the inculcation of certain socio-political attitudes, which some then interpret as either vices or virtues. There was a brief scare in 1970 over 'political indoctrination in the Australian Army'[12], relating to the issue to troops of the AMF booklet entitled 'Pocketbook—South Vietnam'.[13] While this booklet certainly did, as alleged, present the Liberal Party, right-wing and (at the time) establishment view on the Vietnam conflict, this is hardly surprising given the political situation at the time. But as effective, persuasive 'propaganda' the booklet would surely have been a failure; and there seems little evidence that army authorities were ever concerned with the beliefs or attitudes of the soldiers.[14]

On the general question of the socialising effects of the armed forces, the weight of evidence seems to be swinging in a negative direction; ie, researchers here and abroad find very little or no difference between civilian and military populations taken as a whole.[15] There are, of course, exceptions.[16]

The Vietnam experience

There was never any shortage of soldiers wanting a posting to Vietnam or Singapore, where Australian soldiers were also stationed as part of the joint Far East Land Force (FARELF), so most of them probably were 'volunteers'.[17] For career soldiers, particularly officers, a Vietnam tour was a 'must' on the way up the ladder; and for all ranks it provided excitement, interest, and monetary incentives in the form of war-service housing loans, tax free allowances, and duty-free goods. The careful soldier could save all or most of his pay, and thus provide for his future.

Nor was the danger very considerable: in some years more soldiers died while in Australia than in Vietnam (although the per capita rate was higher in Vietnam).[18]

Table 5.5 Deaths—all causes—in forces in Australia and Vietnam

	1967-68	1968-69	1969-70	1970-71	1971-72
Australia	N/A	84	104	103	104
Vietnam	98	95	83	45	8

Source: Army Manning Reviews (AMRs) 1967-72.

Casualties were shared more or less equally between regular and conscript soldiers, bearing in mind that the NS men always constituted less than half the force.

Table 5.6 Australian Army casualties in Vietnam since May 1966 (entry of Task Force)[19]

	ARA	%	NS	%	CMF	%	Total
Killed in action	198	51.3	187	48.4	1	0.26	386
Wounded in action	1156	52.7	1030	47	7	0.3	2193
NBC deaths	37	71.0	15	28.8	—	—	52
NBC injured & ill	396	61.4	249	38.6	—	—	645

Source: *Army Manning Review* 1972

Moreover, not all deaths in Vietnam were directly due to battle. Many were classed as 'non-battle casualties' (NBC), estimated by one source at 'more than one in every nine deaths'.[20]

Nor was a serviceman in Vietnam much more likely to be hospitalised than if he were serving in Australia, New Guinea or Singapore.[21] While Vietnam was the only theatre where battle casualties accounted for any hospital admissions, the largest number in AFV were due to the tropical conditions—ie were gastro-intestinal, skin, malarial, or PUO (pyrexia of unknown origin). Admission rates for psychiatric causes were somewhat higher in AFV than for the army as a whole, but not markedly so.

Psychiatric admissions fluctuated wildly between 1967 and 1972. A nearly threefold increase in psychiatric admission in 1969 was probably due to the appointment in that year of a psychiatrist for AFV; but other annual fluctuations reflect real changes in the mental health of the soldiers or differing policies on the part of reporting and/or admitting officers.

Table 5.7 Psychiatric admission rates April 1969-March 1970

	AFV Cases		PMF Totals	
		Rate per '000		Rate per '000
Psychosis	2	N/A	38	0.8
Psychoneurosis	56		155	3.4
Personality defect	51		360	7.8
Combat fatigue	13		13	0.3
		17.4		12.3

Source: *Army Manning Reviews* 1969-70.

To a large extent, the diggers based in Vietnam were 'living a lie'. They were a small symbolic force, part of an American joint venture with the Saigon government, and so they never had complete freedom of action at the command level as Frank Frost argues elsewhere in this book.[22] The force was not self-supporting, it relied heavily on US logistic, artillery and air support. The Task Force was in a low combat, insurgency area, and yet the soldiers, officers, officials and the public, remained oriented to the view that the diggers were heroic fighters fulfilling a combat mission.[23] This was a reflection of the overall view of the war, and partly a reflection of the traditional view of the role of soldiers and of the previous foreign experiences of Australian troops, who were indeed used as front line combat troops.

Australian tactics
The official political and military view was always that the Australian Task Force had achieved 'great success' in Phuoc Tuy,[24] even though perhaps the war as a whole was not going as well as it might have. But 'successes' in Phuoc Tuy were ephemeral, and depended on use of fairly selective criteria. To some soldiers this was only too obvious—with subsequent reactions on their morale and adjustment.

It seemed easy, for instance, to compare the Australian:Enemy kill ratios and demonstrate the Free World's prowess. There seems to be no reliable overall assessment of the number of Vietnamese who died as a result of Australian activities, but partial figures were consistently in our favour. One journalistic observer estimated that during the years 1966–70 more than 3000 Vietnamese were killed in Phuoc Tuy by the Australians (of a province population of 100,000). SAS teams were credited with a kill ratio of one lost for between 300 and 400 enemy killed.[25] Some battalion histories give casualties for both sides. For example 2RAR in its 1967–68 tour suffered 28 killed in action but claimed 187 enemy killed and 12 captured;[26] in its later tour in 1970–71 it lost 13 for 110 enemy killed and 23 captured or rallied.[27] (To 'rally' or *hoi chanh* meant to desert to the western side, preferably bringing in war materiel as a demonstration of one's *bona fides*.) A year later 4RAR claimed 97 enemy 'eliminations' for their own loss of 8 men killed.[28] The largest single battle which the Australians experienced, at Long Tan, resulted in enemy casualties of 245 killed and an estimated 500 wounded, compared to 17 killed and 21 wounded Australians.[29]

The Australians were highly thought of as jungle fighters. One US general was reported as saying rather backhandedly: 'Aussie troops are so good, we really should be making better use of them.'[30] They relied on small aggressive patrols and made far less use than the Americans of saturation aerial bombing and artillery.[31] However, the Australian technique was seen in a different light by one American ex-marine, who obviously favoured a more aggressive approach:

> The marines rattle around on the trails, making all kinds of noise, spoiling for a fight. The diggers go creeping silently through the jungle, avoiding the trails. You can't help feeling that the diggers are searching the remote jungle for Vietcong while the VC make use of trails, unmolested.[32]

One Australian officer exemplified the low-technology approach: 'Turn the Infantryman loose and let him go after the VC. When the little man jumps into his cubby hole, flush him out with dogs.'[33]

While the Australians did inflict heavy human damage, their main occupation was not fire-fights and killing, but a rather more difficult task of denying the VC access to the non-VC population. This was interpreted both territorially and (more ambivalently) psychologically. By patrolling the jungle and populated areas, the aim was to make life difficult for roving guerillas. In addition, large quantities of foodstuffs, housing and weaponry were destroyed,[34] presumably adding to the VC's logistic burden. There were also some operations 'against suspected NLF cadres by small groups of Australian soldiers and GVN (Saigon) officials'[35] but the VC infrastructure in the province was left largely untouched. In the words of one Australian intelligence officer: 'it's really a police function, and the provincial officials are so implicated no-one wants to find out.'[36]

Civic Action

If strictly military success in Vietnam were to be measured in kill ratios, how was one to approach the problem of 'winning the hearts and minds', ensuring the active allegiance of villagers to the government of South Vietnam? No satisfactory measure could be found, and this created an ambivalence on the part of Australians towards civic action, and a distrust of and dislike for the Vietnamese for whom they were supposedly giving aid, and dying. The rendering of aid (eg., building schools and roads, supply of medical, dental and pharmaceutical services, and improvement of water supplies) usually resulted in thanks, smiles and gifts, Australians were (according to one former CA officer) the recipients of goodwill everywhere in the province. 'This is indicated by the friendly smiles and waves wherever Australians move in the province, the many unsolicited statements of goodwill from Vietnamese of all walks and stations of life and the gifts and hospitality showered on soliders working in civic action.'[37] However, the Vietnamese commitment to and maintenance of most aid projects was unsatisfactory in the longer term, and the friendly feelings were all too unreliable.

The lack of 'real' gratitude shown by villagers relocated to new homes, or by those for whom new schools or new roads had been built, was a source of constant and bitter frustration to many soliders. Alister Brass quotes one of these:

> Why, after six months' determined generosity and bloody hard work, didn't we get any vegetables from Hoa Long? And why aren't the people there prepared to earn themselves a few piastres they could well use by doing our laundry? So far our civil aid activities seem to have achieved bugger all of lasting significance, except in places like Binh Gia. And there they're Catholics, and North Vietnamese into the bargain, so they're on our side already ...[38]

Hoa Long was a village which often caused trouble for the Australians. Its population consisted largely of villagers relocated from Long Tan shortly before the arrival in the province of the Australian Task Force.

The most common epithet used by young Australian soldiers after their one-year tour of duty to describe the long-suffering Vietnamese seemed to be ... 'ungrateful'.

One Australian correspondent, Pat Burgess, reported on how the VC foiled the Australians who built a water system on Long Son Island, off the coast of Phuoc Tuy. The VC stole the crucial pump, so all the rest of the equipment was wasted:

> The tanks cost thousands of dollars ... More important, the sweat of the Australian engineers who built them—almost all of them national service tradesmen—went for nothing. And significantly the people of Long Son don't care.

Burgess quoted Australia's own counter-insurgency guru, Brigadier Ted Serong (the commander of the first AATTV) on the sensible logic of the Vietnamese:

> The Vietnamese doesn't like the cheerful giver. To him the man who gives cheerfully isn't to be trusted. Either he gives because he wants something from you later, or he gives cheerfully because the gift is worthless. If neither of these is true then the man is a fool, and he still isn't to be trusted.[39]

In the case of the cheerful Australian givers, one is tempted to believe that at least the first, often the second, and sometimes the third reason applied.

The resentment on the part of the pacifiers can be attributed to their lack of understanding, lack of education as to the causes and nature of the war, and perhaps the fact that they were somewhat dislocated by the environment and so suspended their more humane values. Partly, too, it was because the modern army gives training and inculcates values which are not appropriate for winning hearts and minds, or absorbing the inevitable slights and failures which come with civic action. Occupation forces do love to be loved, and react badly when they are not.[40]

Not only did civic action workers consider themselves 'used' by the Vietnamese; they were also held in somewhat low esteem by other Australians in the Task Force. Some officers questioned seemed either ignorant of the role of the CA unit or else plain dismissive.[41] Many described it as a joke, a haven for black-marketeers or 'would-be do-gooders', or just a misdirection of resources away from the battalions. (Those working in Psyops suffered similarly.[42]) At its height, civic action used 8% of the Task Force's manpower, and at various times almost all units were engaged in some way in civic action, yet sadly there never seems to have developed any empathy between the overwhelming majority of Australians and Vietnamese. The most common descriptions by Australians of the Vietnamese were 'ungrateful', 'immoral', 'filthy', and 'back stabbing'; while Frost estimates that the single most effective 'civic action' of the Task Force was the negative one of restricting access of its members to the villages and of refusing to allow Vietnamese onto or near the Task Force base area. The Australians were the only foreign troops not to have established bars, laundries and other similar facilities in their vicinity, and this was apparently appreciated by the local Vietnamese officials.[43]

Australians and Americans—'The Australians hate everybody'
The Australians' dislike of the Vietnamese had several components. Many Australians were perhaps racist to begin with; for others the cultural and economic differences were too great to surmount; for others it was too difficult to kill some and trust others. But what was the reason behind the Australians' distrust of and dislike for the Americans?[44]

The psychiatrist Peter G Bourne, a non-Australian who was given the opportunity to join the Australian force in the field and to interview the men when the Australian force was operating under the US 173rd Airborne Brigade at Bien Hoa, offers some interesting answers.[45]

Bourne quotes a saying about the various allied national and ethnic groups that 'The Vietnamese hate the Americans. The Americans hate the Vietnamese. Americans hate other Americans. The local Chinese are hated by both the Vietnamese and the Americans. The Australians hate everybody.'[46] He described the Australians' paranoia as comprised of largely successful 'adaptive measures they have been forced as a group to accept ... to maintain the internal psychological stability of the individual soldiers.'[47] The problem, as he saw it, was that the Australian commitment was only a token force, and the efforts of Australian soldiers were only of symbolic value—'their real military contribution to the war effort is trivial'. In order to give meaning to their efforts, 'they restructured their perception of the environment so that through intense identification with their unit they have made it their sole reference group.'[48] A necessary part of this feeling that they were fighting a private war was a constant competitiveness with and denial of the importance or successes of the US forces. Particularly, the Australian soldiers were critical of certain technical aspects of the US military performance: US officers wasted the lives of the men; all ranks were trigger-happy, extravagant with materiel and even 'soft'; and there was 'a considerable core of anti-Negro feeling ... which was generated by their own sense of hurt and rejection as much as anything'.[49]

Many of these feelings were in evidence among soldiers and officers at the Task Force in 1971. There was the same intense feeling that the whole war in Phuoc Tuy was between the diggers and the VC; and the general Australian opinion of Americans seemed to be that, though they were generous, 'they can afford to be'; and that, as soldiers, they were both undisciplined and unprofessional, and yet also in some way too 'regular'.

One quotable statement summed up these feelings, and also harked back to the World War II adage 'they're overpaid, over-sexed, and over here':

> They're too over-sexed and unrestrained, and if they have a regulation to blow their noses three times a day in the left nostril, they'll do it, no more, no less. They just can't bend, they've gotta stick to the rules. They'd give you the shirt off their back.[50]

Therefore the Australians never really appreciated any of their allies in Vietnam. Certainly the contrast in their life styles was remarkable, but it seems unfortunate that almost none of the American virtues were apparent to the diggers.

Martin Russ, who spent some rather unhappy days with the Australians, contrasted them unfavourably with his beloved Americans, especially the marines:

> (Aussies are) a coarse, cultureless version of the British ... in general ... a pretty lightweight crew. There is no madness in them, no passion, no vulnerability, and worst of all no imagination ... In contrast to loud, friendly, enthusiastic, belligerent, vulnerable, passionate, childlike, responsive, dumb Americans.[51]

But perhaps the Australians would have been flattered by the contrast.

Performance

There has, understandably, always been a preoccupation in military circles with 'what makes an army fight', a concern also of academic research since the Second World War.[52] Only since the involvement of the US Army in Vietnam has it been publicly acknowledged that armies sometimes do *not* fight, that they can 'disintegrate' even though they are the self-proclaimed victors. There have in fact been many instances of quite large scale mutiny in western armies, for example in the First World War, when, according to Keegan, taking a very broad view of the war, a point was reached in every army at which either a majority or a disabling minority refused to go on.[53] Keegan identifies this point as where the number of dead is roughly the same as the number of fighting infantry. With the massive casualties and woeful evacuation procedures and medical facilities of the First World War, this point was not difficult to attain.

But in Vietnam, these objective conditions did not apply. Casualties on the western side were generally relatively light,[54] inflicted mainly by small arms fire or mines, not by prolonged and intensive artillery bombardment; and the time from injury to aid post has been estimated as a mere 15 minutes, immensely raising the odds of survival. Living conditions were, by the standards of war, very good; combat was limited in duration; and the overall tour in Vietnam was maximum of 12 months. But the questions remain. Did something go wrong with the US forces? If so, to what can this be attributed? And were the Australian forces in Vietnam prey to the same problems?

Cohesion and disintegration

A considerable literature now exists on the meaning of 'cohesion', on the factors contributing to and detracting from it, and on the role which it can play in fostering both combat motivation and combat performance,[55] but the concept itself remains highly unsatisfactory, and there seems to be little agreement on how to measure the extent or intensity of cohesion. Nor is the causal link between cohesion and performance clear,[56] since there are many instances where mutiny may result precisely from primary group cohesion; and similarly with 'fragging' (the murder of superiors—from the commonly used fragmentation grenades) and drug use.

Formally, combat is an army's prime function, the means towards the end of defeating the enemy—hence the textbook idea that 'what remains distinctive to the armed forces is their basic orientation towards an image of the battlefield.'[57] But most soldiers in a modern army will not be involved in battle; and for those who are, the goal of 'defeating the enemy' seems to be a secondary one. For those engaged in it, 'with few exceptions, *survival* is the central focus of combat behaviour.'[58] This means that group pressure will, depending on the situation, demand a certain minimal functioning; but it will also discourage unnecessary 'heroics' which might endanger the survival of others. It is easy to see the conflicts between the two goals.

Two controversial American students of the Vietnam experience, Savage and Gabriel, claim that 'by 1969, the American Army began to disintegrate under comparatively minimal stress.'[59] Disintegration is defined by them as 'the emergence of conditions which make effective operations impossible', viz., desertion, mutiny, fragging, and drug addiction; and these conditions are said to result from internal, not environmental factors.[60]

The processes of disintegration here are: the replacement of the gladiator officer type by the managerial, combat non-participant type; the inflation of officer strengths, and the decline in the quality of officers; the destruction of primary groups mainly because of the rotation policies (fixed 12 month term, and replacement and repatriation as individuals, not as units). The picture which emerges is that of an army which began to disintegrate because its soldiers were 'forced to function in a progressively unstructured social and military *milieu*'.[61]

While it is easier to generalise about the small Australian forces than about the large and heterogeneous American forces, it does seem clear that on at least several of these above processes, the Australians differed favourably from their allies. This does not mean, however, that the US forces *did* 'disintegrate' or cease to conduct effective operations, even though there may have been some or even many instances of individual soldiers and entire units refusing to fight, for whatever reasons. No-one has demonstrated the links between, for example, drug use or even unit cohesion (however measured) and combat effectiveness in all situations. Drug-affected soldiers may be very effective killers. As Keegan points out, the use of marijuana:

> may be seen if not as a natural, certainly as a time-honoured response to the uncertainties with which battle racks the soldiers. The choice ... moreover, had local precedents: the pirates of the South China Sea traditionally dosed themselves with marijuana before attacking European ships.[62]

Officers and leaders
Savage and Gabriel (themselves regular officers) allege that the American officer corps as a whole became too large, too careerist, and disloyal. Only the first of these can be demonstrated; officer strength in 1972 reached 14.9 per cent of total force strength in the US Army, after being fairly stable at around 11 per cent during the 1950s and 1960s. While completely ignoring possible technological and organisational reasons for this growth, Savage and Gabriel indict it as being excessive, especially since (they allege) there was a concomitant decline in quality.

For the same period, the proportion of male officers in the Australian Army remained stable at just under 10 per cent; perhaps an acceptable level? In any case, while the number of officers did increase with the introduction of national service and the expansion of the army, this expansion was not very rapid in absolute terms.

Table 5.8 ARA full-time duty male strengths

	ARA ORs	NS ORs	NS Officer	ARA Officer	Total Force	Total Officer	% Officer
1966	20162	8014	105	3209	31490	3314	10.5
1967	20918	15467	276	3459	40120	3735	9.3
1968	22100	15475	317	3669	41561	3986	9.6
1969	22885	15664	343	3840	42732	4183	9.8
1970	23108	15857	351	3888	43200	4239	9.8

Source: Army Manning Reviews 1966–70.

But how can we judge the quality of command and leadership displayed by this important 10 per cent of the army? If we look at what the soldiers, particularly the conscripted ones, thought of their officers, then the result is not very flattering. Some of this might have been mere grouching; and it may not differ substantially from what other subordinates in other organisations would say about their superiors, without telling us anything about how satisfactorily the organisation functions. It might well have been a situation of low commitment, high compliance, and high performance.

Two statistical measurements were made of the attitude of soldiers to their officers—some in Vietnam and some in Australia. Typical items in an 'evaluation of officers' were: 'on the whole, officers in my platoon are popular'; 'If I had to fight, I would feel quite happy about being under my present officers'; and 'Officers tend to look down on the men'. On this measure, as on all others related to the army, opinion amongst the dischargees was less favourable than amongst the new recruits.[64] As a second measure, the discharge sample was asked the open-ended question: 'What did you dislike most about the army?' Several answers related to the men's view of their officers; those coded as discipline, lack of leadership and army hierarchy all contained remarks relating to the quality of officers and senior NCOs. Nearly one third of all complaints fell into these categories. As could be expected, there were more complaints from those serving in technical roles than from those in combat or administration; it was amongst those with relevant civilian skills that the 'interference' of officers was most resented. Perhaps, too, the combat arms with their 'heroic' tradition were more able to inspire their men.

A common set of complaints related to the quality of leadership and the basis of command—domination rather than manipulation. There seemed to be three components to the OR dislike of officers and NCOs. First, that they held their rank purely because of long service, not because they were technically competent. Secondly, that they did not perform their jobs efficiently. And thirdly, that they were undemocratic leaders; they operated by command rather than by group consensus. One conscript complained of 'inept and incapable people in positions purely because of their length of service'. Another thought the officers 'are obviously uneducated (not majority, just enough to cause consistent blunders)'. Many disliked 'the foolish decisions by people not qualified in the field they make the decisions'.

Once in their position, the officers 'lacked leadership', were 'small-minded', 'arrogant', 'drank too much', or were just 'extremely inefficient at administration'. One complained about 'being treated like a little boy by a bunch of would-be-if-they-could-be officers who spent most of their time deciding who's next shout it was at the officers' club and not worrying about what their men were doing'.

The theme of 'being treated like children' (thought by one researcher to be the result of the need of the regular soldiers to re-enact their oedipal conflicts from a position of strength[65]) was common among national servicemen. Many who had been employed in quite responsible civilian positions objected to supervision or interference from their commanders. They tended to feel superior to their officers, particularly if they were technicians, and to obsessively find fault with those ordained by rank to lead and instruct them. Thus they complained of the inequalities of the army hierarchy, the rank structure, the social distinction between 'the animals' (officers) and themselves, the men. 'Arrogant and aloof' said some;

'superior thinking people', said another. 'Petty discrimination between officers and ORs [mess, clubs, uniforms], and lack of feedback from bottom of chain of command.' One NS man disliked 'the way people higher up in rank can make life so miserable for others who serve under them because of personal traits or present day feelings'.

The category of 'discipline' was rather loosely defined to include all complaints relating to interference with personal autonomy. Some were very specific—'all the charges I got'—but more frequently the conscripts complained of 'too much discipline', 'standover merchants', 'being told quote You Will Do This Private ...', or 'bastardisation'. One complained of 'being told to breathe and not to breathe (figuratively speaking of course)', while another condemned 'all the bullshit, regimentation, and drum beating, sabre rattling old bastards who tell you what a great job you're doing for your country!'

A very frequent complaint was that officers and NCOs relied almost exclusively on the use of command and the sanction of charges to exact conformity from their soldiers. A former bricklayer said: 'In my opinion the army's downfall is in its fear of command. Command should be respected not feared and hated.' A former clerk, now in the infantry, wrote:

> What I disliked most: The small-mindedness of little men (who are supposedly leaders of men) who let authority run amok with themselves. I have never in my life been so belittled and not being able to retaliate in any way without fear of losing money.

Some resentment was on the symbolic level of manners. Many soldiers disliked the way they were spoken to (the author's sympathy is entirely with the men on this point); they disliked being told that 'you *will* do this soldier'; and they disliked the lack of comeback at the officers: 'If you tried to get back at officers, you're put on a charge ... But they thrive on your disliking them.'

This interpretation seemed to be largely erroneous: most officers wanted to be liked, but seemed not to know how to achieve this in many instances. One captain said bitterly: 'They don't understand the pips, these nashos—a lot of them don't understand too much.' But from the army command's point of view, the problem was that nashos and probably regulars as well understood *too* much about how the system worked. They were able to exploit the system and get by—'keep your mouth shut and do your two years'—without ever giving their souls to the green machine.

The Australian soldier's alienation from, and resistance to, the army system and its leaders almost always took a passive and purely attitudinal form. There were only two instances in Vietnam of a soldier deliberately causing the death of his officer (in 1968 and 1969), both times by the use of grenades.[66] Interestingly, it is not apparent where these two cases would fit in a table of offences leading to courts martial; the number of charges laid for various offences hardly gives a picture of a force with major disciplinary problems—although it should be pointed out that the overwhelming majority of 'charges' are dealt with summarily by unit commanders and do not go before a court martial.[67] According to the notes on the *Army Manning Reviews*, even drug offences rarely resulted in court martial, one case of marijuana use being recorded under the offence of 'disobedience'.[68]

Table 5.9   Offences leading to courts martial

Nature of offence	Number of charges laid			
	1967-68	1968-69	1969-70	1970-71
leaving unit	—	—	—	4
common assault	3	2	—	—
unlawful wounding	—	1	—	1
wounding with intent	2	—	—	1
theft	3	2	2	3
losing by neglect	1	3	—	—
AWOL	5	3	3	1
disobedience	3	6	4	8
threatening or insubordinate language	5	1	3	—
conduct to the prejuduce of good order and discipline	14	14	6	19
road traffic offences	1	2	—	5
bodily harm by wilful neglect	1	2	—	—
ill-treating/threatening subordinates	—	—	2	—
unlawfully discharging weapon	—	—	2	—
murder	—	—	1	2
other	17	10	1	11
Total charges	55	46	24	55
Number of courts martial held	20	24	10	15
Number of convictions	35	32	22	39

Source: *Army Manning Reviews* 1967-71.

Drugs and psychopathology

Because antipathy of Australian soldiers towards the army hierarchy and its leadership seemed to be restricted almost entirely to the passive attitudinal level, perhaps rather than mutiny or desertion we should expect to find withdrawal, either through drug taking or through psychiatric illness? But here again we search in vain for the sort of figures which have been used to indicate disintegration in the American forces.

The incidence of neuro-psychiatric illness among the American forces seems to have been very low, compared to the levels of Korea and the two World Wars. In the European theatre of the Second World War, for example, annual admission rates for combat divisions were around 25 per cent and even higher in the tropical, Southwest Pacific Area;[69] and a British Army psychiatrist wrote that 'depending on the type of battle, 2 to 30 per cent of all casualties may be psychiatric.'[70]

Many of the conditions of deprivation and stress—especially material ones—which are thought to lead to 'combat-related stress disorders' were avoided by the western forces in Vietnam, but others were present, particularly among the US forces. Most analysts have agreed that the erosion of unit morale caused by constant individual rotations was an important factor in almost all the problems encountered by the US military, the most frequently mentioned drugs. Use of both narcotics and marijuana was extremely high after 1970; but there is in fact no real evidence that this level of drug use impaired the functioning of the forces either in or out of battle. The figures on drug use in the US forces[71] show that while for all types (marijuana stimulants, depressants and narcotics, but not other psychedelics) there was more reported drug use (not necessarily addiction) in Vietnam than elsewhere, this difference is not particularly great; one could speculate that the ease of obtaining drugs meant that drug use there brought with it fewer ancillary problems than elsewhere. Nevertheless, drug use is thought by some psychiatrists to constitute one functional equivalent of combat exhaustion, since it entails a similar 'rejection of the role of combatant'.[72]

In the Australian forces, none of these behavioural rejections of the role of combatant seemed to be present.[73] Psychiatric admission rates were low at around 10 per 1000, though Bourne estimated that at least in 1966 there was a higher incidence of 'major psychiatric disturbances' than among American troops, with fewer milder illnesses,[74] and it is possible that neuroses were dealt with administratively rather than by medical treatment.[75] But the 'functional equivalent' of drug use was never present to any significant extent among Australian forces. Between February 1969 and January 1973 there were a mere 28 discovered cases of use or possession of drugs, and these all involved marijuana only.[76]

It has been falsely alleged that drug use in Vietnam led to currently higher levels of drug abuse in the Australian armed forces,[77] but there is no real evidence to support this. Occasional newspaper reports suggested that 'the use of pot (marijuana) was more widespread in the Australian Army than official charge statistics indicate or the authorities care to admit'[78], but there was actually more concern in the press and among army authorities over the use of alcohol rather than marijuana or narcotics. While alcohol was rationed (a mere two cans of beer per day) for the other ranks, this was relaxed in holiday periods and apparently led to a surge in the court martial rate. One officer reportedly estimated that 80 per cent of all courts martial involved over-drinking.[79]

To what can the apparently negligible use of non-alcoholic drugs in Vietnam be attributed? Several factors have been suggested: the highly selective nature of recruiting of both regulars and conscripts (though whether suspected or admitted drug use led to rejection is not clear); the fact that the 'national habit' was beer not drugs ('perhaps the comaraderie of a couple of beers appeals to him more than does surreptitious drug-taking');[80] the high level of control by officers of their units; and lastly the pressure of peers who thought a drug user would be a 'poor risk' on patrols.

Cohesion—the positive side
So far the evidence presented for cohesion in the Australian force in Vietnam has been of a negative kind. None of the problems associated with the alleged disintegration of the American forces has been found. But there is also some positive evidence from which one could infer a high level of cohesion. There seems to have been a shared latent ideology of 'in-group cohesiveness', acceptance of the war, dislike of the overall army system, and mateship. There were some strains between 'pogos' (those in support roles) and 'sharp-enders' (combat soldiers) and between 'nashos' and 'regs', but these seldom reached the level of overt conflict.

There was an important difference between the rotation policies of the US and Australian forces. The infantry battalions, artillery units and SAS squadron were changed over after a twelve month period on a unit relief basis (although some losses were replaced on an individual basis). It is likely that this policy greatly increased the cohesion of at least the Australian combat units compared to those of the US Army.

Relations with outsiders
There was a considerable amount of Australian paranoia *vis-à-vis* American and Vietnamese allies, but this attitude was not restricted entirely to those of different cultural backgrounds; it was also evident (to a lesser extent) in their defensive relations with the Australian press and public. At times there was a complete ban placed on soldiers talking to the press;[82] at other times just lack of cooperation, reportedly experienced even by an army PR officer attached to a battalion.[83] This uncooperative attitude was endorsed at high levels: for example, in January 1971 the author was asked by the then Task Force Commander: 'What is it exactly you want to do up here?' The answer 'interview national servicemen' was met rudely by 'Well, I'm afraid you're completely wasting your time then, we only have soldiers here.'

To account for this defensiveness we have to look to the domestic political situation. There was never the level of opposition in Australia to the Vietnam War which existed in the US, but the military as a whole seemed to take any signs of opposition to heart. Although it may be accurate to see the soldiers in Vietnam as 'simply the unlucky fall-guys in a chain of political cynicism and ineptitude',[84] the soldiers tended to see the 'lefties'—not the politicians—as responsible for what they saw as the equivocal commitment to Vietnam and ambivalent support for the forces sent there. A popular slogan among the troops in 1971 was 'punch a postie for me' (there had been recurrent postal strikes in 1970), and frequent criticism of 'demonstrators and drug-crazed hippies' was expressed. The bitterness and irrationality is best summed up in a poem popular in 1971, several copies of which were given to the author in Vietnam by soldiers who endorsed its sentiments.

THE BOYS UP THERE

Take a man and put him alone,
Put him 5000 miles from his home,
Empty his heart of all, but blood,
Make him live in sweat and mud.

There is a life I have to live,
And why my soul to the devil I give;
You free boys swing in your easy chair
But you don't know what it's like over there.

You all have a ball without near trying,
While over there our boys are dying;
You burn your draft cards, march at dawn,
Paint your signs on Parliament lawn,
You all want to 'Ban the Bomb',
There is no war in Vietnam.

Use your drugs and have your fun,
And then refuse to carry a gun,
There is nothing else for you to do,
And I'm supposed to die for you.

I'll hate you till the day I die,
You made me hear my best mate cry,
I saw his arm in a bloody shred,
I heard them say "This one's dead."

It's a heavy price to pay,
Not to live another day,
He had the guts to fight and die,
He paid the price, but what did he buy.

He bought a life giving his,
But who gives a damn what a soldier gives
His wife, his mum, maybe his sons,
But there about the only ones.

Shared ideology

Opposition to the war seems to have been a minority view among Australian soldiers, and was voiced in a low key when it did exist. Most soldiers seem to have at least hoped that their presence and actions were worthwhile, although many doubted their effectiveness. They were, at least initially, happy to be in the army. This applied even to conscripts : the majority of NS men reported being in favour of the call-up.[85] I also found a feeling of keenness for combat, as measured by an 8-item scale with statements such as: 'The thought of going to Vietnam to fight doesn't really worry me'; 'It wouldn't be so bad to have to fight', etc.

Among recruits, a keenness for combat was positively correlated with a favourable attitude to conscription, family membership of the Returned Servicemen's League and identification with the army; and negatively with education. Those expecting to vote for conservative parties were also keener to fight in Vietnam. It seems that at some later point in the average soldier's career he became disenchanted with the army itself, so that overall there was a negative view of the army among dischargees and very few reported contemplating a career as a regular soldier.[86] On all measures of favourable disposition to the army there was a markedly lower score among dischargees than among recruits, and soldiers were far more able to articulate what they disliked about the army than what they liked.[87]

On the other hand, most soldiers seemed to think that their performance inside the army was quite acceptable. Dischargees were asked 'how would you describe yourself?'

a pretty good soldier	15.8%
average	75.4%
a pretty bad soldier	8.8%
	N = 228

Most likely to describe themselves as 'pretty good' were those who had been under enemy fire, in a unit which they described as 'tough', or in fighting corps. Soldiers in these categories were more likely to be fulfilling their soldierly expectations, while the 'pogos' suffered from a disjunction between the 'action-excitement' image which the army tried to project and the boring reality which was the lot of most soldiers.[88]

But if it could be said that the average soldier (or at least conscript) disliked the army, it cannot be deduced that there was a problem with unit cohesion. It appears that the strong ethic of mateship among Australian soldiers,[89] was fostered partly by the unit rotation policies of the fighting corps, and a shared ideology of passive acceptance of the war, dislike of those who criticised the army or its presence in Vietnam (the two were equated), and a general 'Australianess.'[90]

Even the combined presence of conscripts and regulars seems not to have caused problems beyond occasional annoyance and name-calling (although the evidence is somewhat equivocal). Most correspondents were struck by the homogeneity of the Australian force in Vietnam:

> Foreign correspondents in Vietnam often complain that the Australian soldier is an unthinking robot; he obeys orders without question. There are no concessions to fashion and one looks in vain for anti-war sentiment, or even for some historical and political knowledge of

Vietnam among Diggers. The ignorance is appalling, but the result is a short-back-and-sides efficient fighting machine.[91]

The opinion of TB Millar that 'the great majority (of NS men), once they are in the army, are keen to do as good a job as possible, and to be and look as much like regulars as possible',[92] can undoubtedly be questioned, but it does seem that conscripts avoided any overt let alone organised opposition to the army. Their presence undoubtedly caused some problems. They considered regular soldiers 'civilian dropouts' who only joined up because of unemployment. And their passive opposition was often quite effective. One regimental sergeant-major who felt uncomfortable with smart-mouthed 'nashos' said 'some of my blokes reckon they can't take much more'. Two comments from officers convey the general view:

> The nashos—they won't bring complaints to the *surface*—but they refuse stripes, won't lead others, even if they have the ability. They want everything done for them, won't help their mates or see a job through.
>
> All regulars are the same, nashos are not. They make the best and the worst soldiers. Best, when they're willing and intelligent; worst, when they're lazy and especially when they're 'short' [ie near the end of their tour].

One correspondent expressed the ambivalence felt by many conscripted soldiers:

> They fitted into the army very well, but not many of the first batch volunteered to stay on ... Many were glad they had gone, but relieved to be home again, alive. Nothing strange about that, of course. But some resented the debasement of discipline and the necessity of having to forget ideals of behaviour and thought and become a cog in a machine whose duty it was to kill other people ... The average conscript was not a conscientious objector in the legal sense, and accepted National Service as a job that had to be done, but many returned appalled, in retrospect, at what they had done in Australia's name.[93]

The atrocity issue

As has often been pointed out, the distinction between war atrocities and the atrocity of war is often merely theoretical. American forces in later years of the war faced constant allegations, and investigation of atrocities against Vietnamese, by individuals and groups at all levels. To attribute ultimate responsibility for these actions, either morally or legally, has been difficult, but it now seems clear that many soldiers were at some time, even regularly, involved in activities which could not be openly discussed for fear of punitive action. That is, they were acknowledged even by the military as being shameful and unacceptable to the civilian public, even though they may have been tacitly or overtly accepted within the military as normal behaviour, or as regrettable but understandable acts. My Lai seems to fail into this latter category.[94]

Occasional allegations of atrocity have been levelled against Australian forces in Vietnam, but only one of these stuck—the water-torture case. Here, too, it was relatively easy to blame the Vietnamese who were also involved in the interrogation.[95] However, some of the policies adopted or at least endorsed by the Task Force could be viewed as atrocious, for instance the relocation of villagers, bombing and defoliation of the country, and killing its civilian inhabitants. There is also evidence that the Australian soldier, like his American counterpart, came to regard the Vietnamese as less than human and therefore outside his normal ethical compass. This is not unusual in modern professionalised warfare:

> The emergence of armed forces into their modern professionalized, disciplined form has had the effect of transforming violence into a mode of order and making its victims appear to be destructive threats.[96]

Everyone is, of course, entitled to be ruthless with threats, but why were there so few allegations of atrocity against the Australian forces?

One answer may be the different political reaction to the war, and another the closed-shop attitude of Australian soldiers to the press and civilians generally. The attitude of one battalion CO is worth quoting:

> The Koreans know just how to handle the Vietnamese ... We are tolerant to a sometimes absurd extent. These people are Asians. They think differently and react differently to Australians. You can't get the respect of the Vietnamese using kid-glove techniques. You've got to think like bloody Asians to get results up here ... I've got the feeling these bastards are laughing at us behind our backs. I lost a good man in there. Even 100 Viet Cong to one Australian soldier is very bad odds to me. I don't know what the satisfactory answer is but we'll have to get tougher.[87]

Due to limitations on their firepower and differences in tactical doctrine Australian toughness never matched that of the Americans. The tighter control exercised over units by Australian officers and NCOs probably meant that there was less likelihood of an unauthorised rampage by soldiers, even if they had been so inclined.[98] The relative infrequency of this type of criticism of the Australian Task Force has perhaps marginally aided the post-war adjustment of its soldiers.

Postscript

Leaving the war back there
The post-Vietnam adjustment of combat soldiers, and their impact on American society, have been matters of continuing concern and research in the US. Starting from the assumption that the soldier does, indeed, 'bring

the war back home', controversies over the nature of the experience and its effects seem to have multiplied with each study.[99] Veterans are variously seen as being 'human time bombs',[100] ready to explode into lethal violence, or as having few problems, being little different in attitudes or behaviour from non-veterans.[101]

There has been too little research in Australia into the adjustment of veterans, either within the armed forces or as civilians, to reach conclusions which are any more than highly speculative. We can point to several features of the American situation which were absent (at least to a degree) in Australia. First, a significant proportion of soldiers—most of those in infantry battalions, artillery units and SAS squadrons—returned to Australian from Vietnam as integral units, and thus continued to function as units for at least a brief period. The battalions paraded through city streets. These parades may have lacked the unequivocal, fervid support of previous victory parades, but they served as some ritual acknowledgement of veteran status. Most combat soldiers did not return home as lone individuals to be discharged or reposted, as in the US.

Secondly, as suggested earlier, the fact that the war and its soldiers were not subjected to such intense criticism in Australia as in the US presumably made the transition to civilian life somewhat easier. In most circles, there seems to be no stigma attached to being a Vietnam veteran, whereas veterans in the US were often subjected to criticism and abuse,[102] even though there the general prestige of the military has remained very high.[103]

Finally, it is quite possible that for the variety of organisational, tactical, and ideological reasons canvassed earlier, the average experiences of the average Australian soldier were less traumatic and more cushioned by group support than were those of his American counterpart. Certainly, for the duration of the war and for many years after the final withdrawal of Australian troops, there was no organised veterans' opposition to the conflict.

Vietnam Veterans' Action Association
An organisation which developed in 1979-1980, the VVAA has been concerned almost entirely with the Agent Orange issue: the alleged deleterious medical effects upon Australian soldiers of various herbicides and defoliants.[104] There has been less concern about non-physical effects of the war. Nor has the plight of the Vietnamese, who were obviously far more seriously affected by harmful chemicals, not to mention conventional weapons, been a matter of agitation by the veterans. This may have weakened the veterans' case in a moral sense, and possibly also politically. Many former opponents of the war in general and Australia's participation in particular would perhaps support a campaign which espoused the cause of Vietnamese civilians as much as those Australian soldiers who, implicitly, must accept the hazards of war whether they were Australian-laid mines[105] or American-manufactured chemicals.

Effects on the soldier and on the army

During the war there was only occasional discussion in the press as to how veterans were adjusting to civilian life. The consensus seemed to be that most did not see this as a problem; those who did were generally concerned with inequities in resettlement benefits, particularly for disabled soldiers.

> For some, the physical and emotional scars are slow to heal and they travel a long, slow road back to a normal life. For most of them, settling back into the community has been relatively uncomplicated. For all of them it is a time they want to forget.[106]

This last sentiment was endorsed in an amusing pamphlet published by some troops, 'Advice on the rehabilitation of a soldier':

> You should appreciate that he is no longer the sweet-tempered angel he was when he left Australia ... he is now older, probably leaner, wiser in the ways of the world, and probably a little strange ... so get the women off the streets, hide the grog, chain the fridge, lock the cow in the barn ...[107]

The pamphlet also mentions that the soldier must be re-accustomed to 'blond and respectable' women, flushing toilets, civilian manners, ordinary food, and Australian traffic. 'ABOVE ALL, HUMOUR HIM ... the Viet Cong couldn't shatter his composure, BUT CIVILIZATION MIGHT!'

This advice naturally seems far distant from academic analyses of the psychological aftermath of the Vietnam war as an effort to deal with a sense of betrayal 'by a nation, a government, by specified political leaders, or by the older generation in general ... (and) ... also a sense of self-betrayal.'[108]

There remains, however, the possibility that effects of combat or Vietnam service may be latent, surfacing months or even years later in behavioural or psychological problems.[109] Not only is the effect of Vietnam service on individual soldiers intrinsic interest and importance; we also need to look at its effects on the army as an organisation. Here, too, there has been little investigation in Australia apart from an occasional press article mentioning factors such as the expansion and then contraction in the army's size, readjustment to peacetime activities, realisation of the problems of logistics and joint force operations, and the problems associated with being oriented towards one function, namely, the Vietnam commitment.[110]

Conclusion

One inevitably compares the Australian soldier in Vietnam to two other models, the GI in Vietnam and the figure of the bronzed Anzac of the First and Second World Wars. In contrast to American soldiers, the Australians in Vietnam seemed to constitute a homogeneous force, whose style was bland and inward-looking, whose behaviour and attitudes seldom betrayed any gross dissatisfaction with the army or the war. Their discontent was directed more towards their allies and towards those at home who did not provide the support or freedom of action which they would have liked.

They appeared more ill at ease with their foreign environment than did the extroverted Americans, and seemed only too anxious to slip back into civilian life. The Australian experience of Vietnam does not possess the cumulative social effect that it does for the US as a nation, nor for the individuals involved.

The modern Australian soldier in action also provides a contrast with the folk-images of the digger myth, so popularly accepted in the earlier wars which Australian citizen armies have fought.[111] Like his Anzac forebear, the Australian soldier in Vietnam was credited with a fine performance, but in the new context of a regular professional army, whose effectiveness was seen as reflecting thorough training and firm discipline. To find the rip-roaring, civilian-at-heart soldiers celebrated in the Anzac myth, one tends to look at the American rather than the Australian camps in Vietnam. Many Australians serving in Vietnam, it is true, were uneasy at their designation as 'soldiers', but this derived more from their non-combatant activities than their distaste for the image of professional soldiers.

In other respects the Australian soldier of the 1960s and 1970s seemed far removed from earlier diggers. Though the forces seemed cohesive and there was some mention of mateship in battalion histories and soldiers' poems, this mateship had lost its aura of sanctity and emotional brilliance in comparison with earlier AIF soldiers. Perhaps this was because of the high (by military) standards of living, the discontinuous nature of combat, the low casualty rate, and the vastly superior medical and support services which the diggers in Vietnam enjoyed—again, in relative historical terms. Soldiers appeared, too, to be somewhat deferential to their college- or academy-trained officers. They often resented their officers' exercise of authority, particularly their resort to formal 'charges' to enforce discipline, but the resentment seldom rose above grumbling and go-slow tactics. But in terms of the standards set by the original diggers, the average officer hardly seemed to qualify as a 'leader' of his men.

Nevertheless, the officers were entitled to and revelled in their many privileges. Egalitarianism among soldiers of differing social backgrounds may have been strong, but the officers appeared highly conscious of rank and social background, though it is doubtful whether these feelings ever manifested themselves in overt behaviour, say, in combat situations. The officers were also rather derogatory about their men, and generally expressed surprise when the author stated as her intention 'finding out what the soldiers think'. 'Do they really think? *We* can give you much better information' was their frequent response. It seems unlikely that the Australian Army will be required to undertake any comparable ventures on a similar scale to the Vietnam operation in the foreseeable future. The 'lessons of Vietnam' (some of which, such as those provided by Agent

Orange, are slow to emerge and assess) may be absorbed neither by the military organisation nor by its political masters. It is depressing that so many will be so little the wiser for the experience.

6   The resisters
A history of the anti-conscription movement 1964-1972
MICHAEL E HAMEL-GREEN

In seven years of war, well-meaning American and Australian youth were sent year by year to play an obscene game of search-and-destroy—setting fire to an entire country with bombs, bullets and napalm. They returned home morally and physically scorched—if they returned home at all.

If intelligent young Australians had been asked whether they wanted to go to Vietnam—if the government of the day had been compelled to appeal for them to enlist—they might have wanted many questions answered. Why was the 'free world' supporting a regime that eschewed the elections called for in the 1954 Geneva Accords? Why had the insurgents such overwhelming support from the rural population? Why had the Diem regime tortured and gaoled even its non-communist opponents? ... But they were not asked. They were conscripted. And instead of facts they were fed anti-communist axioms: 'If we don't stop them in Vietnam, we will find them at our own doorstep.'

Conscription was to bring the issue of the war home to countless families across Australia, either because a son, friend, or relative was called up and sent to Vietnam, or because he was amongst the many who refused to go.

Conscription is not an everyday institution in Australia, nor is it entirely novel; it has intermittently existed for over half the period since Federation, for 42 out of 80 years. The first scheme was introduced in 1911 and took the form of a military training programme for 12 to 16 year-old youths. After the outbreak of the First World War, the Hughes government tried to widen conscription to include a call-up of 21 to 34 year old single men for overseas service—but was defeated at the 1916-17 Conscription Referenda. The youth training programme, nevertheless, continued through the war, and did not end until 1929.[1]

Ten years later the Federal Labor government reintroduced conscription during the Second World War. All unmarried males were called up. Conscripts were not initially required to serve outside Australia's own territories, but in 1942 the boundaries were extended to include the whole of the Southwest Pacific. The scheme ended with the end of the war.[2] Then in 1951 a the Liberal-Country Party government scheme called up 18 year old males for three to six months. Although Australia was sending troops to the Korean War at the time, conscripts were not required to serve overseas. The scheme was reduced in scope in 1957, and was abandoned in 1959.³

The most recent scheme was introduced by the Menzies government in November 1964 to upgrade Australian military preparedness for intervention alongside America in Vietnam. It consisted in a selective (birthday ballot) call-up of 20 year old males for two year periods, with no restrictions on sending conscripts overseas.⁴ By June 1966 conscripts comprised one quarter of the Australian task force in Vietnam; by March 1968, almost one half.⁵ The chances of a 20 year old being chosen in the ballot were approximately one in ten; balloted tertiary students could have their call-up deferred until the end of their studies.⁶ Exemption through conscientious objection provisions was extended to absolute pacifists but not to particular war objectors.⁷ Penalties for non-compliance consisted of fines and/or one to three weeks' gaol for failing to register, burning a registration (draft) card, or failing to attend for medical examination; and two years' gaol for failing to report to an army induction centre after receipt of a call-up notice.⁸ The scheme operated for the entire period of Australian intervention in Vietnam and was brought to an end in late 1972 by the Labor government.

Only during 1911–17 and 1964–72 did conscription arouse great controversy, widespread opposition and resistance in the Australian community. An obvious explanation is that at both times conscription was associated with an unpopular overseas war that did not territorially threaten Australia. The First World War was one of imperialist rivalry. After an initial wave of public enthusiasm, it became increasingly unpopular as casualties mounted with no apparent end in sight.⁹ The Vietnam War was more a case of imperialist repression: the attempted subjugation of an indigenous revolutionary uprising that posed specific and general threats to American economic hegemony in the Pacific Basin region.¹⁰ The initially uneasy support of Australians for the war turned into majority opposition as it became apparent that no quick victory could be achieved and as the facts and injustices of the war became increasingly understood.

One period of opposition to conscription does not fit the pattern. At the very outset of the 1911 conscription scheme, three years before the start of the First World War, 'fewer than half the boys supposed to register did so; more than 20,000 parents exposed themselves to possible prosecution.'¹¹ No doubt the suspicion that conscription was instituted for aggressive, jingoistic purposes was an important element in the 1911, non-compliance, but more important was the novelty of such state coercion in Australia. Many working-class parents, unionists, and pacifists saw the scheme as an unprecedented interference in their lives—and feared that the scheme could be used for strike-breaking purposes and to convert youth to militarism and chauvinism.

Opposition to the 1964 scheme unfolded in marked contrast to the 1911–17 anti-conscription movement. In 1911, defiance and resistance was immediately apparent. In 1964, however, there was merely verbal opposition to the new measure; even those who opposed the scheme acquiesced in the registration periods, or counselled youth to do so. While the earlier opposition became largely channelled into electoral avenues—the 1916–17 referenda—the opposition to the 1964 scheme moved from electoral campaigns aimed at bringing the ALP to office in 1966, to campaigns of resistance and non-compliance that meshed with the wider political opposition to Australian intervention in the Vietnam War.

This account is written from the standpoint of one who actively participated in the anti-war, anti-conscription movement from 1965 onwards.[12]

The introduction of conscription in 1964

The initially passive response to the scheme's introduction reflected both the legitimacy which conscription had acquired during the Second World War and the fifties, and the manipulative manner in which the Menzies government chose to introduce the measure. Officially, the decision to bring in conscription was presented in terms of the need to meet troop strength targets set down in the 1963 Defence Review: voluntary means had failed, so conscription was required. But this obscures the wider context in which increased troop levels were considered neccessary.

According to the Pentagon Papers, the Kennedy administration drew up plans as early as April 1961 for American ground intervention in Vietnam 'to prevent communist domination' of the area. In November 1961 Kennedy noted that further escalation would require the support of 'other nations'.[13] From the early sixties onwards, and especially during the Johnson administration's secret planning in 1964, the Americans gave frequent signals to allies such as Australia that they should prepare themselves for possible military intervention in Vietnam.

These American concerns found a sympathetic audience within the Menzies cabinet and among right-wing Liberal backbenchers as Wilfred Kent Hughes and John Jess; the Democratic Labor Party and National Civic Council; TB Millar and other 'threat experts' close to the government; and the Returned Servicemen's League, which had long cherished the hope of making conscription a permanent part of the Australian way of life.

In March 1962 Wilfred Kent Hughes introduced a conscription bill before Parliament, citing the threat posed by 'increasing pressure of Communist infiltration, subversion and guerrilla aggression in South-East Asia.'[14] After its narrow win in the 1961 election, however, the Menzies government did not care to take such a controversial step without first gradually laying the groundwork.

The first move was to send thirty army advisers to South Vietnam in

June 1962, to establish the principle and precedent of Australian military assistance to the regime. In April 1963 the government announced a five-year defence programme which entailed a £41 million increase in expenditure. 'Acute problems in South Vietnam' were cited amongst the reasons for the upgraded programme.[15] In July the government announced that army target strength would be raised to 28,000 men by 1967. The RSL and various Liberal Party branches enthusiastically followed this decision with a vigorous campaign for the introduction of conscription as a way of meeting the new target.

When Johnson assumed the presidency in late 1963, American planning for substantial air and ground intervention in Vietnam was intensified, but kept secret for fear of political repercussions during the 1964 election. Johnson was standing against Barry Goldwater and was concerned to appear as the 'peace candidate'. 'We don't want our American boys to do the fighting for Asian boys', he affirmed during the 1964 campaign,[16] and repeatedly declared that he sought 'no wider war'.[17] But as the Pentagon Papers clearly show, the Johnson administration began planning air and ground escalation in Vietnam as early as January 1964.[18]

In the interregnum before the presidential election, the administration began giving fresh signals to Australia and other potential allies that they should prepare for an expanded war in Vietnam. In February 1964, Roger Hilsman, Johnson's Assistant Secretary of State for Far Eastern Affairs, visited Australia for an Australian Institute of Political Science Summer School. There we urged 'increased participation of the nations of Asia in their own defence', for 'only through such participation can all forms of aggression be checked at their roots.'[19] In the same forum the Australian academic, T B Millar, strongly urged the introduction of conscription to facilitate such increased participation.[20] Later, he presented his ideas in an article 'Two Years National Service ... And the Sooner the Better?'[21] which showed either extraordinary prescience or inside knowledge: it set out all the substantial features of the conscription scheme that was subsequently adopted.

Millar contended:

> If we are committed to operations on the mainland of South-East Asia, it would be highly desirable, for reasons of effectiveness, logistics, and of playing our full national part, that we should provide a whole division at the initial stages, with a strong follow-up and reinforcement capacity.[22]

Conscription was his key to providing the 'follow-up and reinforcement capacity'. Early in 1964, Wilfred Kent Hughes was advancing a similar line of argument.[23]

At the 13 April SEATO Council meeting, the American Secretary of State, Dean Rusk, spelt out American policy in Vietnam for SEATO members, warning of the 'strategic danger which would exist if communism absorbed Southeast Asia's peoples and resources.'[24] Sir Garfield Barwick 'welcomed and supported this great statement of policy' and noted that the council had decided to 'remain prepared to take further concrete steps' in Vietnam.[25]

In May 1964, the Australian government received an aide-memoire from the Johnson administration indicating various directions in which Australia should increase its 'assistance' to Vietnam.[26] In June, Menzies visited Washington, reportedly under strong pressure to increase Australia's troop commitment in Vietnam.[27] This he did in late June with the dispatch of 30 more military advisers and six Caribou transports to South Vietnam—an action which won extravagant praise from President Johnson.[28] Meanwhile, the RSL. right-wing Liberal backbenchers, and the DLP continued to campaign for the introduction of conscription.[29]

In August 1964, the Johnson administration made use of the Tonkin Gulf incident to secure a congressional resolution which authorised 'all necessary measures' in Vietnam—a blank cheque for future escalation of the war.[30] During a debate on the incident in the Australian Parliament, the Opposition Leader, Arthur Calwell, challenged the government: 'We do not desire to see another eighth division of Australian troops sucked into an Asian jungle or swallowed up by the quicksands of Asia. If we are to be committed, we ought to know the extent of the commitment.'[31] But Menzies declined to be drawn, and merely referred in a general way to Australia's SEATO obligations to assist South Vietnam.[32]

Curiously—or perhaps not so curiously—the Menzies government denied any intention of introducing conscription right up until the moment of the first announcement. November 10, 1964 was the last date compatible with introducing the necessary bill in the final session of Parliament before the December Senate election. In January, July, August and even as late as October 26, Federal ministers had denied that the government was planning to introduce conscription.[33] On October 26, the Army Minister, Dr Forbes, stated that 'The Federal government does not intend to use conscription at present to build up the strength of the armed forces.'[34] Concealment was no doubt designed to lull the Labor Party and other potential opponents into thinking that conscription would not be introduced, while simultaneously permitting backbench Liberals, 'threat experts' and the RSL to soften up public opinion. To have announced conscription long in advance might have encouraged the mobilisation of extensive opposition to the scheme or forced the government into a premature admission of how it planned to use the conscripts.[35]

T B Millar observed in his August 1964 *Bulletin* article that 'For political and other reasons, the voluntary system must be squeezed dry. The Federal Opposition and some others, who are now belabouring the government over defence matters, would not in any case react kindly to the introduction of compulsory training.'[36] By introducing the measure just prior to the Senate election, the government sought to claim the election outcome as a 'mandate' for conscription; Menzies had no intention of repeating W M Hughes' mistake in holding referenda on the issue. The public was to be neither consulted nor forewarned—merely presented with a *fait accompli*.

Lyndon Johnson was confirmed as President on 3 November. On the same day a new White House inter-agency group under William Bundy, the Assistant Secretary of State, met to begin implementing the administration's long-planned air and ground escalation in Vietnam.[37] Two days later, Bundy drafted a memorandum which noted that 'The President is clearly thinking in terms of the maximum use of the Gulf of Tonkin rationale', and recommended consultations with the UK, Australia, New Zealand and Thailand before the final decision on escalation: 'We would hope for firm moral support from the UK and for participation in at least token form from the others.'[38]

At a White House strategy meeting on 1 December 1964, Johnson gave final approval to the bombing of North Vietnam and stated that he wanted 'new, dramatic effective' forms of assistance from several allied countries, specifically mentioning Australia, New Zealand, Canada and the Philippines.[39] On 4 December, William Bundy flew to Canberra to give the Australian government 'the full picture' of the planned escalation of the war, and to 'request additional contributions by way of forces in the event the second phase of US actions were entered.'[40]

The *dénouement* of these secret November-December decisions and negotiations came five months later. Secure in the knowledge that the new conscription scheme could provide the necessary reinforcements, Menzies announced on 29 April 1965 that Australia was committing a battalion of combat troops to Vietnam. In his 10 November announcement of the new measure, he had cited a 'defence emergency': 'The range of likely military situations we must be prepared to face has increased as a result of recent Indonesian policies and actions and the growth of Communist influence and armed activity in Laos and South Vietnam.'[41] He said, it was necessary to build up the army's strength, since 'we expect a continuing requirement to make forces available for cold war and insurgency tasks'.[42] Voluntary means had failed—so conscription was required.

Replying for the Opposition two days later, Calwell contended that nothing had happened in the previous six months to suddenly create such an 'emergency'. He condemned the ballot system as a form of 'Russian roulette', and disputed that the voluntary system had really failed.[43] Neither he nor his deputy, Gough Whitlam, challenged the assumption that it was desirable 'to make forces available for cold war and insurgency tasks'. Whitlam thought that 'in all probability there will be no war in this area' (Southeast Asia)[44] The only Labor parliamentarians who appeared to have any real grasp of what was going on were L R Johnson, K Beazley, J F Cairns, and C Cameron.[45]

In the year before the 1964 introduction of conscription there was no anti-conscription or anti-Vietnam war campaign to speak of—certainly nothing to match the pro-conscription campaign. The first specifically anti-Vietnam war protests in Australia took place during the annual Hiroshima Day Commemoration marches of 9 August 1964, when many of the 2000 marchers in Sydney carried 'No war in Vietnam' banners, and a group of 200 in Melbourne demonstrated outside the US Consulate to protest American bombing raids on North Vietnam during the Tonkin Gulf episode. But there were no other street demonstrations against either conscription or intervention in Vietnam ... nor were there any at the time conscription was announced or in the Senate election campaign that followed.[46] This was understandable in the context, yet it was a measure of the left's weakness that it allowed itself to be lulled into inaction. Throughout three years of official and right-wing preparations for conscription and a new intervention in Southeast Asia, the left and ALP generally (with the notable exceptions of Eddie Ward, C Cameron and Jim Cairns) rarely diagnosed the trend in government policy. They certainly did not attempt to mobilise people against that trend. The scheme which logistically paved the way for Australia to intervene beside America in a genocidal war was created with a minimum of public disturbance.

From passivity to dissent 1964–66

Enactment of a law is one thing, its legitimacy is another, and enforcement it is yet a third step. If the government had successfully caught the left and ALP unawares with conscription in 1964, this did not mean automatic public acceptance for the measure, nor that it would be able to enforce the law in the face of large-scale defiance by those subject to it.

It was open to the Labor Party and others on the left to call for total defiance of the new measure in the same way that the IWW had called, with considerable success, for defiance of the 1916 conscription proclamation.[47] Instead, the ALP quibbled over the sudden policy reversal, the lottery system, and the merits of the voluntary system. No-one in the ALP or peace organisations or on the left issued a call for parents and youth to defy the new measure—no-one seemed prepared to attack the very legitimacy of the scheme.[48]

In contrast to the one in two of eligible youth who did not register in the first years of the 1911 scheme, and the one in three who did not respond to the 1916 Proclamation, less than one per cent failed to register in the first ballot of the 1964 scheme,[49] and none of these seemed inclined to take a public stand on their non-registration.[50] As the Wobblies might have put it, while people were merely *talking* about voting out conscription at the ballot box in 1966, the government was *acting* to create the machinery for slaughter in Vietnam—and consolidate it as a normal and acceptable part of Australian life.[51]

It is true that at the first anti-conscription meeting convened to protest the new measure, organised by the Sydney University Labor, Liberal and

ALP Clubs on November 11 1964, one participant remembered: 'The main plea of the speakers was that we should not let this issue be yet another which has been passed over and accepted; there should be a mass refusal to register'[52] But this note of militancy soon evaporated. At subsequent anti-conscription meetings in the Sydney State Theatre on 22 November[53] and at Sydney Town Hall on 29 November,[54] the main concern was electoral work on the ALP's behalf during the impending Senate election campaign. No street demonstrations were called; the chief activity consisted of handing out leaflets condemning the government for its sudden turnabout on the conscription issue and urging that people vote for the ALP.[55]

At the 29 November meeting, however, a move was made to form a youth organisation to oppose conscription. The Conscription Protest Meeting Committee which had convened the meeting circulated a list among the predominantly young audience of 600, asking for people to put down their names if they wished to take part in a campaign against conscription. This became the initial mailing list of the committee—which subsequently renamed itself the Youth Campaign Against Conscription (YCAC).[56]

The first registration period, the last week of January and the first week of February 1965, passed completely unchallenged, permitting the government to claim that 'young men were anxious to do national service training'.[57] That this was not entirely true was indicated in the remarks of some young men interviewed in one of the first batches to attend compulsory medical examinations. 'They say this is a free country', said John Wighton, a truck driver, 'and then slam you into gaol for two years ... No, I definitely don't want to go. I am dead against it. I'll try every way I can to get out.'[58] John Duke, a cutter, felt that 'If you've got to do it, then that's it, but if I can get out of it, I will'.[59]

When the realities of the Vietnam war exploded in the public consciousness in March-April 1965 (the start of American bombing of North Vietnam and large-scale commitment of American and Australian combat troops), anti-conscriptionists took part in rolling demonstrations outside US consulates. It was not until June that YCAC took its next major step: an advertisement in *The Australian* on 19 June, signed by 144 potential conscripts, saying (in part):

> The undersigned young Australian male citizens, being of an age making us liable for military service, declare that WE OPPOSE OVERSEAS CONSCRIPTION because:
>> We believe that we may be sent to fight in Vietnam ... This would be a moral wrong and an unjust call upon our lives by the Government of our country. We share a fundamental belief that to safeguard the future of our nation, Australia's role in these perilous times is to seek an end to South East Asian disputes, through negotiations for peaceful settlements—not to pursue the murderous path to world conflict

through prolonging the slaughter in Vietnam.

The advertisement concluded with an appeal for fellow 20 year olds to sign and send in a pledge: 'I support the campaign against overseas conscription.'

This first manifesto, with its strong emphasis on opposition to conscription for *overseas* service, and on a negotiated settlement in Vietnam, aligned the leadership of YCAC with corresponding ALP policies. This remained the stance of YCAC in all States until the 1966 election. In almost all YCAC branches the leaders tended to be active ALP members. Internal pressures from pacifist members to persuade YCAC to take a stand against conscription *as such*, and from radical members to take a stand for immediate withdrawal from Vietnam and to use more militant tactics were generally subordinated to the electoral strategy of ending conscription through an ALP victory at the next election. Militant or civil disobedience tactics were seen by the YCAC leadership as likely to endanger Labor's chances.[60]

Hundreds of young men from all over Australia responded to YCAC's advertisement in *The Australian*, thereby furnishing active constituencies for YCAC branches in every State.[61] Another kind of anti-conscription group was formed at about the same time. Initiated by Joyce Golgerth and Pat Ashcroft at a meeting in Sydney on 5 June 1965, the organisation was called Save Our Sons (SOS) and consisted of 'mothers joining together to voice their opposition to the conscription of their sons for the slaughter in Vietnam'.[62] Similar groups were formed not long afterwards in Melbourne, Brisbane, Perth, Newcastle and Adelaide.[63]

In the latter half of 1965, YCAC and SOS began to make a major impact on the public consciousness through controversial demonstrations such as the 30 June protest at Sydney Central Station as the first batch of NSW conscripts departed for the army's Puckapunyal training camp, and the 28 September demonstrations at conscript intakes in both Melbourne and Sydney.[64] The YCAC-SOS campaign intensified in the following year with a wave of draft card burnings in four cities (Sydney, Melbourne, Brisbane and Perth); a sit-down during the Melbourne Moomba Parade; vigils outside Prime Minister Holt's Melbourne home; and continued demonstrations at army induction centres.[65]

By the middle of 1966, YCAC had effectively made the point that, far from eagerly complying with conscription and the war, a significant proportion of youth was vigorously dissenting from the scheme. If so, then the government had won an ironic victory of its own. It had successfully established the credibility of conscription's punitive sanctions and the legitimacy of personal exemption or deferment. It was scarcely troubled that conscript-age dissenters were seeking and gaining temporary or permanent exemptions, so long as the inherent coerciveness of the system was adequate to guarantee the requisite supply of conscripts, and so long as the scheme exacted compliance even from those most opposed to it.

The anti-conscription movement consciously or unconsciously deferred to these purposes. With rare exceptions, the movement's advice to young men at the time was to seek personal exemption through the legal conscientious objection provisions of the scheme. The public draft card burnings of early 1966 represented the form but not the substance of resistance because few, if any, of the burners carried their resistance further into non-compliance with registration procedures, compulsory medical examinations, or army call-up notices.[66] Even groups with a remembered tradition of civil disobedience, such as the Quakers and the Federal Pacifist Council, spent most of 1965 and 1966 setting up 'conscientious objection advisory groups' rather than conscientious resistance groups analogous to the 1912 New Zealand Passive Resisters' Union (PRU) and the 1915 Australian No-Conscription Fellowship (NCF). Contrary to the intentions of their organisers, the CO Advisory Groups undermined the potential of solidarity between those subject to conscription: they oriented members' thinking towards their own personal exemption rather than collectively overthrowing conscription and ending Australian participation in the war.[67]

During the final months of 1966, the YCAC-SOS-ALP campaign against conscription reached its peak with frequent demonstrations, numerous meetings and rallies, and strident protests at Prime Minister Holt's election campaign meetings. No-one wished to think what would happen if Labor were defeated. Those who had reacted with healthy outrage towards the Vietnam war and conscription could scarcely bring themselves to believe that the majority of Australians would not feel similar outrage and vote accordingly.

Amidst all the protests and incessant campaigning in the pre-election months, two events stand out as carrying significance for future developments within the anti-war, anti-conscription movement. One was President Johnson's tour in October of several Australian cities, designed to boost the Liberals' election campaign and reward their support of America's Vietnam policy. The other was the decision of Sydney schoolteacher, Bill White, to refuse a 18 July notice requiring him to report for duty at an army induction centre.

The massive demonstrations that followed President Johnson in Australia were widely reported not only within Australia but in America itself, and successfully contradicted the image of the down-under ally as one hundred per cent loyal on the issue of Vietnam. At the same time, the over-reaction of local police and American security agents gave Sydney and Melbourne protesters the same baptism in police brutality which Queensland anti-conscriptionists had already experienced earlier that year when a street parade was broken up by police on 24 March. This experience was one factor in the rise of a militant student anti-war and anti-conscription movement.

Bill White's decision to defy a call-up notice was equally significant: it was the first occasion when one subject to conscription publicly engaged in an act of resistance likely to incur a lengthy gaol sentence. An absolute pacifist, White was eligible for official conscientious objection status and sought such classification. Only when his conscientious objection case failed and he confronted the prospect of induction did he begin to resist. He said at the time:

> I am opposed to a State's right to conscript a person, I believe very strongly in democracy and democratic ideals—and I believe that it is in the area of the State's right over the life of the individual that the difference lies between totalitarian and democratic government. My opposition to conscription, of course, is intensified greatly when the conscription is for military purposes. In fact the National Service Act is the embodiment of what I consider to be morally wrong and, no matter what the consequences, I will never fulfill the terms of the act.[68]

But he did not, apparently, see himself as complying with the terms of the Act by registering or filing for conscientious objection status; even after he was gaoled (just before the 1966 election) he continued to seek CO status, eventually succeeding at a second case on 23 December 1966.

The prevailing attitude among objectors at the time is evident in the aims of the Bill White Conscientious Objectors' Defence Committee (formed in August) which somewhat narrowly focussed on assistance to that miniscule proportion of 20 year olds who happened to be absolute pacifists and thereby eligible for CO status:

1. To render assistance to Bill White, teacher and conscientious objector, in whatever ways possible.
2. To seek by amendment of the National Service Act and regulations thereunder the removal of harsh provisions as applied to conscientious objectors.
3. To assist at the discretion of the Committee any other conscientious objectors who may suffer from the *National Service Act* 1951–1965.[69]

In the context of the movement in 1966, however, what mattered far more was the spirit that White himself had shown in defying conscription to the point of going to gaol. In Brecht's words, 'so much is already won when only one man stands up and says no'. Most of those who began to resist in the ensuing years, myself included, would acknowledge some debt to the example of Bill White. If one person's refusal to cooperate could create such a public impact how much more might have been achieved if YCAC had adopted a similar stand at the very outset.

In the final weeks before the 1966 election, a coalition of anti-conscription groups in Melbourne launched a 'Vote No Conscription Campaign' based upon extensive television, radio, and press advertising:

We aim to turn the Federal Election into the Referendum on Conscription denied the Australian people. We need only to persuade 10% of Liberal voters, mainly women, that their vote means life or death to hundreds of young men—and conscription will be defeated. We will reach the electors through the mass media of press, radio, and above all, television.[70]

In the event, of course, a sizeable majority voted for continuance of the Liberal-Country Party Government.

This was not a case of people disagreeing with the anti-conscriptionists—opinion polls at the time showed a majority of Australians opposed to sending conscripts to Vietnam[71]—but rather a case of (anomalous) persuasion by an effective government and mass media campaign that dramatised the supposed communist 'threat from the north' and the so-called logic of the 'domino theory', by which Thailand, Malaysia and Indonesia would all 'fall' if South Vietnam went communist.

Nevertheless, the anti-war and anti-conscription movement was partly responsible for the election defeat: a movement reluctant to incur the risks of civil disobedience and gaol was scarcely in a position to communicate the life-or-death urgency of the fact that a whole land and its people faced destruction under the bombing, napalm, defoliation and technological onslaught of the world's greatest military power. Also, the movement's narrow emphasis on the demand 'No Conscripts for Vietnam', to the detriment of the more far-reaching 'Withdraw All Troops' and 'Abolish Conscription Now', failed to alert people to the inherent injustices of the war and conscription system.

From dissent to resistance 1967-69

Following Labor's defeat, YCAC branches quickly disintegrated in all States. No thought had been given to an alternative strategy. Despite daily escalation of the war and conscription's integral part in Australia's involvement, virtually no demonstrations were organised in the whole of 1967.[72] But if the Laborite anti-conscription groups, not to mention the ALP itself (led no longer by Calwell but by Gough Whitlam) had temporarily ceased their opposition, this did not mean that nothing happened, for 1967 saw the beginning of an entirely new kind of challenge to conscription.

Three 20 year olds facing registration in the January-February 1967 registration period independently decided to publicly refuse to comply, a course that made them liable to automatic call-up, and ultimately, if they refused call-up notices, to two years' gaol. The three, Mike Matteson and Chris Campbell in Sydney, and Errol Heldzingen in Melbourne, may well have been influenced by the example of White in late 1966 and the growing draft resistance movement in America. Moreover, each drew strength from direct action traditions in their political philosophies: anarchism, pacifism, and radical socialism respectively. In the July-August registration period, they were joined by John Paull, Mike Jones, and the Mowbray triplets, David, Robert and Graham; and in 1968 by Len Truscott, Jonathon Hicks, Stephen Townsend, Sean Foley, Jeremy Gilling, Graham Jensen, Karl Armstrong, Tony Dalton, David Bissett, and Laurie Carmichael Jr. Others who regretted their earlier registrations began to resist at the medical examination stage. In July 1967, Brian Ross of Orbost, Victoria, refused to attend the compulsory medical; and Geoff Mullens of Sydney took a similar stand in February 1968.[73]

The significance of these non-compliers' action lay in their courageous refusal to seek personal exemption, whether through the ballot, medicals or conscientious objection provisions (for which most were quite eligible to apply). They were the first to publicly place themselves on a collision course with the government as a deliberate means of discrediting conscription and the war for which it was being employed. After Bill White, they were the first to take the issue of the war and conscription seriously enough to risk two years' gaol in protest.

Brian Ross, the first of the group to receive and refuse a call-up notice (requiring him to report to an army induction centre on 17 August 1968), explained his stand in the following statement:

> Non-cooperation with the National Service Act shows a willingness to forfeit personal liberty and underlines a faith in human dignity, and a determination to bring evidence of this faith before the general public. To dismiss such action as irresponsible is a greater disservice to mankind (and to our society) than the apparent defiance of the law. This Act applies to every twenty-year old. The rest of the community may wash its hands, but one would hope that these acts of non-cooperation might remind many people of their individual responsibility for the actions of the state.[74]

The government appeared in no great hurry to prosecute these early non-compliers but moved more rapidly in the cases of several who had sought conscientious objection status, were denied exemption, and then refused to comply with the military.

Two such cases, Denis O'Donnell and Desmond Phillipson, were already in the army, having decided to seek CO status after being conscripted; another was a journalist, Simon Townsend, who refused to comply with a call-up notice after being denied exemption at his CO hearing. All three were sent to Holsworthy military prison and their cases became the focus of considerable public outcry and demonstration, particularly aroused by the brutal treatment they received there.[75] This outcry caused the National Service Act to be amended in May 1968 to transfer custody of national service defaulters from military to civilian gaols. Later that year, a fourth unsuccessful conscientious objector, John Zarb, a Melbourne postman, became the first to be sent to a civilian gaol after refusing to comply with a notice. He spent over a year in Pentridge

Prison in Melbourne.

No doubt encouraged by these stands, a new group sprang up in Melbourne early in 1968, the Draft Resistance Movement (DRM). Its aims and actions were distinctly more militant than its YCAC predecessor:

> The DRM has not been formed to oppose conscription, it has been formed to wreck it. We are opposed to the war in Vietnam and we intend to resist the conscription of Australian youth for this war by *all* available means. We will hold demonstrations of various kinds with the aim of making conscription as ineffective as possible; we will supply information on how to fail medical exams and other methods of resisting the draft and we will encourage people not to register. By these means we will help those 20 year olds who do not wish to be conscripted for any reason.[76]

In the first DRM demonstration, at the February conscript intake, four members chained themselves across the Swan Street army barracks gates while 50 DRM and SOS supporters staged a sit-down in front of them. A second vigorous demonstration was held when Prime Minister Gorton spoke at the Caulfield Town Hall on 13 February; and a further sit-in at the Federal Parliamentary Offices on 26 April.

Although the DRM as an organisation lasted no more than a few months, its stress on mounting levels of resistance was carried on by increasingly militant student groups, including Students for a Democratic Society (SDS) and the Pacifist Society at Melbourne University; the Labor Club and the Pacifist Society at Monash; SDS at Sydney; SDS at Tasmania; and Students for Democratic Action (SDA) at the University of Queensland.

Throughout 1968 and 1969, these groups, especially in Melbourne and Sydney, mounted extensive resistance, in the form of numerous sit-ins and impromptu raids on government offices. They intensively campaigned to incite 20 year olds not to register: urging young men not to register was not only vital to broadening the draft resistance movement but in itself an act of civil disobedience, since it violated the incitement provisions of the Commonwealth Crimes Act.[77] In moving from protest to resistance, the students were increasingly joined, not only by members of the established anti-conscription, labour and peace organisations, but also by large numbers of academics, writers, artists, and churchmen. Over the same period, the Congress for International Cooperation and Disarmament (CICD), Amalgamated Engineering Union (AEU) and several other Melbourne unions instituted vigorous solidarity campaigns on behalf of gaoled objectors: John Zarb at Pentridge, and, later, Brian Ross at Sale Prison. Demonstrations and vigils outside the gaols were almost weekly events and 'Free Zarb' and 'Free Ross' slogans became a common sight on walls and railway sidings around Melbourne.

The developing resistance to conscription was closely integrated with more general actions such as the militant 4 July and 25 October 1968 anti-war demonstrations in Melbourne. Draft resisters did not see themselves as being anti-conscription *instead* of being anti-Vietnam war but rather *because* of being anti-war, an approach subsequently recognised in the dual anti-war anti-conscription aims of the Vietnam Moratorium.

The first intensive 'Don't Register!' campaign was launched during the 1969 January-February registration period, following a combined SDS-Draft Resistance Conference in Carlton, Melbourne, on 28–29 December 1968. On the first day of the campaign, seven students were arrested, two on charges of 'incitement' under the Crimes Act and the rest under a Melbourne City Council by-law (By-law 418) prohibiting the handing out of leaflets. As news of the arrests spread, the numbers handing out leaflets on the steps of the Melbourne GPO snowballed—so that by the following Saturday there were over 500 people handing out 'Don't Register' pamphlets.

Faced with this epidemic of criminality, the Commonwealth Police were highly selective in making arrests under the Crimes Act. They concentrated on a handful of student 'ringleaders' rather than on more prominent or powerful members of the community. City Council parking officers were less fussy in their policing of By-Law 418. By the beginning of March, over 100 people had been thus arrested, including, J F Cairns, MHR (who became national chairman of the Vietnam Moratorium in the following year). Many arrested under the By-Law refused to pay their fines and were gaoled for five or seven day periods, and the number facing gaol grew larger every week. As a result, this relatively minor free speech issue was fought to a successful conclusion within the space of ten weeks: on 9 April the City Council repealed the law.

Controversy over Crimes Act arrests continued, however, and generated far-flung declarations of support. In Melbourne on 7 and 25 March, Sydney on 7 and 13 March, Canberra on 24 March, and Brisbane on 1 May, students held large demonstrations in support of those arrested and handed out 'Don't Register' leaflets. By the end of March, over 1000 students had thereby exposed themselves to the risk of 12 months' gaol (the maximum penalty for incitement).[78] The overworked duplicating machine at SDS headquarters in Carlton ran 24 hours a day in an effort to meet the demand for updated 'editions' of the leaflet, carrying more and more signatures.

In the two-month period to the end of April 1969, 302 people were arrested in anti-conscription marches, sit-ins, and occupations across the country. On of the most notable was dubbed the 'Battle of Sydney' by the press. On 11 April, 600 Sydney University students marched from the campus to the city, a familiar, almost weekly, pilgrimage in that period. But this time, when they reached Castlereagh Street, they broke into a full-scale charge, racing towards the Federal attorney-general's office. Arriving before the police, they successfully occupied the office—compelling the police to drag them out laboriously, one by one. 110 were arrested. A far smaller but equally militant act of resistance took place on 23 April when a draft resister, Louis Christofides, sat on the railway line at Wollongong holding up a train that was about to take conscripts to Sydney[79]

In June, civil disobedience spread from students to academics and from academics to the boarder community, an important broadening of the movement which owed much to the courage of three Sydney University academics, Professors Charles Birch and Charles Martin, and Dr Terry Smith. At a university meeting they made speeches supporting draft resisters and publicy encouraged young men not to register. This received widespread coverage in the press. *The Australian* reported that the Acting Minister for National Service, Mr McMahon, called for an immediate report on suitable action against the professors.[80] Within days, over 120 fellow academics had pledged their support; by the end of the month more than 500 academics across the country had signed similar 'incitement' statement.[81]

Early in July, a Committee in Defiance of the National Service Act was formed, and issued a 'Statement of Defiance' pledging 'whole-hearted support, encouragement and aid' to draft resisters.[82] 'The signing of the Statement of Defiance,' wrote Ken McLeod, a founding member of the committee, 'marked the end of token support for non-compliers, and began a new escalation of the anti-conscription movement in Australia'.[83]

Following the extraordinary wave of support that developed around the actions of Birch and Martin and the Committee in Defiance, the government quickly backed away from plans to prosecute them. In late June, McMahon denied that he was considering prosecution of Birch and Martin, while on 26 August Attorney-General Bowen told Parliament that he was inclined to think a prosecution 'would not succeed'. That the government could quite easily and successfully have prosecuted all Statement of Defiance signatories was later demonstrated by the committee's successful self-prosecution in NSW and Victoria in late 1969 and early 1970.[84] What inhibited the government was not its ability to prosecute but rather the crisis that would result if it were to gaol those who had signed the statement—8000 by late November 1969.[85]

Even in the case of the hundred or so who successfully prosecuted themselves, the government carefully refrained from enforcing the usual gaol sentence for refusal to pay fines. A government that had no qualms about sentencing 20 year old draft resisters to two years' gaol clearly felt highly diffident about gaoling better-known citizens for even a few days. The self-prosecutions valuably exposed the cynical selectivity of the government's sanctions and helped undermine conscription's earlier aura of legitimacy.

In the period leading to the 1969 July-August registration, student resistance continued. Among the more notable actions, in terms of public impact, were the temporary imprisonment of Mr Snedden, then Minister for Labour and National Service, in his Treasury Place office in

Melbourne; a barricaded occupation of the Victorian headquarters of the Liberal Party; a sit-down in front of the Sydney University Regiment as it paraded before the NSW Governor, Sir Roden Cutler; a further occupation of the Sydney office of the Minister for Labour and National Service; a raid on the Adelaide offices of the National Service Department in which the office was wrecked and pigs' blood poured over the files; and a 16-hour sit-in at the Newcastle office of the Minister for Defence, Mr Fairhall.[86] Draft resisters were becoming both more organised and more numerous, holding two interstate conferences in May and August.[87] At several universities, including Latrobe, Flinders, and Sydney, as well as the National Union of Australian University Students (NUAUS) August Council, student unions and offices were offered as sanctuaries for draft resisters.[88]

In September, several Victorian unions organised a series of demonstrations at the court cases of four draft resisters, the largest demonstration being the Williamstown court case of Laurie Carmichael Jr, son of the Federal Secretary of the Amalgamated Engineering Union. Workers from the nearby naval dockyard went on strike to attend, swelling the courthouse crowd to about 500 in all. When Carmichael appeared outside the court, he was suddenly 'kidnapped' by supporters. In what proved a useful experiment in the feasibility of 'underground resistance', his supporters succeeded in keeping him underground for a week before he voluntarily gave himself up. The action greatly increased the confidence of anti-conscriptionists that they possessed the power to resist the actual *enforcement* of conscription.

Meanwhile the authorities showed extraordinary inertia in their prosecutions of the original 1967 and 1968 draft resisters: six, nine or even twelve months intervened between failure to register and prosecution for non-registration; between prosecution for non-registration and being asked to attend a medical; between prosecution for not attending a medical and receiving a call-up notice to report to an army induction centre; and between failure to comply with a call-up notice and prosecution for failing to comply. On 29 October 1969, however, the authorities finally gaoled one of the original group of resisters, sentencing Brian Ross to a two year term in Sale Prison in south-eastern Victoria. CICD, SOS, and several unions organised a 'Freedom Ride' to Sale gaol to dramatise the fact of his imprisonment.

In mid-December, angered at Ross's gaoling, 200 shop stewards and delegates from 27 Victorian unions issued a controversial mutiny call:

> This meeting of Shop Stewards and Delegates issues a call to all young workers to refuse to register and refuse to comply with the National Service Act.
> > We encourage those young men already conscripted to refuse to accept orders against their conscience and those in Vietnam to lay down their arms in mutiny against the heinous barbarism

perpetrated in our name upon the innocent, aged, men, and women and children.[89]

This mutiny call was widely publicised, and roundly condemned by both press and government. *The Age* noted that the maximum penalty for such incitement was life imprisonment.[90] The Prime Minister, Mr Gorton, attacked the call as 'lawless'[91]—yet the government betrayed the same reluctance to gaol the unionists as it had earlier shown towards the Committee in Defiance.

Two years of resistance to conscription and intervention in Vietnam had apparently changed the climate of opinion. It became politically difficult for the government to prosecute any but the most convenient scapegoats—youthful draft resisters, and student radicals. As we shall see, the government became increasingly selective in its treatment of these groups.

From resistance to collective power 1970-72

The impact of the anti-war and anti-conscription movement was not only evident in the cautious behaviour of the government but also dramatically revealed in public opinion polls.

By mid-1969 the minority opposed to keeping troops in Vietnam had turned into a majority: a Gallup Poll taken in August 1969 showed 55 per cent in favour of bringing Australian troops home compared to 40 per cent in favour of the troops staying.[92] All previous Gallup Polls on the same question had shown a majority in favour of fighting on; all polls after August 1969 were to show a majority in favour of bringing the troops home.[93] And a majority of Australians had always opposed the sending of conscripts to Vietnam.[94] By 1969, polls on the validity of the conscription system itself (based on questions that artificially divorced the scheme from its use in Vietnam) showed a downturn of approximately 10 per cent for those who would continue with conscription as compared to those who would end it. With the exception of the September 1971 poll (taken just after the announcement that conscription was being reduced from two year to 18 month service terms) public support for conscription dropped from the 63-70 per cent range in the period April 1965 to August 1969 to the 53-58 per cent range in the period October 1969-June 1971.[95]

1969 was thus the watershed year for public opinion on the war and conscription. Although the Liberal-Country Party coalition was returned to office in the 1969 Federal election, its majority was severely reduced, reflecting in part the increasing public distaste for government policies on the war.

The war raged as cruelly as ever. A greater tonnage of bombs had already been dropped on the Vietnamese countryside than were dropped by either side in the Second World War. With the prospect of another three years of a government that showed no sign of reversing its Vietnam policy, many in the wider anti-war movement began to take more seriously the extra-parliamentary direct action that had been pioneered by student groups, draft resisters and the Committee in Defiance over the previous two years. The sit-ins, incitement campaigns, and draft resistance actions of 1968–69 contributed importantly to a sense that the war and conscription were each and everyone's responsibility; that there were more ways of influencing events than through the ballot box; and that one had to act *immediately*—inaction meant complicity in the continuing destruction of the Vietnamese people.

In contrast to the sense of hopelessness that paralysed many in the aftermath of the 1966 election, the mood after the 1969 election was one of renewed spirit and determination to mount such massive protests and resistance as could scarcely be ignored by the government.

At a national meeting in Melbourne in early 1970, anti-war groups from across the country reached agreement on the concept of a moratorium—a halt to business as usual as a means of protesting the war.[96] The dual demands of the Moratorium were 'the immediate total and unconditional withdrawal of all United States and allied troops from Indo-China', and 'the immediate abolition of all forms of conscription'.

The idea produced an unprecedented response in schools, universities, colleges, offices, factories, churches and local communities. On 8–9 May 1970, over 200,000 people took part in moratorium demonstrations in cities and regional centres all over Australia. The Vietnam Moratorium both revealed and fostered a new sense of community amongst those opposed to the war and conscription. It was a profound warning that when a government defies the feeling of its people on a serious enough issue, personal interests and private concerns can be subordinated to the necessity of common protest—even when the government and media define such protest as illegal.

After the Moratorium, government strategy in Australia, as in America, was chiefly determined by political necessity: to try to placate the moderates while holding out against the radicals. Partial withdrawal was promised but immediate and complete troop withdrawal refused. The Nixon strategy during this period was to 'Vietnamize' the war by progressively transferring combat responsibilities to the South Vietnamese troops under an umbrella of intensified bombing of North Vietnam, Laos and NLF areas, and the abortive invasion of Cambodia (aimed at NLF 'sanctuaries' near the border). Even the moderates in the anti-war movement, however, were undeceived by the cynical ploy of 'changing the colour of the corpses'. Far from subsiding, the anti-war movement continued to maintain pressure on the government with a second national moratorium in October 1970, and a third in June 1971.

On the issue of conscription, the government had already recognised the political dilemma posed by the small but growing number of declared draft resisters. If it gaoled them all, the whole scheme might have had to be abandoned as a decisive electoral liability. But to gaol none would create the impression that the system was a paper tiger. The temporarily successful solution was simply to delay prosecution of the majority of resisters in the hope that the psychological strain of waiting to be gaoled would induce compliance, quiescence, or desperation (such as escaping overseas), while one or two resisters could be gaoled to give the appearance that the government was 'enforcing' its law. Thus, of the original eight resisters who had publicly declared their non-compliance in 1967, only one had received a call-up notice by August 1968; and only a further three received a call-up notice by the end of 1969.[97] Only one of the eight had been gaoled by the end of 1969.[98] Yet, in the handful of cases of unsuccessful conscientious objection applicants who continued their objection to the point of resisting a call-up notice, the government could move fast. In late 1968, Zarb, Beddoes and Reisenleiter were gaoled for two-year terms less than two months after they disobeyed call-up notices.

The rationale of this policy was tacitly admitted by Mr Snedden, Minister for Labour and National Service:

> We refrain from prosecution until we are satisfied the young man has had every opportunity to think the thing out. We want him to know the alternatives and to consider them. Given time to examine the issues in this way, a number do change their minds.[99]

Snedden did not, of course, mention that draft resisters were being given *years*—rather than months—to 'think things over'. The strain did tell on some,[100] but the considerable increase in new resisters more than compensated for this. By the end of 1969, over 60 liable young men had publicly declared their resistance in the form of declarations and letters to the government and press.[101] By September 1970, this number had more than trebled.[102]

Less than two weeks after the first Moratorium, the Minister for Labour and National Service revived a previously-discarded plan for civilian service for draft resisters; and on 27 May Cabinet approved the scheme. The idea was not that draft resisters could be persuaded to accept such an alternative,[103] but rather to render the gaolings of resisters more acceptable to the public. The journalist David Solomon interpreted Cabinet's motive as:

> concern .. with the effect of the (90 to 100 potential) gaolings. With the public getting sicker of the Vietnam commitment, with the knowledge that some troops are coming out of Vietnam anyway, it is not the best time to have to face a large scale assault by protesters on the national service scheme ... In this instance, what the Government proposes is to make the application of the penalty for breaking the law more palatable—not to people who break the law, but to the public. So, military prison becomes a civilian gaol, civilian gaol becomes a choice between gaol or labouring. It isn't an alternative to national service, it is an alternative penalty for dissenters.[104]

Two weeks later, several of the more conservative backbenchers, including Jess, Greenwood, Wedgewood, Bonnet, Calder and Cormack, successfully reversed the Cabinet decision at a combined meeting of the government parties.[105]

But rejection by hardliners of an alternative penalty for draft resisters did not mean that the more politically sensitive Liberals had given up hope of avoiding a confrontation. The Minister for National Service immediately foreshadowed new procedures to automatically refer draft resisters to the courts for determination of their conscientious objection status.[106] This procedure, which came into effect in August 1970, was evidently designed to reduce the number of non-compliers who would have to be gaoled by making the more pacifist or religious draft resisters submit to compulsory court examination. From August 1970 to the end 1972, forty four resisters were compulsorily referred to courts under this procedure. Most refused to cooperate, but some did and were duly exempted. In at least two cases, draft resisters were exempted *despite* their refusal to cooperate with the court proceedings.[107] In all, 20 were exempted under the procedure to the end of 1972.[108]

At the same time, the government continued the policy of protracted prosecutions and token gaolings. Despite the dramatic increase in draft resisters during 1969–70 only four resisters received call-up notices in the whole of 1970.[109] Of the over 60 public resisters to the end of 1969, a mere eleven had received call-up notices by the end of 1971.[110]

Several Melbourne resisters felt that a new and separate draft resisters' organisation had become not only viable but an absolute necessity if the government's cynical prosecution policy were to be exposed. On 20 June, 1970, an all-day conference of 45 Melbourne draft resisters at La Mama Theatre, Carlton, resolved:

> That there be an organisation known as the Draft Resisters' Union. Membership shall be open to all persons who have refused to comply with the National Service Act together with those intending future non-compliance who are willing to sign a statement to this effect.[111]

From the outset, the Draft Resisters' Union sounded a note of radical militancy, both in its aims and practice. Its guiding principles were 'immediate repeal of the National Service Act and the immediate end to Australian support for American imperialism rather than simply the release of particular gaoled objectors,' and it called for the 'setting up [of] an effective underground and sufficient draft sanctuaries to provide the basis for a sustained public campaign immediately police are in pursuit of draft resisters'.[112] Two participants later characterised the DRU's formation as the development of a 'collective conscience rather than an individual conscience'.[113]

The formation of the DRU and similar, though autonomous, groups in New South Wales, Queensland, Canberra, Western Australia, and South

Australia[114] was crucial in giving resisters a sense of solidarity with each other and with the broader anti-war, anti-conscription movement at a time when the government was doing its best to demoralise them with appeals to self-interest and the strain of waiting to be prosecuted. The DRU also gave fresh impetus to the 'Don't Register' campaigns and to demonstrations at resisters' and inciters' court cases, then regularly organized by student, SOS, unionist and Moratorium groups.

Most importantly, the DRUs developed effective ways to force the government to confront the issue rather than continuing its low-profile policy of bureaucratic delay in prosecution. Through vigorous representations to incumbent Attorney-Generals (first Hughes, then Greenwood), challenges issued at public meetings addressed by government ministers, letters to the press, and constant communication of the statistics on selective prosecution, the DRUs brought increasing pressure on the government to increase its rate of prosecution.[115] That these efforts were not without success is indicated by comparison of official figures for 1972 and 1971: 2738 were denied the benefit of the ballot in 1971 for failing to register at the proper time; of these, 327 or 12 per cent were prosecuted for failure to register.[116] By contrast, in the first half of 1972, 1238 were denied the benefit of the ballot for failing to register—and 880 or 71 per cent were prosecuted! In terms of summons or warrants for public resisters who refused call-up notices, almost as many were issued in 1972 alone as in the whole preceding four years: 25 in 1972 compared to 28 during 1968-71.[117]

If the government was finally being forced to implement its conscription laws for fear of the whole thing becoming a national joke, then it was equally important for anti-conscriptionists to show that the very act of enforcing the law would generate such community resistance that the government would have to abandon the scheme or face a more general crisis of confidence in itself. With the formation of the DRUs, resisters began to rethink the question of mobilising public opposition to conscription and the war. Before 1970, they had tended to make a fetish of their own act of individual non-compliance and to believe that their own witness in gaol would automatically generate public opposition to the Act. Certainly the first gaolings of Bill White, John Zarb and Brian Ross had generated such opposition, but it was simplistic to believe that all further such gaolings would generate equivalent momentum. On the contrary, there was a danger of demoralisation by repeated demonstrations outside prison walls, merely calling for the release of particular resisters instead of an end to conscription and the war. Such action seemed impotent to achieve even the lesser goal. In a sense, the gaoling of resisters was serving the government's purpose more than the gaoled resisters' purpose.

At the same time, draft resisters began to sense another contradiction in their own position. How could they refuse to comply with one aspect of the system,—the induction notice—while complying fully with its underlying guarantor—the penal sanctions? On the other hand, resisters well knew that if they did not turn up at court hearings, the authorities might try to ignore their challenge altogether.

A solution to the dilemma was the concept of an 'underground resistance', which had been current for a number of years but only in the sense of helping those who simply failed to respond to a court summons and wanted to keep out of sight. As early as 1967, SOS and other anti-conscriptionists combined to help one particular Melbourne 20 year old remain underground. The new element in the 1970 idea was an underground network to actively challenge the whole system rather than simply help young men escape or avoid the scheme. The week that Laurie Carmichael, Jr, spent underground in late 1969 had shown the feasibility of the idea. In the following year, the movement anticipated keeping resisters underground for long periods during which they would make frequent public appearances in circumstances where the government could only arrest them with great difficulty, if at all.

In contrast to the liberal version of civil disobedience whereby one is under an obligation to 'accept the consequences' of one's lawbreaking, the underground resistance concept represented a radical challenge to both conscription and the more general sense of the state's legitimacy in the eyes of the people.[118] Previously the anti-conscription movement had contested the *right* of the government to enforce conscription; now it began to contest the *power* of the government to enforce conscription.

Before 1970, draft resisters had exercised a kind of monopoly over resistance. This was partly due to the government's repressive tolerance in refusing to prosecute the Committee in Defiance and anti-conscription trade unionists; and partly to the resisters' own mistaken, elitist belief that it was sufficient to resist and leave to others the orchestration of resistance by placard parades, letters to the press, and other legal forms of support. In the waiting game being played by the government, many resisters looked for ways to serve their gaol sentences as soon as possible rather than extend the psychological uncertainty still further. Yet the possibility of widening the social circles of resistance depended precisely on the resisters' willingness to live under constant stress, never knowing when or where they might be arrested, continually trusting others rather than determining the outcome wholly for themselves.

The underground resistance concept provided the means for broader sections of the community to challenge the government's authority. It was the logical answer to the government's policy of deferred and selective gaolings, since any attempt to gaol even one resister would encounter the collective resistance of the sheltering communities; moreover, the government could not afford to ignore defiant public appearances by underground resisters.

In September 1970 an Underground Fund Committee was set up in Melbourne, with representation from the DRU, SOS, the Moratorium and

Catholic Worker group,[119] and the beginning of a network of contacts and 'safe' households was established. On 7 October 1970 the DRU newspaper, *Resist*, announced that the underground had become operational. The first resisters to use the network were Ian Turner and Paul Fox of Melbourne, for whom warrants had been issued on 23 September 1970 for refusal of call-up notices. In January 1971, a West Australian resister, Gary Cook, joined the underground; and in mid-1971 two more Melbourne resisters joined.[120]

The first major underground resistance action took place at the Melbourne moratorium 30 June 1971. Several days before, four underground resisters announced publicly that they would appear openly at the Moratorium.[121] The four resisters duly addressed the crowd of 80,000, which then marched from the city square to Parliament House. From there about 5000 demonstrators escorted the four back to the relative safety of Melbourne University in what proved a tense and agonisingly long march. Commonwealth police hovered at the edges of the march all the way. At the time police disclaimed any intention to arrest the resisters, but the Attorney-General subsequently revealed on a television programme that the police had in fact intended to make arrests when the march dispersed; on seeing 'thousands of people surround the men', they decided otherwise because of the likelihood of a 'civil disturbance'.[122]

Encouraged by the success of this first action, the DRU and other anti-conscription groups sought ways to expand the resistance. They were particularly spurred by the government's August decision to retain conscription after the completion of Australian withdrawal from Vietnam at the end of that year. Notwithstanding that conscription had been introduced primarily to support the Vietnam commitment, and that Defence Minister Gorton in mid-1971 announced that Australia faced no foreseeable threat to its mainland for ten years, the government evidently sought to make conscription a permanent feature of Australian society. In this new context, the DRU and other anti-conscription groups viewed the attempt to retain conscription on a long-term basis with the deepest suspicion, contending that the its basis lay in a wish to retain the capacity to intervene against further threats to western and Australian economic imperialism in the Pacific Basin area—perhaps in Papua New Guinea, Thailand or Cambodia.

Following discussions between Melbourne DRU and RAM,[123] and decisions taken at a two day National Conference of Draft Resisters at Melbourne University (18–19 September 1971) it was decided to hold a week-long resistance commune at that university which was one of the many whose student bodies had passed 'sanctuary' motions. Several underground resisters would publicly take part in the action and be protected from arrest; at the same time the action would serve as an organisational basis for launching a fresh campaign of resistance to conscription. Accordingly, five underground resisters, three from Melbourne and one each from Sydney and South Australia, announced on the final day of the DRU conference that they would so act.[124]

In a raid at 4.55am on 30 September, three days after four of the underground resisters had taken up residence in the Melbourne University Union, over 150 Commonwealth police, personally led by the chief commissioner, surrounded the building. Smashing their way through locked plate glass doors and barricades erected by the resisters' supporters, the police attempted to arrest the resisters and shut down a pirate radio station which anti-conscriptionists had been operating within the building. Two of the resisters were sleeping in another building on the campus. The two sleeping in the union building were on the third floor and quickly hid in a prearranged hiding place behind one of the walls.[125] Police finally arrived at the room twenty minutes later. Failing to find the resisters, but correctly convinced that they were still in the building, police spent the next four hours smashing their way into all the likely hiding places there, but without discovering the resisters. We remained in our hiding place for the next ten hours.

Meanwhile, the supporters who knew before the police arrived at the third floor that the four resisters were safe, offered no resistance to the police but simply staged a sit-down at the top of the stairs. In frustration at finding neither the resisters nor the pirate radio, the chief commissioner implausibly accused the students of violently resisting police.

In the controversy that followed, the Attorney-General Ivor Greenwood said that he had 'concurred in what was proposed to be done' and complained that, on the one hand, the draft resisters had challenged police to arrest them, and on the other, they were 'not in attendance when police arrived'.[126] This was not quite accurate: the resisters had never said they wished to be arrested; they actually denied the right of the government to arrest them. The point in appearing publicly was not to invite arrest them but to challenge the *power* of the police to arrest them. The aim was both accomplished and seen to have been accomplished. A mere 300 anti-conscriptionists successfully frustrated an apparently carefully-planned attack by over 150 police led by the head of the force. They showed that the 30 June Moratorium incident could be repeated by far smaller communities of people.

In the remainder of 1971, and throughout the following election year, underground resistance actions were executed frequently with considerable success. In November, Mike Matteson, one of the four who had eluded police at Melbourne University, appeared live on an ABC-TV This Day Tonight programme simultaneously with Attorney-General, Senator Greenwood, speaking 'on line' from another state. Greenwood immediately ordered police to the Sydney studio but Matteson escaped through a back window. In December, Tony Dalton addreessed marchers at Melbourne University before they went to blockade the offices of the National Service Department. Early in 1972, a Melbourne resister, Barry Johnson, was nominated as the official ALP candidate for the Hotham electorate in the forthcoming Federal election. Not long after he was issued with a warrant for refusing a call-up notice, and continued his candidature from underground—a stance which simultaneously tested the government and the sincerity of the Federal ALP leadership's opposition to conscription, and served as a constant focus for the raising of the conscription issue throughout 1972.

In April 1972, a crowd of several hundred Sydney University students spontaneously gathered on the campus when it became known that two Commonwealth police had arrested Mike Matteson. Police had followed a car in which Matteson was returning from a press interview, stopped it, and jumped into the backseat, handcuffing themselves to him. The astute driver immediately headed into the university grounds and sounded the alarm. With the help of boltcutters, students separated Matteson from his captors and guided him to safety.[127]

Besides these more publicised actions, the growing number of underground resisters, 23 by the end of 1972, was involved in frequent but less dramatic appearances at small meetings of workers, students and local community groups; press and television interviews; and the preparation of booklets, newsletters and other material on conscription and draft resistance.[128] Morale was highest amongst those underground resisters who lived and worked together. The efficiency of the underground's resistance methods were described in the 1971–72 Annual Report of the Commonwealth Police Force as having occasioned 'extreme difficulties ... to investigating police'.

Throughout the whole 1970–72 period, opposition to conscription and support for draft resisters expanded in the ALP and spread to new sections of the community. On 14 June 1970 the Victorian State Conference of the ALP unaminously passed a motion stating that the ALP 'supports and encourages all young Australians to refuse to be conscripted to fight in the dirty war in Vietnam'.[129] In July the Labor Premier of South Australia, Don Dunstan, announced that he would refuse to register if he were of conscriptable age. At the June 1971 Launceston Conference of the ALP it was stated firmly that 'a Labor government will repeal the present National Service Act and annul its penal consequences'; and on 17 June the ALP Federal Executive declared its support for draft resisters.

On 16 June 1970 the headmaster of a 107 year old Methodist GPS School, Newington College, wrote as follows to the Sydney Morning Herald:

> I am loathe indeed to be forced publicly to advocate (non-violent) civil disobedience. But the Cabinet's reversal of its decision re alternatives to gaol for honest National Service dissenters means gaol for many who, when deep loyalties clash, must serve God rather than Caesar ... As an ex-Serviceman, a private citizen and a man of law and Law, I publicly

encourage 20 year olds, in good conscience and in loyalty to God rather than Caesar, to defy the National Service Act.[130]

For this stand the Rev. D A Trathen was subsequently forced to resign by the Newington College Council.[131]

In other developments, the 1971 General Assembly of the Presbyterian Church of Victoria declared its support for 'conscientious non-compliers with the morally questionable National Service Act';[132] and two well-known Presbyterians, the Rev. Professor R Anderson, Principal of Ormond College, and Rev. K̃ Wootton, Minister for Urban Strategy and Action, publicly declared their willingness to give concrete assistance to resisters.[133] In May 1972, a group of 24 Catholic priests wrote to the Federal Attorney-General expressing similar sentiments.[134]

And in August 1972 anti-conscription sentiments were voiced in the most unexpected quarter of all. The NSW Governor, Sir Roden Cutler, confessed 'to doubts about the need for national service' and added 'certainly I am doubtful about its efficacy. The ballot system—with its introduction of lottery effects on the career of a young man—is something to which logical objections can be raised.'[135]

By 1972, public opinion had begun to turn decisively against the existing form of conscription, despite the fact that all Australian troops had been withdrawn from Vietnam by the end of 1971. An Australian Sales Research Bureau poll taken in February 1972 found that only 26 per cent of Australians wanted to continue the existing scheme of overseas service compared to 41 per cent who preferred a scheme where conscripts were barred from serving overseas, and 33 per cent who wanted to abolish conscription altogether.[136] A Gallup Poll taken two months later on the question of selective versus universal conscription revealed a different form of dissatisfaction with the existing scheme: only 11 per cent wanted to see the existing selective system continue compared to 63 per cent who preferred a short-term universal system and 23 per cent who wanted an end to conscription altogether.[137] A similar Gallup Poll question posed again in October 1972 found as few as 7 per cent wanted the selective system continued, compared to 66 per cent for universality and 24 per cent for total abolition.[138]

Not only had Australians acquired a marked dislike for the overseas service and selective aspects of the scheme, they also began to show a corresponding distaste for its penal aspects. A Gallup Poll in February 1972 showed that only 5 per cent of Australians thought draft resisters should be gaoled, compared to 26 per cent who thought they should be given non-combatant duties, 18 per cent who wanted to see them work on civilian duties, and 19 per cent who thought they should not be penalised at all.[139] The public had clearly rejected the government's attempt to stigmatise draft resisters as 'criminals'.

It was not surprising therefore that it became a major issue in the 1972 election campaign. Whitlam drew the loudest cheers at election rallies when he pledged a Labor government to end conscription and release all imprisoned resisters; on the other hand, government ministers appeared almost apologetic when defending their administration of conscription. After winning the election, the Whitlam government immediately made good its promises to end conscription and release imprisoned resisters. That the ALP's pledge to end conscription was one of the main elements in its victory was suggested by an ANOP survey in February 1973. Asked the question, 'In which two of these areas do you consider the Federal Labor government had done the best job since coming to power?', 49 per cent or nearly one in every two people mentioned conscription as one of these areas.[140]

Formal Liberal ministers subsequently acknowledged the change in public attitudes on selective peacetime conscription. In the May 1974 Federal election, the Opposition Leader, Mr Snedden, pledged that conscription would not be reinstated by a Liberal government; and former Army Minister, A J Forbes, noted that "National service will not be used by a Liberal government in peacetime as a means of supplementing regular forces numbers'.[141] Such reversals in Liberal policy were tribute enough to the effectiveness of the draft resistance campaign in changing the public climate on the issue.

It may be assumed that even if Labor had not won the 1972 election the Liberals would have been forced by pressure from below to abandon conscription in any case. Over the last two years of the scheme the numbers of draft resisters increased dramatically and the government was finally provoked to more rapid and systematic prosecutions. Rapid increases in the number of resisters facing 18 month sentences could have resulted in massive confrontations between the government and the harboring communities. Given the public disillusionment with conscription and sympathy for the resisters, such confrontations would almost certainly have forced relinquishment of the scheme.

What, briefly, did the draft resistance movement achieve or fail to achieve? Like the broader anti-war movement of which it was a part, draft resistance was a more middle-class than working-class movement. This was partly due to DRU neglect of working-class constituencies and partly to intermittent union involvement in the campaign. A greater involvement of young workers in the campaign might well have led to an earlier end to conscription. Secondly, the DRUs failed to develop continuous liaison with conscripts after they were called up. Nor did they try to develop anti-war groups within the army, as was done so effectively in America that it became an important factor in bringing about an American withdrawal. Of course, the higher proportion of American youth affected, and the very size of American army camps, made this a more feasible strategy than in Australia.[142]

On the other hand, much was accomplished. Draft resistance

contributed significantly to the heightening of public consciousness of the Vietnam War, American imperialism, and the illegitimate exercise of authority. As an integral part of the wider anti-war movement it helped bring about the eventual withdrawal of troops from Vietnam. Moreover, it spurred people to take responsibility for their own lives rather than abdicate their freedom to the state, and offered a working example of how illegitimate authority could successfully be defied by face-to-face communities of people who showed solidarity with one another and attempted to overcome their factional differences.

For draft resisters themselves, the movement proved a profoundly radicalising experience, a personal encounter with life on the under-side of the system, which engendered an immediate affinity with all excluded and oppressed groups.

For the broader peace movement, draft resistance campaigns provided a baptism in the practice and efficacy of direct action and civil disobedience. Hundreds of thousands of Australians from all social backgrounds succeeded in shaking off the incubus of fear and self-interest which had contained and vitiated dissent throughout the fifties and early sixties.

No doubt, as America shifts to the authoritarian right with the 1980 reimposition of draft registration, Australian conservatives within and outside the Liberal Party will contemplate once again the reintroduction of conscription. But if they do, they will find themselves confronted with an anti-conscription movement whose thinking and practise resumes where the last movement left off.

7 Public opinion and the politics of the polls
MURRAY GOOT AND RODNEY TIFFEN

It is part of the conventional wisdom that western public opinion constrained the conduct of the war and that public opinion against the war contributed greatly to the political misfortunes of the governments who waged it. In Australia there was clearly fierce partisan debate and a considerable movement against the war. Yet what most Australians thought about the war—even when we arm ourselves with the available public opinion research—remains problematic.[1]

A public opinion poll is a peculiarly dependent, fragile and at the same time artificial and limited form of social knowledge. Nothing else gives such an authoritative map of the sentiments, values and attitudes of the nation. But its only reality is limited to a set of responses to doorstep interviews usually designed to provide short, simple stories for the press. Typically, it does not distinguish between those with an interest in the question and those without; between intense and casual opinion, or informed opinion and the ignorant. Nor does it probe the qualifications and contingencies which may attend answers to seemingly straightforward questions. The picture of opinion can vary markedly with apparently minor changes in the wording of questions, with the ways in which responses are channelled into pre-determined categories and in response to changes in events. No set of data ever represents a comprehensive or 'pure' view of public opinion, and in interpreting poll results close attention must be paid to the timing of polls and the nature of the questions asked.

Moreover, because of the status accorded public opinion in democratic rhetoric and because political fortunes are tied to both the reality and appearance of public opinion, the processes by which opinion is produced and made public are themselves politically important. Each step in the construction of public opinion, as a list of numbers against a set of alternatives, involves strategic decisions about both the production of knowledge—which aspects of which issues to pursue and which to ignore, the phrasing of questions and the formulation of responses—and its presentation—how the polls are to be interpreted and whether, when and with what prominence they are published. The story of those decisions is in many ways as important as the content of the opinions they reveal.

Patterns of polling

The Vietnam war straddled a strategic period in the development of Australian survey research. When Australia first committed combat troops in 1965 only one major commercial organisation was regularly probing public opinion; academic surveys were scarce; and polling by parties was primitive and haphazard. By the war's end in 1975, there were four market research agencies taking regular soundings of the public's political views.[2] Survey research was no longer a novelty for Australian political scientists, and the major political parties commonly commissioned their own polls.

In the 1960s Australia's only national opinion poll was the Morgan Gallup Poll, affiliated to Gallup International and produced for the Herald and Weekly Times group of newspapers. Conducted five to eight times a year and based on interviews with some 2000 voters, each poll covered a dozen topics with one question, occasionally two. Between 1965 and 1970, questions touching on Vietnam, conscription or Australian attitudes to Southeast Asia formed part of nearly every Morgan poll. Results were reported in terms of the total sample, and usually in terms of one or other of a number of demographic and other variables: sex, age, occupation and intended vote.

By the 1960s, market research had also discovered the teenager. In 1965, 1967 and 1968 Morgan conducted separate surveys among the 15–20 year age group. The first and second of these surveys included questions on conscription; the second and third, questions on Vietnam. Australian Sales Research Bureau (ASRB) surveys among 16–25 year olds were conducted in 1964 and 1966. From 1971, when the prospect of a lower voting age loomed larger, the sample base for the Roy Morgan Research Consumer Omnibus Survey (into which the Morgan Gallup poll was incorporated) was redrawn to include those aged 16 and above.

In 1971 Morgan's virtual monopoly was broken. The Melbourne *Age* and the *Sydney Morning Herald* commissioned a public opinion poll from ASRB, first based on Melbourne and Sydney voters, later run nationwide. In the same year Rupert Murdoch created Australian Nationwide Opinion Polls (ANOP) for his flagship, the *Australian*. These new polls, run by less conservative men for less conservative newspapers, were conscious of the need for more sophisticated polling—perhaps covering fewer topics, but with greater depth. In 1973, when the Morgan poll shifted to the *Bulletin*, McNair Anderson Associates took over the contract with the Herald group to constitute Australia's fourth national opinion poll.

The rise in the number of polls coincided with a decline in the pollsters' interest in Vietnam. Morgan, now completing a survey every second weekend, averaged only two questions a year on Vietnam compared with about a dozen a year in the late 1960s. McNair, polling six times a year, produced a similar number. ASRB in the field about four times a year produced only a handful of items. ANOP conducted a special defence survey in August 1971 but little of relevance thereafter. For the polls the war wound down much more rapidly than it did in Vietnam.

The Vietnam War also coincided with a boom in the social sciences. Survey researchers produced a number of studies which, though smaller in size and regional in spread (80–150 interviews in Melbourne and Sydney being the rule), covered a wider range of issues with more sophisticated techniques than would ever be attempted in polls designed for the press.

The first academic surveys date from 1966: Western and Wilson's study of attitudes to conscription in Canberra; Hughes' PhD on the relationships between psychological dispositions and political attitudes among 400 voters in Melbourne and Sydney; Clarke's survey of adolescents in Melbourne's workforce; and Altman's examination of the importance of foreign policy issues in the electorate of Isaacs.

The only study similar in size to the opinion polls, to touch on Vietnam, was Aitkin's national panel study of 1967 and 1969. In between came Berry's surveys of the Sydney peace marchers, carried out in 1967 and 1968; and Connell's PhD, based on a 1968 sample of Sydney children, which provided through highly sensitive, open-ended interviewing perhaps the most fascinating data of all.

As with the commercial polls, the academic data on Vietnam thinned out after the Australian decision in December 1969 to commence withdrawal. The only later surveys are Mann's 1971 study of how attitudes to authority among 1435 Sydney residents affected their responses to the My Lai massacres; an investigation in the same year by Connell and some of his students into the relationship between attitudes of young Sydneysiders and attitudes of their parents; and Tiffen's 1972 survey of Melbourne voters' attitudes to Asia.

Surveys on university campuses were not only conducted by academics. At a number of universities student councils latched on to surveys not only as a means of identifying opinion but of organising it. The Vietnam war, and especially conscription, an issue which directly affected so many students, triggered a volley of campus polls.

The political parties relied more on the polls published by the press than on any they produced themselves. Roy Morgan was personally close to Calwell (who, according to Morgan, helped his election to the Melbourne City Council by organising the Labor vote against the Civil Group's favourite son), and also to Holt, whom he met occasionally at the Flemington races. Both used to ring Morgan 'continually' (Holt also ringing on behalf of Menzies). Together with Curtin, they had been the 'only politicians to care'. McMahon, of course, rang 'a hell of a lot'. But not Gorton and certainly not Whitlam.[3]

Throughout the sixties, Labor's private research—largely undertaken by Marplan, the market research offshoot of their advertising agency, Hansen

Rubensohn-McCann Erickson—concentrated on state elections and state issues. A few surveys on Federal issues, initiated by individual candidates, were undertaken in individual electorates.[4] Liberal research during this period consisted of (equally) crude questionnaires, administered across a number of states, and mostly carried out by Young Liberals under the supervision of the party's administrative officers.[5] By the seventies, when the major parties had placed their research on a professional footing, the people designing the polls rarely considered Vietnam and conscription to be important issues.

The final and most intriguing source of data on Australian attitudes are the surveys commissioned from Roy Morgan Research by the United States Information Service (USIS) and its successor the United States International Communication Agency (USICA). Questions about Vietnam were not often raised in international surveys until after the collapse of Saigon and Cambodia in 1975. Once the war became a political liability the agency was given to understand that the state of international public opinion was not something about which President Johnson wanted to know.

Under these circumstances the United States was forced to rely for most of its monitoring on published polls. Morgan Gallup Polls were received on a regular basis by the US Embassy; and by Lloyd Free and Hadley Cantril at the Washington and Princeton-based Institute for International Social Research where, from about 1967, international opinion was monitored 'to encourage the United States and other governments to pay more attention to psychological and social factors in formulating their policies'.[6] In addition, the Foreign Affairs Division of the Legislative Reference Service of the Library of Congress used Morgan's data in a 1966 report on the American image abroad, as did Dr Gallup for a presentation to a 1968 Congressional Committee.

Although Australian born, Roy Morgan was a champion of American interests. An honorary member of the Princeton University class of 1948 he named his second son, born in the United States, after Cordell Hull, Secretary of State under Roosevelt. When a Professor Goldman from Princeton, was appointed Special Consultant to President Kennedy, Morgan wrote (in vain) pressing his services and his connections with Gallup, Cantril and the USIA.[7] In 1962, after Free and Cantril had omitted Australia from a list of countries in which they intended to commission research on a regular basis, Morgan was forced to acknowledge that Australia was 'too faithful as an ally to need study'. Was it 'right to assume', he asked in 1967, 'that Australia has been excluded because Uncle Sam has no problems here?'[8]

Whether it was the advent of the Labor government or an unrelated change of policy, the USIS was far more active in polling Australian opinion in the seventies than in the sixties; and their reports remain the source of valuable data, not least on attitudes to the United States.[9]

While the Morgan organisation had some impact on the polling of the USIS (changing questions here, adding a question there) its major impact was in the public domain. Indeed, to write a history of public polling on the Vietnam years is to write largely of the work of the Morgan Gallup Poll.

Vietnam

Morgan's interest in Australia's involvement in Indo-China dates back to the last stages of the French occupation. In 1953, the government's decision to give 'out-of-date military equipment' to France was supported, according to the Morgan poll, by half the electorate; the other half being either opposed or undecided. 'The high percentage without opinions' the Morgan report observed, 'reflects widespread haziness on this subject, particularly among women'—but not so hazy, apparently, to obscure the headline in the subscribers' report, 'Australians approve aid to Indo-China', or its cold war battledress. Morgan also offered the touching reassurance that 'much opposition was expressed simply because of the fear that the equipment might be too old to use'.

In May 1954 Morgan Gallup bounced back to declare 'Indo-China is our business'. Asked 'If the French are driven out of Indo-China, do you think Australia will be greatly affected?', 37 per cent said 'yes, greatly'; 17 per cent, 'yes, a little'; 16 per cent said 'no'; and 30 per cent had 'no opinion'. The proportion with 'no opinion' was even higher than the last poll. This passed without comment, as did the possibility that haziness also characterised many of the positive responses. More curious was the decision to count those who had said Australia would be only affected 'a little' as if they had said 'yes', without qualification. Some 70 per cent in the same survey agreed that 'if watersiders again refuse to load munitions given to the French for use in Indo-China' then 'troops should do the loading'. This probably said less about their feelings for the French than about their views on industrial relations.

Getting Australia in
The first Australian poll on Australian or American forces in Indo-China was conducted in April 1961. Voters were asked:

> If American forces go to Laos—a small country in Asia between China and Thailand—to fight the Communists, do you think Australian soldiers and airmen should or should not also go there?'

The question made no attempt to distinguish those who might have heard of Laos and developments there from those who had not. The attempt to situate Laos implicitly acknowledged the electorate's interest or knowledge might be minimal. The language—'a small country' (David) versus the communists (Goliath)—and the geo-political allusions to China and Thailand may have prefigured a positive outcome, but in fact the 41:43

division was no greater than if voters, out of ignorance or uncertainty, had divided at random.

In April 1962, voters were asked:

> If America goes to war against the Communists in South-east Asia to defend Thailand, do you think Australia should also fight there, or keep out of it?

The vote was 35:50 in favour of keeping out. Strangely, this result was only released to subscribers as an addendum to a June poll headlined 'Sending forces to Southeast Asia approved'. This item found a 61:27 majority approving the government's decision to send token forces to Thailand and Vietnam to support the Americans. The Morgan release argued that the figures showed 'a big swing of opinion since April', at best a naive interpretation. They asked different questions: going to war is one thing, sending token forces another. Moreover, the first item canvassed hypothetical future options; the second examined approval for a *fait accompli*. Poll results often show the public more willing to acquiesce in government decisions already taken than to approve possible future commitments.

In June 1963, five months after Prime Minister Menzies won a general election he had called on the grounds of the 'international crisis', Morgan Gallup reported a convincing 64:16 majority for keeping a 30 man team 'helping train local anti-communist forces in South Vietnam, a small country between Thailand and China'. The support was doubtless boosted by the small commitment and the non-controversial presentation of their task. (No reference was made to possible combat or to any of the controversial aspects of the Diem regime which were then a matter of great western concern.) Finally, in the reference to China and Thailand, politics triumphed over geography. There is no physical sense in which Vietnam lies between Thailand and China, although the description conjures the image of dominoes falling to communism.[11]

In April 1965 the government announced the sending of 800 combat troops. In May and again in July, Morgan Gallup found majorities favouring the decision. Support remained high in September, when a 56:28 majority approved Australian troop numbers being raised from 1100 to 1450.

Morgan showed prescience in February 1966 when, anticipating his friend Harold Holt's announcement by a few weeks, he asked whether respondents favoured or opposed increasing the Vietnam force from one battalion to two. Support was slightly down to a 48:35 plurality. The final government decision in late 1967 to increase the number of troops was actually opposed. Opinion was 46:37 against increasing 'our forces from 6300 to 8000'.

Morgan Gallup asked only one question over a period sufficiently long to illuminate trends in opinion on the war: 'Do you think we should continue to fight in Vietnam or bring our forces back to Australia?' Asked ten times over a period of five years, this question constitutes our best single index of support for the war. (Table 7.1)

Table 7.1 'Do you think we should continue to fight in Vietnam or bring our forces back to Australia?'

Month/Year	9/65	9/66	5/67	10/68	12/68	4/69	8/69	10/69	10/70	10/70
Continue	56%	61%	62%	54%	49%	48%	40%	39%	43%	42%
Bring back	28	27	24	38	37	40*	55	51	45	50*
Undecided	16	13	14	8	14	12	6	10	12	9

Source: Morgan Gallup Poll: APOP Subscribers' reports.
* 'bring back now'

Support for a continuation more than doubled opposition between September 1965 and May 1967. Other measures of support during this period also show solid majorities behind the government. In July 1966, 64 per cent said they supported Mr Holt's statement that 'we would go all the way with America in the defence of South Vietnam and Southeast Asia.' Similarly, around 70 per cent approved the visit of Vietnam's Premier Ky to Australia in January 1967.

There is a very long gap of 17 months before the continue/bring back question was asked again. By October 1968 there had been a noticeable growth of opposition, but we can only guess when opposition began to build. This was a tumultuous period, marked by the Tet offensive and sharp political disputes in the United States. Indeed by late 1967, there was evidence of considerable public unease. In November, Morgan Gallup found that more opposed than supported the recent government troop increase; opinion evenly divided over American bombing; and only a plurality (48:25) was prepared to agree that the South Vietnam government had their support, even after being cued that 'our Prime Minister, Mr Holt' had 'told the President of South Vietnam that the South Vietnamese Government had the "active sympathy and support of the government and people of Australia" '. (Holt was cited by the poll as 'our' Prime Minister in a way Whitlam never was; and in preambles to questions Morgan Gallup never cited a critic of the war or a pessimist, or 'balanced' items with competing claims.)

A clear break in support occurred in mid-1969, a few months before Gorton's post-election announcement that he would soon start withdrawing Australian troops. The proportion favouring withdrawal rose 15 points between April and August, a staggering figure in the absence of any particularly dramatic developments. After this, there were always more who preferred withdrawal to continuation.

This series of items affords the best opportunity to examine how Morgan

Gallup treated swings in opinion. Seven of the ten times warranted separate headlines in Morgan releases. These included the first six each of which showed more people supporting the continuation option. Of the others, three which showed majorities to bring the troops back were released with minimal comment, buried among results on several other election issues. The headings were 'Some ALP planks could be net losers'; 'ALP planks had little power left'; and 'New Laws Approved for Demonstrators'. On six occasions there was a 'shift' of 5 per cent or more choosing one of the two options. Two were in a hawkish direction, and each time the swing was highlighted in either the heading or the story, and comparisons were made with earlier findings. Of the four occasions when support for involvement declined only one was so highlighted. Indeed the two biggest swings (a rise of 14 per cent for the 'bring back' option in October 1968, and of 15 per cent in August 1969) passed without comment, and without any comparison with earlier figures. Even in August 1969, when there was both a dramatic swing of opinion and—for the first time—a decisive majority against the war, the item was buried.

The Americans

In 1964 Roy Morgan advised an inquirer that 'it would be presumptuous for us to measure Australian public opinion on American Presidents'.[12] But before year's end, the Morgan poll had asked whether Australians wanted Johnson or Goldwater as the next president. Not until May 1965 did Morgan first probe Australian opinion about US policy in Indo-China. Interviewers reminded voters that President Johnson had said 'the US would settle for no less than assured independence for South Vietnam', and asked whether 'American forces should remain in Vietnam, or get out?' The response was 64:20 for remaining. This was probably inflated by the preamble (proclaiming ideals without any hints of possible costs or the transgression of other values) and the use of the stark 'get out' (a slogan then commonly found on railway embankments) rather than 'withdraw', 'pull out', or 'bring home' favoured by American Gallup.[13]

Even at this stage support was probably more qualified than the previous item suggests. For the first and only time, the Morgan Gallup Poll in February 1967 raised the question of war aims and the desirability of seeking a compromise solution, asking whether America and her allies should fight for a complete victory in Vietnam or seek a compromise peace. A resounding 62:27 majority wanted a compromise. The American Gallup Poll had quizzed Americans on an assortment of peace proposals from as early as 1964, and continued to do so until the end of the war. Both internationally and domestically it was an important focus of political debate, but like the Australian government, Morgan Gallup evinced little interest in the question of peace, which was never raised again.

One other question never asked in Australia was whether Australia or America had made a mistake in sending troops. From May 1966 onwards, the American Gallup poll replaced a series on whether America should or should not 'have become involved with our military forces in Southeast Asia' with a series on whether 'in view of developments since we entered the fighting in Vietnam' the United States had 'made a mistake sending troops to fight'. By early 1968 a majority was saying 'Yes'.

In 1970, Roy Morgan took the unusual step of sending to Dr Gallup's son, who was then in charge of the poll company, a note of complaint. The 'mistake' question, he argued, included 'three biasing phrases, each of which would tend to produce "Yes" answers ... '. To Morgan the question seemed 'to suggest that the interviewer is implying that all developments have been adverse', and second, it suggested 'that the US did make a mistake'; and thirdly, there was no alternative as in 'approve or disapprove' questions, only the alternatives yes and no. Morgan suggested that Gallup run a split ballot (something Morgan himself had never done on Vietnam or any other issue), with half of the sample asked something like: 'In your opinion was the US right or wrong in sending troops to Vietnam (between 196__ and 196__)?'[15]

Whether or not Morgan's three points have any substance (and all three are open to challenge), his solution was to ask a rather different question. The term 'mistake' is much less harsh than 'wrong': the first connotes miscalculation, the second moral culpability. In the event, Gallup did not follow Morgan's suggestion, and neither did Morgan.

Early in September 1966, Roy Morgan had replied to a request from American Gallup for a question on US involvement in Vietnam in the following terms:

> Normally we would not ask people what they think another country should do. However as you want us to ask it we will do so. You ask if there are any other questions we would like you to ask. I think it would be interesting to have a worldwide Gallup Poll on punishment for minor offences.[16]

The Vietnam question asked in September 1966 in Australia, the USA, Canada, West Germany, Britain and France was

> Just from what you have heard or read, which of these statements comes closest to the way you, yourself, feel about the war in Vietnam?
> A. The US should begin to withdraw its troops
> B. The US should carry on its present level of fighting
> C. The US should increase the strength of its attacks on North Vietnam.'[17]

In Australia only 21 per cent wanted the US to begin withdrawing; and the combined proportion for the other two options, 67 per cent, was higher than everywhere except the US.

A year later the question was repeated, this time in nine countries. Morgan Gallup, apparently without the Americans knowing, asked a rather different question:

> Do you think America and her allies should increase their war effort in Vietnam for a quick victory; or hold things about as they are; or get out of Vietnam soon?

This question differed from the one asked in the other countries in several important respects. As in 1966, Morgan presented the withdrawal option last, not first. The question referred to America and her 'allies' not just America (The US then had around 500,000 troops in Vietnam; the only other foreign troops were 8000 Australians and 50,000 South Korean, both clearly following the US lead in all war policies.) 'Begin to withdraw' was replaced by 'get out soon'. Most importantly the escalation option was changed. Mention of North Vietnam, the enemy, was dropped in favour of 'increase their war effort', a phrase with less suggestion of violence, aggression or risk; and crucially, the phrase 'for a quick victory' was added. Morgan's apparent military omniscience quite outrageously led it to guarantee an outcome. (No mention was made of the possibility of a bigger, bloodier stalemate, or the risk of China entering the war).

This skewing of alternatives no doubt helped boost the escalation option from 24 per cent to 37 per cent, but overall the combined support for escalation and holding things as they were had dropped from 67 per cent to 55 per cent. American Gallup published the results of the international survey as if the Australian question and those asked elsewhere had been identical. Unlike the previous year's four-country survey, Morgan Gallup did not publish the international comparisons. These showed that in nine of the eleven countries surveyed, those opting for withdrawal outnumbered the combined support for the two continuation options. Only in the US and Australia was there a majority for continuing.

The Australian results were not included on subscribers' sheets until after a further poll in December showed that the combined proportion for the two continuation options had risen from 55 per cent to 63 per cent. This report was headed 'More say "Fight on in Vietnam" '. The following February this had dropped to 58 per cent. The report's heading 'Most say "Fight on in Vietnam" ' made no mention of the slippage. This latest poll was taken in the immediate aftermath of the communists' huge Tet offensive. Opinion polls in the US showed no immediate increase in anti-war feeling, but a delayed reaction (in March and April) showing declining support for the war.[18] Unfortunately, there was a hiatus in Australian polling on Vietnam in this period.

February 1968 was the last occasion when any commercial pollsters probed Australian opinion about general American policy. However, the USIA—through Morgan research—did so in 1972 and 1975. When asked in 1972 to give their opinion of the current policies and actions of the US in Vietnam, 44 per cent (of the 95 per cent 'aware' of the Vietnam 'situation') chose very or somewhat favourable, and the identical proportion said somewhat or very unfavourable. This balance of opinion was more favourable to the US than in any of the other eight countries surveyed. After the fall of Saigon, six countries were asked whether the US 'did or did not do all it should to meet its commitment in South Vietnam?' In Australia the wording substituted 'could' for 'should'. Some 43 per cent said they had, 39 per cent said they had not. Australia was the only country where favourable opinion outweighed the unfavourable.

The other questions about American involvement focussed on the bombing of North Vietnam. In May 1965, Morgan Gallup asked voters whether they approved of 'the American bombing of military targets in North Vietnam'. Just over half did so, about as many as approved the sending of Australian troops; although, in contrast, only 29 per cent rather than 37 per cent disapproved the bombing.

In July 1966 Morgan Gallup took the unusual step of first asking whether voters had heard of 'the American bombing of Hanoi and Haiphong [pronounced HI PONG] in North Vietnam, a couple of weeks ago?' Nine out of ten said they had. The interviewers then proceeded:

> Our Prime Minister, Mr Holt, then said he *accepted* the military judgement of the United States that it was *necessary* to bomb those oil dumps in Hanoi and Haiphong. Do you approve or disapprove Mr Holt's statement?[19]

Again the question was loaded: only one point of view is mentioned, and the emphasis is on technical military necessity rather than civilian casualties. Perhaps the 56:24 approval was no more than expected. After all, 1966 was a vintage year for the government.

Fourteen months later voters were asked, quite simply, whether they favoured or opposed bombing North Vietnam. Only 39 per cent were in favour and 43 per cent were against. The report to subscribers was headed 'Indecision on bombing N. Viet'. November 1967 brought the embroidery back:

> Should the Unites States *continue* bombing North Vietnam or *un*conditionally stop it?

But it made little difference. Opinion was divided 40:38 for the bombing. In subscribers' reports the results did not earn their own headline.

In June 1968 the question was again re-formulated, now for the last time. Taking its cue from President Johnson's diplomatic and political shuffling, Morgan Gallup asked:

> In your opinion, should America *resume* bombing *all* of North Vietnam —or keep bombing only the *southern* half of North Vietnam—or *stop* all bombing of North Vietnam?

Even with two pro-bombing and only one anti-bombing option, with bombing the southern half almost presented as a 'moderate' option, it made little difference. The combined support for both bombing options was only 44 per cent with 40 per cent opposed. Yet the Morgan release conjured the headline: 'More support for bombing'. A table comparing this result to the two earlier ones omitted any mention of the differences in wording. The writing was on the wall. Although American bombing continued sporadically until Christmas 1972, there were no more polls on the subject.

Getting Australia out
After polls in August and October 1969 had shown that more Australians favoured bringing our troops back and after President Nixon had announced a policy of Vietnamization in late 1969, the Morgan poll began to explore opinions about the speed of withdrawal. These showed, at first, a considerable degree of public ambivalence. In December 1969, voters were asked:

> 'Which do you favour for Vietnam—a ceasefire now, followed by a quick withdrawal of all American and Australian troops—or the training of more South Vietnamese troops, followed by the gradual withdrawal of our troops?'

A gradual withdrawal was preferred by 65 per cent, with 29 per cent opting for a ceasefire and quick withdrawal. How many hard-liners, however, had been disenfranchised by the question? The following April produced an answer:

> 'Which do you favour for Vietnam. Bring our forces back to Australia now, or bring them back in stages, or keep the same number in Vietnam until the end of the war?'

Exactly half opted to withdraw in stages. The hardliners, 19 per cent, were outnumbered by the doves, 25 per cent.

Both items were highlighted in Morgan Gallup releases. They were recounted in largely unexceptional terms, except that both were described as if the previous results favouring 'bring back' over 'continue' had never occurred. No attempt was made to acknowledge or explain the differences. The key to the puzzle is the difference in the questions. Students of public opinion know that as options multiply, response spreads. The three options in April almost guaranteed that the proportion for withdraw would be less than in the October poll. The difference was predictable, even if not predicted.[20]

In mid-1970, Morgan Gallup probed responses to the new situation in Cambodia, following the overthrow of Sihanouk in March, and the invasion by America two months later. A majority 51:30 approved the US and South Vietnamese troops going into Cambodia, but the same sample was against Australian troops doing likewise by 48 per cent to 37 per cent. Moreover, differently worded questions in August and November found only 30 per cent and 39 per cent respectively willing for Australia to give arms to Cambodia.[21]

Twice, in November 1970 and April 1971, Morgan Gallup asked almost the same question:

> And finally one on Vietnam, where our army is being (has been) reduced from 3 battalions to two battalions. In your opinion, should we keep two battalions in Vietnam, one battalion or none?

In November 1970 only 37 per cent supported the government's decision (including, presumably, those opposed to any withdrawal), with 13 per cent wanting a further withdrawal to one battalion, and 37 per cent wanting a complete withdrawal. The item headline 'Cut Vietnam force to one battalion' suggests a mandate for an option favoured by only 13 per cent. Again no mention is made of the results of the previous month, which found 50 per cent wanting to bring back the troops rather than continue.

In April those preferring a complete withdrawal rose from 37 per cent to 48 per cent, outnumbering the combined total for the other two options (down from 50 per cent to 37 per cent). The release was headed simply 'Support for Vietnam war drops'. This distribution of opinion was broadly confirmed four months later in ANOP's first poll on Vietnam. ANOP asked simply 'Should Australia withdraw its troops from Vietnam?', 58 per cent said Yes and 35 per cent No.

At year's end, Morgan Gallup told its sample that after most Australian troops had come home it was planned to leave 'about 50 instructors to train South Vietnamese troops'. No fewer than 59 per cent favoured the idea. The wheel had turned full circle: the question, and the response, were virtually the same as in 1963. At last an item had produced a seemingly hawkish majority, even if the definition of hawk had become ever weaker.

Curiously, no questions were asked by commercial pollsters on Vietnam in 1972, a year of continuing political conflict over the issue, a major North Vietnamese offensive and important negotiations in Paris.

The Whitlam Labor government, elected in December 1972, removed the last vestiges of the Australian combat commitment to Vietnam. While retaining political relations with South Vietnam, and sending substantial aid, the government also initiated diplomatic relations with North Vietnam. In early 1973 the peace accords between North Vietnam and the United States were signed in Paris. Fewer news stories emanated from Vietnam in the following two years than in more than a decade. Until the final days of the war in mid-1975, pollsters broached issues on Vietnam on only three occasions.

In early 1973 both Morgan Gallup and ANOP asked questions about recognizing North Vietnam, but with very different results. With almost identical wording, ANOP found a 57:34 margin favouring recognition, while the Morgan poll found opinion divided 38:29. The biggest source of difference was ANOP's 9 per cent undecided against Morgan's 33 per cent. There is no immediate explanation for the discrepancy. In ANOP's survey voters were also asked to choose the two areas in which they considered the Labor government had done the best (and worst) jobs. No fewer than 49 per cent named 'conscription and national service' as best (19 per cent as worst): the issue topped both lists. Vietnam was not among the ten issues that ANOP polled.

In February 1975, Morgan Gallup informed interviewees that the Labor Party had decided to allow the communist Viet-Cong of South Vietnam to open an information office in Australia, and asked whether the Viet Cong (the ALP would have called it the Provisional Revolutionary Government) office should be allowed. A 54:32 margin opposed the move.

Conscription

Attitudes to conscription—which Morgan Gallup nearly always called compulsory military training or national service—were polled regularly during the war. Though conscription was introduced by the government only in 1964, Morgan Gallup's soundings had already established its public acceptability. In the early sixties around 70 per cent agreed that 'compulsory military training' or a system ('like the American') of 'two years full-time military training for all young men who are fit' would be desirable.

At the end of 1964 the Gallup poll was able to affirm the same high level of support for 'the government's plan to register all young men of 20 and eventually to call-up 7000 a year for two years full-time service—overseas if necessary'. In September 1965, support for the government's plan to increase the number to 8000 stood just as high, although this question did not mention the possibility of 'overseas service'. At the end of April 1966 (with 1400 national servicemen on their way to Vietnam), and again in July and November, support for the call-up of 8000 men with the possibility of their serving overseas, hovered between 63 and 68 per cent. The higher figure was promoted as showing 'more support'; the lower figure interpreted as little change, or in terms of a different relativity such as '2-to-1 for call-up'. In November 1967, support was 70 per cent; a year later, 65 per cent.

By the end of 1969, as the Vietnam war seemed to turn sour, conscription too seemed a little less attractive.[22] In polls taken in August and October 1969, April and October 1970, and June 1971, support slipped from 63 per cent to 53 per cent. The government's decision, later in 1971, to cut the period of service from two years to eighteen months reversed the drift.

The most controversial aspect of conscription was the policy of sending conscripts overseas to Vietnam. Morgan Gallup asked a question about this on six occasions between December 1965 and July 1967. The question was: If their battalion is sent to Vietnam, should the national servicemen go with it or remain in Australia? Those preferring that they should remain in Australia varied between 49 per cent and 57 per cent, and always outnumbered those wanting them to go to Vietnam. Though an issue of enormous import, Morgan Gallup resisted any temptation to exploit the newsworthiness of its findings. The first poll was included in subscribers' reports only after the second had produced an even more emphatic majority for remaining—itself reported as saying only that the public was 'not convinced'. Twice the findings were tacked onto other findings. On the two occasions when there was some swing against keeping the conscripts in Australia, this was highlighted. Only once was majority opinion highlighted in the Morgan reports. One unfavourable headline from six unfavourable results!

There were two other noteworthy aspects of Morgan Gallup's presentation of results. After the first poll, all subsequent poll reports included some reference to earlier findings. The first poll, finding 52 per cent for national servicemen remaining, was mentioned in every subsequent report. The second poll, which found the highest proportion, 57 per cent, against sending conscripts, was quoted (to highlight the drop in opposition) after the third poll but never again. After the last poll, Morgan Gallup reminded its readers that:

> It should be noted that this vote against sending national servicemen to Vietnam does not mean that Australians are against our fighting in Vietnam. Indeed more than 60% favour continuing there.

This statement was true, but is notable for being the sole occasion on which Morgan, in reporting one item, drew attention to another to help clarify its meaning. This approach was notably absent from items canvassing withdrawal options quoted above. Although conscripts were still sent to Vietnam, the question was not asked again after July 1967. Instead the Morgan poll continued to ask a question on conscription which avoided any reference to Vietnam, preferring the coy phrase 'with possible overseas service.'

The other aspect of conscription which aroused significant public dissent was its selective nature. Morgan Gallup did not examine this directly until November 1971. Of the 69 per cent who favoured compulsory military training, there was a five to one preference for a universal call-up. In 1972 and 1973, perhaps inspired by the prospect and advent of a Labor government opposed to conscription, Morgan Gallup canvassed a number of forms of compulsory military training for different lengths of time. None of these options was actively under consideration by either of the political parties or the bureaucracy. These polls showed clearly that the Australian public favoured compulsory military training but universal rather than selective, for training in Australia rather than combat overseas, and for periods shorter than a year rather than the eighteen months and two years favoured by the Liberal government. A similar conclusion emerged from a 1972 ASRB poll: 32 per cent favoured a system based on volunteers; 41 per cent, conscription by ballot but without overseas service; and only 23 per cent, the current system of conscription by ballot with the possibility of overseas service.

Just as the government saw no alternative to conscription, if it were to send combat troops to Vietnam, neither it seems did Morgan Gallup.[23] Only the advent of the thoroughly modern ANOP in 1971 gave voters a choice between the force of the state and the sovereignty of the market. At the instigation of John Menadue (General Manager of the then pro-Labor News Ltd, subsequently private secretary to Whitlam) voters were asked whether they would prefer to 'continue conscription' or 'increase salaries and conditions by raising taxes' in order to 'maintain the size of Australia's armed forces in peacetime'. Opinion was almost evenly split, with one-third for each of the two options, 9 per cent wanting both and the remaining 19 per cent wanting neither or unsure.

National service appealed as a way of instilling discipline and extracting 'community service'. During the Vietnam years the largest figure recorded in favour of two years' national service was 77 per cent (September 1967), when it was defined to include time spent in the armed forces or working on development projects. A 1969 question of Aitkin's, though it mixed several considerations (universal versus selective conscription, combatant and non-combatant duties, and what to do with conscientious objectors) pointed in the same direction: 41 per cent favoured 'conscription for military service ... for all young men not just for some'; 33 per cent in favour of conscription, with 'those who are opposed to fighting .. allowed to do their national service in other ways'; 7 per cent in favour of the ballot for conscription; and only 17 per cent opposed to 'any form of conscription at all'.[24] In Western and Wilson's 1966 Canberra survey on conscription, the statement gaining greatest endorsement was that which read 'conscription for two years would do the average young man a lot of good'.[25] In Melbourne in 1972 Tiffen found 78 per cent agreed that 'the experience of military life for a limited period does most young men a lot of good'.[26] But this belief in the virtues of military discipline and community service did not extend to combat in Vietnam.

Draft resisters
Against the value of discipline and community service, 'conscience' readily implies the spirit of the insubordinate, the selfish, the slothful. Western and Wilson found the Canberra public evenly divided over whether 'conscientious objection should be grounds for avoidance of national service' and whether 'a person who strongly opposed the government's policy in South Vietnam should be exempt from military service in Vietnam', even though he may not 'object to being conscripted'.

The Morgan poll evinced a more varied and longer-lasting interest in this subject than in sending conscripts to Vietnam. The polls generally found even less sympathy for conscientious objectors. Between December 1969 and March 1973 four surveys (the last by ASRB) suggested that no more than one voter in four thought that those who refused to register should be allowed to do their 'usual work without penalty' or had a 'right to refuse'. Public opinion, however, was also opposed to sending them to jail, and preferred service in a non-combatant unit or two years' work on a civilian project.

In December 1968 less than one respondent in four upheld the right of someone to object to service in a particular war rather than to war in general. William White, a Sydney school teacher who refused to do non-combatant duties when directed to do so by a magistrate, was subsequently granted full exemption by another magistrate. The Morgan poll canvassed opinion on this case in February 1967. A rather improbable 97 per cent claimed to have heard of White. Only one in four would have upheld the full exemption although only one in three thought he should not be 'allowed to teach in front of a class'. The heading on the Morgan report simply read: 'White should do his duty'.

The Australian public was reluctant to acknowledge the issues of free speech surrounding conscription. In August 1970, only 33 per cent said that people publicly stating that 'young men should refuse to register for national service' should not themselves be penalised. In February 1972, only a quarter agreed that it was right to televise an interview with a young man who had refused to register for national service.

Demonstrators

In September 1967, Morgan Gallup found that only 10 per cent thought people should 'be allowed to send money to the Viet Cong, other than through the Red Cross'. Giving money to the enemy, like draft dodging, was clearly beyond the pale. Demonstrating, a traditional civil liberty, was not. In August 1969 and October 1970, Morgan asked whether people who 'disagree with the majority' (in October, less tendentiously, 'disagree with what the government is doing') 'have the right to demonstrate peacefully in the main streets of the capital cities'. Over 70 per cent agreed they had. But less than 10 per cent thought demonstrators had the right to block traffic, and only one per cent thought they had the right to be violent. 'Demonstrate? Yes, but don't disrupt' was the poll's fatherly advice.

A year later the majority of voters thought that 'moratorium marches ... allowed in the capital cities as in recent years' should be stopped. Not for the first time we note a discrepancy between the endorsement of a general principle and the judgement of a concrete political practice.

Asked in 1968 whether the police are usually too hard, about right, or not hard enough when 'dealing with university students and other demonstrators', only 7 per cent claimed they were too hard, while 43 per cent said they were not hard enough. In 1970, two in three agreed that there was a 'need for stronger laws for controlling demonstrators'.[27] It is unlikely, however, that any consensus would have attended actual imposition of specific penalties. On the one occasion when this question was pursued by pollsters, opinion was marginally in favour of allowing a university student on scholarship, who took part in a demonstration and was convicted of breaking the law, to keep his scholarship.

Social and political patterns of support

Altman has contended that until 1968, the 'Gallup Polls recorded considerable backing [on Vietnam] from nearly all strata of the population'; and that Labor's official policy of withdrawal 'was perhaps the clearest case in the party's history of it not representing the views of large numbers of its supporters'.[28] Not only does this reading gloss over the differences among Labor spokesmen before 1968, it imputes a measure of popular agreement about the war which simply did not exist.

After 1965, when Menzies committed troops to Vietnam, the war divided voters in a way which few other issues have done before or since.[29] Labor voters did support the sending of 'token forces' in 1962 and 1963. But every decision regarding combat troops was supported by less than a majority of the Labor vote. Similarly, from 1965 to 1970, questions on whether American and its allies should continue—even escalate—the war, or withdraw from it, produced differences between Labor and Liberal voters of about 30 percentage points.

Again, between 1965 and 1968, while the majority of government supporters backed the Americans bombing the north, Labor voters opposed. The gap between Labor and Liberal support ranged from 15 to 32 points. Although in 1966 most Labor voters were prepared to go 'all the way with LBJ' (as the question put it) at the end of 1967 most confessed they did not support the Vietnamese regime. Among Labor (and Liberal) voters support seems to have been based on the need to 'fight them there rather than here', not on the virtues of the South Vietnamese regime itself.

Even in 1966 the majority of Labor voters did not support the sending of conscripts to Vietnam. On this issue the gap between Labor and Liberal voters grew quickly to over 30 percentage points. Support for conscription itself and opposition to conscientious objection were different matters. Liberal voters were fairly solidly behind the government on these two; so, by a slender majority, were Labor voters. Partisan differences were least marked over attitudes to demonstrators.

The government depended more heavily on the votes of women than of men to keep it in office during the war.[30] Yet more men than women supported Australia's intervention, American policy, conscription and sending conscripts to Vietnam. The differences were often small (less than

10 percentage points) but fairly constant in direction. They were all the more remarkable for cutting against the grain of party support. On some occasions differences were greater. The greatest occurred on the bombing of North Vietnam—the polls' most aggressive option. Most men supported the bombing, most women opposed, and the gap between them exceeded 20 percentage points. Differences of this magnitude between the sexes, on public issues, are rare.[31]

As in most polls on international issues there were consistently more women than men giving 'don't know' responses, usually by a small margin but sometimes by more than 10 percentage points. After 1969 when Morgan Gallup was canvassing withdrawal options, sex differences disappeared. Moreover, on issues not involving combat, women were often 'colder warriors' than men. By margins of more than 10 percentage points women were more likely to think Australia would be threatened in the next 15 years, that the communist takeover of Indo-China would be bad for its people, and to oppose in the late sixties the admission of Communist China to the United Nations.

Support for conscription was weakest, and support for draft resisters and the moratorium marches strongest among those at or approaching a conscriptable age. Voters in their twenties were more solidly proconscription than either those at risk or their parents.[32] What those at risk thought about being conscripted and sent to Vietnam can only be guessed: this was a question the 'youth' polls never asked. Opposition to the sending of conscripts to Vietnam was most highly organised among under-graduates. Surveys in 1966 at three universities (Melbourne, the Australian National and Tasmania) suggested a much higher level of opposition than among voters in general.[33]

The pattern of opposition to the war itself was very different. Support for Australian and American bombing was highest among younger voters. Even student opinion supported American involvement in Vietnam, including the bombing of the north, and Australia's military presence. Surveys at the Universities of Sydney and Tasmania in 1968 suggested, however, that at least on the question of bombing the north, student enthusiasm was waning.

On the evidence of the Morgan youth polls (1966–68), support for the war was actually highest among those still at school or having just left. The Liberals enjoyed a handy lead over Labor among 16 to 20 year olds at this time, which may have been related to foreign policy issues. Suggestive evidence for this comes from a 1966 ASRB survey of youth, which found that of those aged 16–25, 58 per cent thought Labor but only 7 per cent thought the Liberals 'would weaken our alliance with the US'; 28 per cent thought Labor 'strongly anti-communist' (compared to the Liberals 73 per cent); and 37 per cent considered Labor 'keen to build up Australia's defence' (Liberals 78 per cent).

The relatively low level of support for conscription among students (only 50 per cent of students at ANU in 1966 favoured the call-up) had its parallel among professionals as a whole. Their support for conscription was at least 10 percentage points lower than any of the urban occupation categories used by the polls.[34] Professionals were clearly the most progressive group on the rights of demonstrators and related issues. Again these attitudes did not spill over into attitudes to the war itself, where professional support was often higher than the community average.

Leaving aside conscription (where the hostility of professionals narrowed the margin) and the rights of demonstrators (where professional support was sufficiently strong to reverse the general trend), 'white collar' workers were more likely than 'blue collar' workers to toe the government's line on the need to continue the war, to send conscripts to Vietnam, and to support American bombing.

Perceptions

Most survey items on Vietnam sought to ascertain approval or disapproval of immediate policies or actions. They give little insight into the public's perceptions of what was happening in Vietnam, or why; nor do they show how opinion on Vietnam was related to other attitudes, the factors that may have influenced these perceptions, or whether these were enduring and clear-cut, or unstable and ambivalent.

There was little incentive for commercial pollsters to probe these questions. Morgan Gallup ventured into perceptions of Vietnam only once. In August 1968, it asked:

> Some people say the war in Vietnam is resistance to North Vietnamese aggression but others say it is a civil war in South Vietnam. Which do you think is nearer the truth—resistance to North Vietnamese aggression or a civil war in South Vietnam?

A bare majority chose the northern aggression option, the rest dividing between the civil war option and the 'don't knows'. The *Herald* chose not to publish it—a refusal almost without precedent. Morgan took the hint, and this line of inquiry ceased.

After the 1973 Peace Accords, ANOP tested public perception of their likely effectiveness, and found 77 per cent thought that they had not ended the war. Finally, in 1975, McNair asked respondents whether they thought the communist takeover of Cambodia and South Vietnam would be a good or a bad thing on the whole for the people of these two countries. Bad overshadowed good, 42 per cent to 23 per cent, with over a third undecided.

Some light can be thrown on the structure of attitudes to Vietnam by examining relations between different opinion items. It is not surprising that those opposed to the draft were far more sympathetic to the rights of conscientious objectors, nor that they were overwhelmingly opposed to sending conscripts to Vietnam. However, it would be totally erroneous to picture the Australian public as divided into camps with systematically related attitudes to Vietnam, conscription and related issues. As Hamel-Green has noted, the polls show that substantial proportions of anti-conscriptionists believed that moratorium marches should not be allowed and that the conscription laws should be obeyed.[35] In 1966 there was only a difference of 15 percentage points between hawks (those who supported the Vietnam war) and doves (those opposed) in their perceptions of threat to Australia, with significant percentages of both 'threatened' doves and 'secure' hawks. In 1967, a quarter of those who supported the government's decision on increasing troops, and nearly a third of those who favoured the bombing of North Vietnam, were not prepared to say they supported the government of South Vietnam. The same poll on the troop increase and bombing showed that only marginally more than half the electorate were consistent hawks or doves.

Two Australian studies have tried to relate attitudes to Vietnam to more basic psychological dispositions. Hughes found a slight tendency for high scorers on an authoritarianism scale to have more hawkish attitudes on defence issues, including Vietnam.[36] In the context of attitudes to the My Lai massacres, Mann found a strong tendency for high authoritarians to favour 'letting off' without punishment those soldiers who killed civilians, and to profess that they would kill civilians if ordered to do so.[37] More surprisingly, although the Vietnam War debate aroused many racist elements, none of the academic studies by Hughes, Aitkin or Tiffen revealed any positive relation between attitudes to Vietnam and various measures of ethnocentrism and racial prejudice.[38]

The only study using depth interviews is Connell's study of Sydney school children. He found considerable support for Australia's involvement. Although they condemned the war, the children also believed that Australia was under threat. The more horrifying the war, the more important that it be fought there rather than here.[39]

Tiffen probed the interaction of attitudes and perceptions. His small Melbourne sample was given ten statements on possible reasons why the war in Vietnam had 'lasted many years longer than most people thought it would', and respondents were asked to rate their importance. If they thought a statement was not true, they said it was of no importance. Five of these statements were 'dovish' in that they challenged the moral justifications for involvement (eg 'The South Vietnamese government was corrupt and dictatorial and lacked the support of the Vietnamese people'). The other five reasons were 'hawkish' in that they gave 'technical' reasons, endorsement of which was consistent with support for the war (eg 'The Viet Cong and North Vietnamese were better organized').

More people ranked eight of the ten items as a major or fairly important reason than as of minor or no importance. This suggests a degree of acquiescence by respondents, and a fairly low level of strong attitude patterning. The two items receiving strongest endorsement were both 'hawkish': 'The Russians and Chinese gave the North Vietnamese supplies and technical assistance' and 'The South Vietnamese Government and army lacked experience and technical know-how.' The two statements most clearly rejected were 'dovish': 'The Vietnamese people saw the Americans as foreign invaders, not protectors; and so nationalist sentiment was on the side of the Viet-Cong', and 'The South Vietnamese government was more interested in enriching itself than in fighting the war'. All five statements designated 'dovish' produced statistically significant differences betwen supporters and opponents of our involvement. However there were few differences on the 'hawkish' statements.

The proportion of 'don't know' responses averaged 25 per cent. Partly this was due to the difficulty of the judgements required. But similar questions on reasons for Aboriginal and for Asian poverty generated much lower proportions of 'don't knows', despite the fact that Vietnam had been far more consistently and prominently in the public eye. Partly the 'don't know' responses represented a 'don't want to know' orientation. They were highest on items which most sharply challenge conventional legitimations, and lowest on the least controversial items, a pattern also found in questions on Aboriginal and Asian poverty.[40]

In sum, opposition to Australian troops in Vietnam had only haphazardly developed into a more thorough opposition to the nature and rationale of intervention.

Vietnam and the vote

Whether an individual voted Liberal or Labor certainly had a substantial bearing on where he or she stood on Vietnam, but did attitudes to Vietnam in turn affect voting choice? There are conflicting conventional wisdoms. In one version, Vietnam cost Labor dearly in 1966, while waging an unpopular war contributed to the Liberal decline in 1969 and 1972. Aitkin goes so far as to suggest that Vietnam may have delivered to Labor an extra 4 per cent of the electorate, or nearly 'half of the party's gain through conversion in the period 1966 to 1969'.[41] The alternative wisdom holds that Vietnam had little effect. Some political scientists have declared the electorate divided over Vietnam, but not in a way that affected their party allegiance. As one put it, 'the war has been a vital political issue to the activists rather than to the voters' and would 'lead to little electoral change'.[42]

Certainly the war coincided with unusually sharp electoral changes. Until 1963, the average shift in Labor's share of the vote in the post-war period had been 3 percentage points. Yet between 1963 and 1966, Labor's vote dropped by 5.5 per cent. In 1969 Labor improved its vote by no less than 7 per cent and a further gain of 2 per cent in 1972 carried it into office. The period also saw the birth of the Liberal Reform Party and later the more significant Australia Party, an anti-war party which gained over 2 per cent of the vote in both 1970 and 1972, mainly from professionals.[43] A realignment of age groups also took place. In 1966, younger voters were the least likely to vote Labor; in 1972, the most likely.

A major change in the occupational pattern of party support was also underway. Measured by a series of Morgan Gallup polls, and averaged across the periods, 'white collar' support for Labor dropped from 36 per cent in 1960–64 to 31 per cent in 1965–69. At the same time 'blue collar' support had dropped from 65 per cent to 56 per cent. But whereas the period 1970–74, marked by Labor's temporary dominance, saw 'white-collar' support for Labor rise to 38 per cent, it never recovered among 'blue collar' workers. The gap between 'white collar' and 'blue collar' support for Labor—the conventional index of 'class voting'—slipped from 29 to 25 in the first two five year periods, before plummeting to 19 in 1970–74.[44]

A connection between the rise of foreign policy issues in this period and a shift in the occupational composition of the vote was first suggested by Altman. He argued that in 1966, 'most voters perceived foreign policy as the crucial issue' and that this led 'to a large shift in votes that tended [sic] to erode slightly the class basis of party support.'[45] Hamel-Green was later to point to the 'relative lack of correlation between occupational class and attitude towards conscription', warning that as the ALP 'becomes increasingly middle-class in membership and policies, manual workers could be expected to become politically 'homeless' and either adopt apolitical attitudes or come under the hegemony of the dominant conservative ideology.'[46]

Probing the effect of issues on voting intention poses a set of the most vexed and intractable problems in opinion polling. The first problem is to identify those who may potentially change their vote. The second is to measure the salience of issues, to ascertain patterns of support for the different parties' policies, and to analyse their role in the complex of reasons which contributes to the final voting decision.

Morgan Gallup attempted to tackle the problem in September 1966, during the run-up to the election, when it presented voters with a list of ten issues and asked them to nominate the one, two or three 'likely to be important issues to you personally, when you cast your vote'.[47] Hospitals and medical services, and education were each nominated by about one in three; Vietnam and conscription each by less than one in four; and housing, unemployment and wages by fewer still. The question (with VIP flights as an eleventh alternative) was repeated in November with no shift in result. Unfortunately, there was no attempt to distinguish first choices from third choices; nor is there any way of estimating the extent of 'double counting' (eg the number of voters who nominated both Vietnam and conscription). The Morgan report, released after the election, was headed: 'Vietnam was not chief issue'. But this begged the issue. There was no attempt to link party preference to the priorities on issues. In both surveys respondents had in fact been asked their voting intention, whether they might change their mind, and if they did change for which party they would then vote. While there were no data on who had changed their vote from 1963, or the intentions of those newly enrolled, these surveys permit some revealing comparisons.

The only two issues which even 5 per cent more Liberal than Labor voters ranked as important were education and Vietnam. On three issues there was no difference between the party supporters—hospitals and medical services, housing and conscription. The other, mostly lesser, issues were ranked more highly by Labor supporters — pensions, unemployment, wages and working hours.

Among those indicating a possible change of vote—about 8 per cent in September, 4 per cent in November—the proportion which saw Vietnam as an important issue rose from 26 per cent to 36 per cent between the two surveys, while the proportion mentioning hospital and medical services, and prices, fell. At November, substantially more of these who indicated they might change to the Liberals nominated Vietnam than any other issue apart from education.

Further evidence indicates that Vietnam was an asset to the Liberal cause. In November those who favoured national service and sending national servicemen to Vietnam ranked Vietnam (but not conscription) more highly as an issue than did those who opposed national service and sending national servicemen to Vietnam.

In short, Morgan's claim that 'despite the efforts of politicians, conscription and Vietnam were relatively minor issues' is only a half-truth. Conscription may not have helped the Liberal Party but Vietnam was as important as any other issue. Hospitals and medical services may have 'topped the poll' but, as an issue, it lacked cutting edge.[48]

Morgan Gallup repeated this approach in the 1967 Senate election, and reached similar conclusions. Slightly more Liberal than Labor voters continued to give Vietnam a high priority, but now a greater proportion of those who said they might change to Labor than of those who said they might switch to non-Labor gave Vietnam priority. Even at this stage Vietnam was no longer an advantage for the government. Aitkin's 1967 survey bolsters this argument. Among those who nominated Vietnam as one of the 'most important problems the federal government should do something about', Labor held a 28 percentage points margin over the Liberals as the party most likely to do what voters wanted.[49]

By 1969, Vietnam was definitely damaging the Liberals. Some months before the election, Morgan Gallup asked voters to nominate 'the chief election issue' as far as they themselves were concerned. There was a large spread of response, with 28 per cent failing to nominate any issue, but 14 per cent nominated Vietnam, more than twice as many as any other issue.

Morgan Gallup changed their approach in August and October. The poll ran through attitudes to a number of issues—Vietnam, national service, Australian troops in Malaysia, the F-111, housing, the financing of medical services, etc-and then asked voters whether they felt so strongly about any item that they 'would definitely vote for a party which promised it'; and whether there were any issues they felt so strongly about that it could affect their vote. This is a much more stringent measure of issue salience than that used in 1966 and 1967. However, Vietnam was singled out by more voters (16 per cent in August, 17 per cent in October) than any other issue; and chosen by three times as many wanting to bring the troops back as to continue military involvement. Not surprisingly, among those who wanted to bring the troops back, Labor voters outnumbered those still intending to vote Liberal by about five to one.

On both occasions the results were reported to subscribers in a way which obscured the fact that Labor's positions generally attracted more 'decisive' support than the government's. The possibility that Labor's policies might already have encouraged Liberals to switch their vote to Labor passed without acknowlement. Readers were only invited to consider the much smaller group who 'would [still] probably vote L-CP but could be switched' by particular issues. Sounding like a government pep-talk, the report announced that Labor's positions 'could be net losers' (the August headline) or 'had little power left' (October); and that the government could counter the residual attraction of Labor policies among Liberal voters simply by more fully explaining its own policies. Readers guided only by these reports would have been surprised that Labor scored its most dramatic swing in a generation.

The most searching examination of the relation between attitudes to Vietnam and party support is in Aitkin's analysis of his 1967 and 1969 surveys. The question (with results) was:

> As you know, there is a lot of discussion around Australia about what we should be doing about Vietnam. Which of these statements comes closest to what you yourself feel should be done? If you don't have any opinion about this, just say so.
> A. We should have troops fighting in Vietnam, including conscripts
>   [1967: 28 per cent; 1969: 24 per cent]
> B. We should have troops in Vietnam, but only volunteers
>   [1967: 43 per cent; 1969: 43 per cent]
> C. We shouldn't have any troops in Vietnam, and only send civilian experts
>   [1967: 7 per cent; 1969: 12 per cent]
> D We should stay out of Vietnam altogether.
>   [1967: 16 per cent; 1969: 18 per cent]
>   No opinion/don't know [6%, 3%]

The results 'suggested a stable division of opinion, with perhaps a very slight move in 1969 towards withdrawal'. At the same time the panel data reveal 'considerable individual movement: only 55 per cent stuck to the position they had adopted in 1967, while 25 per cent were more "dovish", and 20 per cent were more "hawkish".' While there was slight movement against the war among supporters of all parties, this was greatest among Labor voters. Moreover by 1969, 'the parties were seen in sharp relief: 87 per cent correctly identified the government as supporting involvement, including conscripts, and 78 per cent had the Labor Party in favour of complete withdrawal or at least a position of civil aid only'. Despite these clear perceptions, the single most popular option among supporters of both major parties was the policy of neither, namely sending volunteer troops.

Aitkin's consideration of causal links is properly cautious and qualified. However the overall thrust of his position is that although 'the issue was manifestly of small moment to most of the electorate', and 'although we cannot from this evidence say confidently that the change in attitude to the war caused the change in vote', 'we can say that, on balance, changing attitudes to Vietnam in the period 1967–69 were a material aid to the ALP. ... we are left with an estimate of about 4 per cent for the contribution of the Vietnam issue to Labor's increase in support—or rather less than half of the party's gain through conversion in the period 1966–69. No other domestic or foreign issue had the apparent importance of Vietnam in the period under study ... '[50]

We differ from Aitkin's conclusion in two principal ways: aspects of his data suggest a weaker interpretation of the link between attitude to Vietnam and the swing to Labor; conversely, his data tend to underestimate the growth of opposition to military involvement in Vietnam.

Aitkin's claim about causality is limited, relating only to those in the panel who changed their mind about both Vietnam and their party vote. Judged in the larger context of the pronounced swing to Labor between 1966 and 1969, it seems implausible that Vietnam accounted for half of the conversions. While Labor was well ahead of the government on Vietnam, Aitkin's argument underplays the fact that it was well behind (24 percentage points) on defence. His net figure for all foreign affairs and defence issues gave Labor the lead by a mere four percentage points. Domestic issues came more to the fore in the political agenda, during this period, a change which the Labor leadership was keen to promote.

One puzzle is the contrast between Aitkin's and Morgan Gallup's findings, apparently stemming from differences in the question format. The Morgan polls most adjacent to Aitkin's surveys show curious similarities and differences. In 1967, both found 24 per cent saying in effect that we should not have troops in Vietnam. However in Aitkin's four option format, only 28 per cent were willing to send conscripts to Vietnam, whereas 42 per cent of a Gallup sample said they should be sent. Morgan's data from 1965 to 1967 suggest strongly that many voters were prepared to back the government on Vietnam even though, from the outset, they were (separately) opposed to the sending of conscripts. Most importantly, by 1969, Morgan Gallup had registered a doubling of support for withdrawal (from 24 per cent to 55 per cent), while Aitkin found a rise of only 6 per cent, and now recorded a figure 25 percentage points less than Morgan.

If nothing else, these findings suggest the lightness with which opinions were held by large numbers of the electorate. However it also seems that Aitkin's question minimised the amount of opinion change. His four option format is balanced in offering two options favouring military involvement and two opposing it. However, three of the four options favour some support for the South Vietnamese government. This may have had the unintended effect on some, whose opinions were casually or tentatively held, favouring the volunteer option in Aitkin's question but opting to bring back the troops when faced with the sharper choice posed by Morgan Gallup.

Ironically, Aitkin's own data have been used by Read to argue the unimportance of Vietnam, but we are even less convinced by Read. She supports Aitkin's question over Morgan's. She argues (against the evidence) that Vietnam was less salient in 1969 than in 1967. Among those who by 1969 switched to Labor she is only prepared to count as 'Vietnam switchers' those who saw Vietnam as 'the most important problem' facing the federal government.[51] While Aitkin exaggerates the importance of Vietnam, this kind of analysis surely underestimates it.

For the 1970 Senate election, Morgan Gallup adopted the approach of 1969, listing eight issues (including seven of the ten used in 1969), using the same format to determine voters' views on each; and then asking voters whether there were any issues where they would definitely vote for the party which took their stand. In 1969 no fewer than 80 per cent had nominated an issue that would affect their vote, but this time only 39 per cent did so. Again, the overall conclusion was that 'no one issue had much potential for swinging people from the LCP to the ALP'.

ALP research in mid-1971 (conducted through small groups by Spectrum International) revealed that 'the only things that are clear about ALP policy are the basic stances on Vietnam and conscription.'[52] Remarkably, in Morgan Gallup's list of ten issues before the 1972 election, neither Vietnam nor conscription appeared. For this election, Morgan Gallup returned to their 1966 approach, asking voters to select the three issues that would be most important to them. In an election day survey in Sydney, McNair also omitted Vietnam and conscription from their list of eleven 'key issues' on which voters compared the parties. Still, among those who had voted Labor, more advanced Vietnam and conscription as a reason for their vote (4 per cent) than any other single issue.[53]

Impact of Vietnam: threats, defence and the American way

What effect did the Vietnam war have on attitudes to related issues such as defence, the American alliance, and other Southeast Asian countries?

Perhaps the main prop of public support for intervention was the 'domino theory', that the war in Vietnam was part of a communist thrust towards Australia and it was better to stop 'them' there than here. In May 1965, following the announcement of the first Australian troops for Vietnam, Morgan asked 'what would happen to Thailand and Malaysia if the United States left Vietnam'. Some 64 per cent said they would be taken over by other countries, and only 16 per cent said they would remain as they are. To the question 'Do you think Australia would eventually be in danger from China if the United States pulled out of Asia?' 72 per cent said yes; again a recalcitrant 16 per cent said no.

At the end of the war, in May 1975, McNair showed respondents a list of nine countries and asked whether they thought the takeover of Vietnam would lead to attempts at a similar communist takeover in any of the nine. Only 19 per cent said it would lead to no such attempts while 70 per cent named at least one country. The most commonly nominated were Thailand (59 per cent) and South Korea (49 per cent); 29 per cent chose Australia. After the dramatic communist victories in Indo-China, the domino theory was alive and well.

Willingness to intervene in other Southeast Asian conflicts seemed barely diminished. In a wide-ranging survey of attitudes to defence in August 1971, ANOP found 58 per cent favouring withdrawal from Vietnam, but the identical proportion thought Australia should provide military assistance if a Southeast Asian country asked us to defeat a communist rebellion. In April 1975, Morgan asked:

> If forces from Vietnam and Cambodia enter Thailand, and America sends forces to keep them out, in your opinion should Australia send forces to Thailand to help the Americans or not?

Opinion was evenly divided with 46 per cent saying not to send forces, and 44 per cent saying send them. This is not significantly different from a similar item in 1962, cited earlier in this chapter, which showed a majority against sending forces to Thailand.

A survey for USIS in September 1975 illustrated the public's ambivalence. Some 43 per cent thought Australia had too little influence in Southeast Asia, 35 per cent the right amount and 6 per cent too much influence; yet 39 per cent thought we should play a more active role in Southeast Asia and 49 per cent thought we should not. To achieve more influence while being no more active would have set Australia's policy-makers a challenging task indeed.

The sense of external threat to Australia has remained high. In November 1967, June 1968, and April 1969, Morgan Gallup found over half agreeing that there were countries which were a threat to Australia's security, around 30 per cent nominating China. In 1976 and 1978 Morgan found less than half believed Australia was threatened, around 15 per cent again nominating China.[54] In February 1970 and April 1975, Morgan Gallup found 54 per cent and 58 per cent respectively who thought that Australia was 'likely to be menaced by (some) country in the next ten years, requiring more spending on defence'.

The more stringent question asked for the USIS reduced those perceiving a threat to a minority: Do you think any countries will pose a military threat to the security of Australia in the next five years?' 41 per cent in 1975 and 35 per cent in 1978 answered yes. The country most often nominated (25 per cent and 17 per cent) was China. In contrast, when the *Age* poll in April 1977 listed eight Asian countries, only 23 per cent did not judge at least one of them likely to be a threat to Australia. In this poll China remained our favourite threat. Other polls (Morgan, 1976 and 1978) put Russia equal with China;[55] and the *Age* poll of April 1980 put Russia well ahead.

The most valuable source here is a series of ANOP surveys which asked 'Will Australia be threatened from outside its borders in the next 15 years?' (Table 7.2) On this evidence, our sense of threat apparently diminished slightly between 1971 and 1974—possibly under the influence of Whitlam and the ALP, and the increased public disrepute of western involvement in Vietnam. But since 1975—under the influence, perhaps, of defeat in Vietnam and the rising political fortunes of Malcolm Fraser's Liberals—the perception of threat has risen again, and indeed was higher in 1980 than for any survey during the seventies: ANOP's figure for October 1980 is almost identical to that of the *Age* poll's for April 1980.

Table 7.2 'Will Australia be threatened from outside its borders in the next 15 years?'

	Aug.'71	Feb.'74	March '76	Sept.'77	April '79	Oct.'80
Yes, it will	42%	36%	51%	47%	51%	64%
No, it won't	45	51	38	41	39	28
Unsure	13	13	11	10	10	8

Source: *Australian Financial Review* 13 October 1980.

Accompanying this fearful view of the world has been a constant voter desire to have more spent on defence. The first item explicitly probing increases in defence was from Morgan in 1967. The question was rather loaded, offering two 'increase' categories and only one 'decrease', while respondents were cued by the preamble: 'If Britain carried out its plan to *withdraw all* its armed forces from Southeast Asia within 10 years ... '. 46 per cent thought our armed forces should be increased a lot and 21 per cent thought they should be increased a little.

A similar picture emerged from a battery of ANOP questions in August 1971. Faced with only two alternatives, 59 per cent thought the size of Australia's armed forced should be increased, and 19 per cent that they should be reduced. On defence spending 46 per cent said it should be increased; 40 per cent left as it was; and 10 per cent, decreased. However the ignorance in which these views were held was illustrated by a third item, where 66 per cent underestimated the size of the defence forces. The actual size was 90,000, but fully 50 per cent estimated 49,000 or less.

The advent of the Labor government did not significantly change the distribution of opinion. An *Age* Poll in March 1974 found 71 per cent of people perceived the ALP government as spending less money on defence than its Liberal-Country Party predecessors. Two months later, McNair found 51 per cent thought Australia was not spending enough on defence, and again in the last months of the Whitlam government, 59 per cent told interviewers working for the USIS that Australia was spending less than it should.

According to three McNair polls, the Fraser government has fared little better. Perhaps it has generated expectations it has been unable to meet. In mid-1976 exactly half the electorate thought the government was not sufficiently concerned with defence. Only 12 per cent thought it showed too much concern. In October 1978, the proportion thinking the government was spending too little was 58 per cent; in 1979, in Aitkin's follow-up survey, 57 per cent; and in March 1980, McNair again found 80 per cent agreeing that defence spending should be increased. In January 1981 Morgan Gallup told interviewees that the president of the RSL has said that 'it was urgent to upgrade and re-equip Australia's army, navy and air-force'. Although this meant 'we would spend a lot more money on defence', 77 per cent were agreeable.

Guns before butter? Not entirely. In a workforce survey conducted by McNair early in 1981, a sample of 800 was asked to assume that they had to cut $1000 million from government spending, then asked to nominate the amount they would cut from programs for the poor and other disadvantaged groups, health and education programs, programs for environmental and consumer protection, and military defence programs. Those interviewed were least willing to cut health and education, and programs for the poor. While 18 per cent were prepared to cut $600 million or more from defence almost no one wanted cuts of this size in any of the other programs.[56]

Public attitudes to the United States have remained overwhelmingly positive. In 1972, 70 per cent of voters in a USIS survey thought the United States had made 'very great' or 'considerable' efforts to promote peace. In June 1970, 67 per cent 'regardless of how much you may like or dislike' the United States, had 'great' or 'considerable' respect for it; a proportion that rose to 77 per cent by 1972.

In September 1975, 82 per cent of Australians judged that the basic interests of the United States and Australia were 'very much' or 'fairly well' in agreement, a marginal decline from 90 per cent in March 1972 and 93 per cent in early 1963. In the same 1975 survey 69 per cent nominated the United States when asked if there were any countries with whom it was very important for Australia to have close political ties. The next highest were Britain (33 per cent) and Japan and Indonesia (25 per cent). Further, 76 per cent thought Australia's relations with the United States were already very or fairly close. In 1967, 1969 and 1979 Aitkin found a high proportion who thought ties with the United States should be either 'very close' or 'fairly close' (88 and 89 per cent) with the proportion saying 'very close' declining slightly (49, 44, 41 per cent).[57]

In 1975, USIS reported that 72 per cent could name no major problem existing between the two countries. Both 1975 surveys asked: 'In the event of Australia's being threatened by some other country, how much trust do you feel Australia can have in the United States to come to our defence—great deal, a fair amount, not very much or none at all?' Some 75 per cent in May and 77 per cent in September expressed a 'great deal' or 'fair amount' of trust; 79 per cent in 1978. These were down slightly from the 83 per cent in March 1972.

Commercial polls report similar findings. In April 1975, 73 per cent of a Morgan sample said our treaties with America were of real value to Australia, while only 13 per cent felt that they were of so little value they should be ended. This differed only marginally from the 77 per cent affirming the treaties in 1970. Morgan Gallup's extreme wording—complete acceptance versus complete rejection—produces a misleading picture. It should be qualified by an ANOP finding of 1971 where a majority thought we would have to rely increasingly on ourselves rather than depend on the United States; and by a 1978 survey conducted for the USIS which found only 34 per cent who had both heard of ANZUS and knew that the United States was a member.

In April 1972, Morgan reported 64 per cent wanted the United States to use our naval base in Western Australia. In March 1980, McNair found 59 per cent thought we should encourage the United States to strengthen its bases here. According to a Morgan poll of July 1980, a similar proportion agreed with the suggestion that the 'United States station some of their planes in Northern Australia'. But in January 1981, when Morgan asked about B-52 bombers which 'the United States wants to be able to land at Darwin airport'—but which 'may carry nuclear weapons'—support was virtually halved. Even when airstrips in northern Australia 'a long way from towns' was offered, barely half of those interviewed favoured the proposal.

An *Age* poll in June 1975 found 78 per cent saying the friendship and goodwill of the United States was important to Australia, placing it slightly ahead of Japan (75 per cent), Britain (63 per cent) and the other seven countries listed. When McNair asked its sample in September 1980 to name Australia's best friend, 55 per cent named the United States and 24 per cent the United Kingdom.

None the less, confidence has sometimes been disturbed. In March

1972, when respondents in a USIS survey were asked to nominate recent actions that had given a favourable or unfavourable impression of the United States, a number named the policies and actions in Vietnam: 18 per cent favourably; 13 per cent unfavourably. However, Vietnam responses comprised one-fifth of the positive total and one-half of the much smaller negative total.

The September 1975 survey found a majority who thought the United States took Australia's view into account either not very much or not at all. In addition, although out-numbered by those wanting closer cooperation (39 per cent) and those wanting to maintain the present relationship (26 per cent), a significant minority (26 per cent) thought it would be better for Australia to act more independently of the United States. In 1976, while 31 per cent said they would be 'very concerned' if 'the United States' role in military and security affairs in Asia' declined, 32 per cent thought they would be 'not very' or 'not at all' concerned. While 46 per cent (down from 57 per cent in 1972) thought the United States was the strongest country in the world, only 32 per cent thought it would be in five years time.

In 1963, 41 per cent had a 'very favourable' impression of what the 'United States has been doing in international affairs recently'; in 1972, this number had dropped to 23 per cent. Two other sets of items also suggest Vietnam may have farnished the US image somewhat, both showing a decline in the first half of the 1970s and a rise again by 1978. The first item asks: 'How much confidence do you have in the ability of the United States to deal wisely with present world problems? A great deal of confidence, a fair amount, not very much, or none at all?' To our knowledge the USIS has asked that question seven times in Australia. Net results, taking the proportions answering 'not very much' or 'none at all' from those answering 'a great deal' or 'a fair amount', are reported in Table 3.

Table 7.3 'How much confidence do you have in the ability of the United States to deal wisely with present world problems?' (percentage points difference between a great deal/fair amount and not very much/none)

	March 63	June 70	Jan 72	March 72	Feb 74	May 75	March 78
Net Positive	54	33	28	52	17	21	60

Source: USIS (see footnote 9)
Note: Up to 1972 the positive alternatives were very great/considerable.

A dip in favourable attitudes to the United States in the early 1970s is also suggested by a USIS item simply asking respondents to nominate the category which best describes their general feelings about the United States—very good, good, neither good nor bad, bad, very bad. In 1963, the net favourable (the difference between the first two categories and the last three) was 68. In 1972 it was down to 17, and in 1978 had risen again to 34. Similarly, the proportions answering 'very good' were 34 per cent, 9 per cent and 15 per cent.

Figures from other countries on changes in US prestige suggest an almost universal trough in mid-1970, following the invasion of Cambodia, and a similarly spectacular peak in early 1972 following Nixon's visit to China. The final defeat in Indo-China seems to have occasioned less disillusionment than the Cambodian invasion.

Four months after 'the US evacuation from Vietnam', 59 per cent of the Australian electorate thought it 'very' or 'fairly likely' that 'The United States' role in military and security affairs will *decline* in Asia'. By 1978, 'looking ahead over the next year or two', only 7 per cent thought it likely that 'the United States' attention to military and security affairs in Southeast Asia and South Pacific region' would decline.

USIS polling manifested an interest in Australian public opinion overall and in 'elite' or educated opinion, particularly in the kinds of people the State Department sees as 'opinion makers', with access to the higher reaches of business, government and the media. Almost all USIS reports record separately the opinions of those who either finished secondary school or matriculated (whether or not they proceeded to University or some other form of tertiary education). One survey in 1971 was confined exclusively to 'educated opinion'.

As our earlier analysis of the somewhat narrower group of University students and professionals suggested, this interest is not without cause. Where there are differences it is the better educated who emerged as less well disposed to United States' interests than those whose schooling stopped early. This seems especially true of of 1972, the crest of a wave which brought Labor to office.

Aftermath: Vietnam and the Indo-China refugees

Vietnam has not completely disappeared from Australian debate. Vietnam's invasion of Kampuchea and its border war with China created headlines. Most importantly, the enormous exodus of refugees in the years 1977–79 engendered strong negative feelings.

Immediately after the war, an *Age* poll offered respondents a list of ten countries. North Vietnam ranked worst on both the questions asked. Only 11 per cent thought its friendship and goodwill were important to Australia, while 42 per cent thought it unlikely to be friendly to Australia, compared with the USSR 39 per cent, and China 29 per cent. Almost two years later, from a list of eight Asian countries, Vietnam was ranked as least important to Australia, least democratic and least trustworthy. Some 27 per cent thought Vietnam was aggressive, slightly less than nominated Indonesia or China. Again, 15 per cent saw Vietnam as a threat to

Australia, putting it fourth in a list topped by China (41 per cent).

Nor has the Australian public been keen to give aid to post-war Vietnam. A USIS poll in September 1975 found two-thirds in favour of Australia's giving aid to Southeast Asia, but only one-third approving aid to Vietnam. In February 1979, McNair found most voters in favour of the Fraser government decision to suspend aid to Vietnam.

Faced with the problem of Indo-Chinese refugees, the Australian public was generally unwilling to admit sizeable numbers. At the end of the war, some goodwill was apparent. In April 1975, Morgan found most voters in favour of bringing Vietnamese orphans here, and a slender majority for allowing permanent Vietnamese refugee settlement. In September 1977, as refugee numbers began to build, the *Age* poll asked voters which type of migrant they wanted most: those who have skills we need; those who are 'like the majority of Australians'; refugees who need a country; or those who have relatives here. The question forced a choice of priorities which may have been unreal for many. It attracted a figure of 12 per cent for refugees, and with it the curious remark that 'there was little support for refugees who are now making up a large part of the annual migrant intake'. The latter claim is dubious at best, and the former is a *non sequitur*. As Kenneth Rivett argued, 'proof that a man loves his wife most does not even tend to show that he feels tepid towards his children'.[58]

Three times Morgan Gallup asked another unsatisfactory question: 'About refugees from Vietnam. Would you allow any number of them to live permanently here—or limit their number—or stop them from staying here.' The results did show that the number wanting to stop refugees rose from 20 per cent in November 1977 (when the number of refugees was lower) to 32 per cent in March 1979 but predictably, the majority rejected both complete prohibition and a completely unregulated flow. Around 60 per cent settled for the middle option each time. Since, in February 1979, 80 per cent could not say where to place the limit, the question was not particularly useful.[59] In mid-1979 Morgan dropped this question and instead handed respondents a list of eight possible numbers of refugees to be allowed to settle here. One quarter opted for none, and over a third wanted some number less than the then policy of 10,000 per year. Experience suggests, however, that offering interviewees a large range of numbers, without guidance to their meaning in terms of current practice or proposed policies, encourages a spread of fairly meaningless responses.

A 1978 McNair poll showed 80 per cent of Australians against taking more migrants from Asia and Africa than at present; but the alternative of maintaining the present intake was not offered. The same poll showed 77 per cent disagreed with the proposition that 'we should give special preference to people from Vietnam'.

More satisfactory were questions framed in terms of current policy. McNair's questions in February and September 1979 obtained almost identical responses. On each occasion a majority wanted fewer or no refugees, and about 30 per cent accepted the planned number. A mid-year *Age* poll, with a different set of alternatives, found even less goodwill. Only 7 per cent said accept more; 23 per cent wanted the same number, 30 per cent wanted fewer and 37 per cent none. A mid-1978 telephone poll, in which respondents were asked whether Vietnamese refugees should be allowed to stay in Australia produced 24 per cent Yes; 9 per cent Yes, but with qualifications; and 57 per cent No.

The couple of thousand 'boat people' who landed in northern Australia touched a fear almost as old as white occupation of Australia. Morgan Gallup broached the general question first in late 1975, before any boat people had actually landed. Drawing respondents' attention to the attempt by 350,000 unarmed Moroccans to march into Spanish Sahara in an unsuccessful attempt to take it over, Morgan Gallup asked: 'If hundreds of thousands of unarmed people from the north landed in northern Australia from small boats, should we let them stay, or force them to leave?' In the circumstances, the 58 per cent-19 per cent majority to 'make them leave' seems the least that could have been expected.

In September 1978 and 1979, McNair offered three alternatives: allow them to settle, send them back, or get some other country to take them. Opinion was evenly split in three ways. There was no probing of the second preferences of those who had opted for the unrealistic solution of finding a third country to take them. In mid-1979, Morgan gave respondents a sharper choice: to accept the refugees or put their boats back to sea. This produced a 53 per cent-28 per cent vote for accepting them.

It is easy to say that the hostility to Vietnamese refugees stems from Australian racism, but on our evidence the motivation is more complex. On the one hand, a 1971 *Age* poll showed Asian immigrants to be the least desired; and McNair, in 1976, found 79 per cent who rejected the idea that we invite big numbers of 'coloured' people to Australia, and 69 per cent who said that their arrival would reduce our standard of living. On the other hand, 75 per cent of a 1972 *Age* poll agreed that 'coloured' migrants are as acceptable as any other migrants. In late 1975, McNair found 36 per cent who thought there were too many Asian migrants, but almost half the sample thought there was about the right number. The response was slightly more favourably than for an identical question on non-English-speaking European migrants. The 1976 poll cited above found 57 per cent thought the adoption of Asian children by Australian couples should be encouraged. Most remarkably, a two-thirds majority told McNair in September 1979, that they would welcome Vietnamese refugees settling in their area.

The second half of the 1970s, a period of rising unemployment, saw a decline in the popularity of all migration to Australia. In 1977, half the *Age* poll sample thought we should not be concerned if population growth slows: only a quarter thought we should encourage more migrants.

Conclusion

The public stance of opinion pollsters suggests that they are merely the recorders of opinions which exist independently of their activities. But polling is neither politically neutral nor passive. The Vietnam War provides a compelling illustration of this. The principal organisation, the Morgan Gallup Poll, made decisions as to when to start polling and which questions to ask, how to interpret the results and how to disseminate them, when to stop and what questions not to ask, in ways that often boosted the appearance of support for intervention, and undercut any sense of public opposition. Although hardly unique, the issues surrounding the Vietnam War provide one of the most sustained, wide-ranging and clear-cut cases of the manufacture of opinion. In a politically loaded way.

From the severely limited data available on public opinion the following general picture emerges. The Australian and American intervention in Vietnam enjoyed clear majority support in 1965 and 1966. In 1967 and 1968, general support was maintained, but with more qualifications. From mid-1969 majority opinion favoured withdrawal, at first tentatively, but with increasing consistency and strength in the following years. Opinion on conscription shows no such trend. Although support faltered somewhat late in the war, a majority continued to support it. An equally emphatic majority, however, opposed sending conscripts to Vietnam. Attitudes to anti-war demonstrators, to conscientious objectors and draft resisters, and to the civil liberties questions raised, were consistently negative. Although equivocal and incomplete, the evidence suggests that Vietnam was an electoral asset to the Liberals in 1966, and a limited electoral advantage for the ALP from 1969 onwards. On issues related to Vietnam—defence spending, the American alliance, attitudes to Southeast Asia — few changes in public opinion seem to have resulted from the war.

8 News coverage of Vietnam
RODNEY TIFFEN

The deep and many-sided divisions over the nature of the Vietnam war, and over Australian and American involvement in it, inevitably extend to opinions about news coverage. The role of the western news media raised questions for those wanting to understand and affect political outcomes, and for those whose prime interest was to understand and improve media performance.

Did news reporting, through undue concentration on the inevitable ugly aspects of war, unduly constrain western conduct of the war, as some hawks allege? Or, as many doves charge, did the media prolong public acceptance through distorted reporting based on an ideological framework which justified western intervention? What were the main virtues of coverage and its main defects? And what were the causes of both? Did news reporting improve during the long course of the war?

This chapter proceeds in three parts. The first considers the general influences on the content of news about Vietnam. The second examines news coverage from the Diem period to the final communist victory. The final part attempts to evaluate the quality of news coverage and to determine its effects.

Influences

Critics of the media sometimes write as if news content were the product of a single coherent viewpoint, designed to maximise ideological effectiveness, without constraints of time, cost, access or audience. The political views of proprietors and editors, and of reporters and sub-editors do influence news presentation, and do so to varying degrees in different news organisations. But this is only a very partial explanation. News content is best understood by examining how news is made. This involves three main elements: an analysis of the routines of news organisations, including their division of news-gatherers into particular 'rounds' or 'beats'; the process of information-gathering within each news round; and the ideas of 'news values' and 'audience demand' which structure reportorial and organisational priorties.¹

All other aspects are dependent on staffing policies. Although some papers sent correspondents for lengthy periods, none ever had a permanent Vietnam correspondent. For most of the period, the Melbourne *Herald*, *Australia's largest press group*, and *The Age* each had a Singapore-based correspondent whose extensive commission included Vietnam. Similarly, the Australian Broadcasting Commission (ABC) had several correspondents based in Singapore who were able to cover Vietnam when required. The Melbourne *Herald* and *Sydney Morning Herald* also used the roving freelance correspondent Denis Warner.

The most constant source of material for Australian newspapers came from the international news agencies.² Some papers were also able to draw on material syndicated from Britain and America. Our politically subordinate role and relatively tiny military presence were matched by a disproportionately smaller commitment of journalists. More intangibly, Australian editorial decision-makers adopted a less serious, less probing interest than their US counterparts.

The primary factor affecting the patterns of news content was the many-layered influence of the western governments. There is a world of difference between the news coverage of Vietnam we received and what we would have received if the news media had simply been official propaganda organs, or subject to official censorship. Nevertheless, news was most deeply influenced by the media's relations with officialdom.

The most direct form of influence was the reporting of government statements and actions. Occasionally news became simply a conduit for government views, for instance during the Tonkin Gulf crisis, and in the official reports of bombing missions to which journalists had no access. Governments can exploit their news-producing initiative in the timing and staging of dramatic announcements. Official releases of information are the most prolific and routine source of news, and few journalists can afford to ignore them. Even though widespread scepticism led to the Saigon daily briefings being dubbed 'the five o'clock follies', they were always heavily attended and resulted in the filing of countless stories without further checking.

Less directly, journalists' judgements of importance are very sensitive to official concerns and priorities. Cohen wrote that the press 'may not be successful in telling people what to think, but it is stunningly successful in telling its readers what to think about'.³ In turn, the government may not succeed in determining news media viewpoints, but is more successful in setting their agenda.

The biggest impetus to critical reporting in international affairs is division and conflict within officialdom, or inconsistencies between official positions. Institutional sources are not monolithic: different agencies have different tasks and orientations; subordinates have different problems and pressures from their superiors; and individual ambitions clash. Despite President Nixon's claims that the 1971 incursion into Laos was a success, news reports based on the almost unanimous views of lower officials conveyed its failure. A similar dynamic was a spur to critical reporting of the Diem regime.

In most adversary situations, the government possesses a considerable arsenal of formal and informal sanctions. What the government says and does is still news, so there remains scope for influencing coverage, including public denunciation of the news media. The routines of reporting become more difficult and unpleasant if the reporter's sources act abrasively or resentfully.[4] Lack of access is a potent punishment. Sometimes news organisation executives may stand firm during a public confrontation, but seek a quiet accommodation later. *Newsweek's* Francois Sully was expelled from Vietnam in August 1962 for his critical reporting of the Diem family. The following December *Newsweek* published a highly complimentary cover story on Madame Nhu.[5]

Another major influence on news content is editorial and audience attitudes, and conventional news values, which together define the demand for news. Vietnam reporting was notable for the narrow range of interests, and for the news organisations' fear of controversy. TV has the most centralised decision-making among the news media, and its necessarily brief items force extreme selectivity. An NBC News vice-president proclaimed: 'it's not a Vietnamese war, it's an American war in Asia, and that's the only story the American audience is interested in'. Such network policy ensured that only the most sporadic attention was given to Vietnamese politics and society. Similarly, a Sydney press executive once told a correspondent to regard Southeast Asia as Australia's backyard.[6]

Mass media shy away from stories which do not, in Walter Lippmann's phrase, capture the easy interest, whose significance and meaning are not immediately apparent to their audience. To make a society as remote, unfamiliar and complex as Vietnam intelligible and interesting was a challenge which most news organisations failed to acknowledge, let alone to meet.

The news media are often painted as revelling in controversy, but more often media executives prefer comfortable mediocrity.[7] Sharply critical stories raise acute questions of accuracy and trust, because they may confront political vested interests and strong public prejudice. Nearly all the instances of critical reporting cited later in this chapter were accompanied by considerable nervousness and reluctance among news executives, which sometimes proved justified by the political and public aftermath.

Finally, the situation of correspondents and conventional news practices also influenced content. Most journalists, especially those 'firemen' who only visited Vietnam during major stories, had very restricted contact with Vietnamese society, either because their news organisations had very narrow interests or because, like most correspondents, they themselves could not speak Vietnamese.

News is concerned with reporting fresh developments, its focus is tan gible events. This has a pervasive but less obvious influence on its content. History and stable conditions may be included but usually only to 'background' breaking stories. As David Halberstam wrote:

> The problem was trying to cover something every day as news when in fact the real key was that it was all derivative of the French Indo-China war, which is history. So you really should have had a third paragraph in each story which would have said, 'All of this is shit and none of this means anything because we are in the same footsteps as the French and we are prisoners of their experience'. But given the rules of newspaper reporting you can't really do that. Events have to be judged by themselves, as if the past did not really exist. This is not usually such a problem for a reporter, but to an incredible degree in Vietnam I think we were haunted and indeed imprisoned by the past.[8]

News coverage

Evaluation of the conflicting viewpoints about news coverage is difficult because the war was so protracted and complex, and news coverage so voluminous, raising different concerns and issues for different media at different times. No single episode or period is indicative of the whole. It is desirable to trace through in some detail the dominant themes in coverage of each of the war's major stages and crucial espisodes.

News coverage of the Diem period is notable for the initially glowing accounts of his rule, and for the pivotal role of the Saigon press corps in later tarnishing that image and possibly acting as a catalyst for his overthrow in 1963.

The Tonkin Gulf incident of August 1964 marked a major escalation of American involvement, and is the most powerful example in modern times of an American administration's capacity to dominate and manipulate news coverage in an offically-proclaimed crisis.

The Australian government's escalation in Vietnam was a marked political success, partly sustained by its ability, through astute management plus media acquiescence, to secure overwhelmingly favourable news coverage. The politics and press coverage of escalation in Australia differed greatly from that in the USA.

The offensive by the North Vietnamese and Viet Cong during the 1968 Tet holiday has come to be viewed by many as the turning-point of the war. Controversy surrounds charges that news accounts, through their excessive 'pessimism', helped convert the offensive into a political success for the communists, despite their military failure.

The era of Vietnamisation produced a strange combination of trends in American reporting: a lessening of media interest due to the perceived warweariness of the public and diminished attention to immediate military developments were mixed with more acute, informed reporting of major developments and a broader range of critical or interpretative commentary.

NEWS COVERAGE

Australian reporting partly paralleled these trends, but there is less evidence of either growing expertise or growing scepticism.

Australian press coverage of the communist victory in 1975 reflected an unprecedentedly intense concern for refugees and orphans, sympathy for the US government and criticism of the Australian Labor government, a marked lack of interest in examining reasons for the west's defeat.

Diem

There were two sharply contradictory press images of Ngo Dinh Diem. The first, essentially unchallenged from his installation as president in 1954 until the early 1960s, was an incorruptible democrat, courageously and successfully struggling against communism. The second view which became increasingly prominent in 1963, was Diem as a remote, ineffectual leader of a corrupt, dictatorial and divisive regime, inexorably losing Vietnam to communism.

Diem in 1954 was the perfect Asian leader for American public consumption. He was untainted by collaboration with the French colonialists, spoke earnestly of nationalism and of nation-building, led an austere personal life, and was a staunchly anti-communist Catholic—ideal ingredients for building what was later dubbed the Diem myth.

Many American politicians praised him lavishly; Vice-President Johnson was perhaps the most eulogistic, describing Diem as 'the Winston Churchill of Southeast Asia' (1961). The news media dutifully recorded such views, and were independently enterprising: 'doughty little Diem' (*Time*, 1960), 'one of Asia's ablest leaders' (*Newsweek*, 1960), 'Thomas Jefferson would have no quarrel' with Diem's definition of democracy (*New York Times*, 1957).

Australian ministers were equally glowing. External Affairs Minister Casey strongly defended Diem's refusal to hold national elections in 1956, and maintained that this action had not violated the Geneva agreements of two years earlier. The period 1954–57 was one of strengthening relations between Australia and South Vietnam, climaxed by Diem's visit in September 1957—one of the first visits to Australia by a foreign head of state. *The Age* called him 'incorruptible and intensely patriotic'. *Herald* coverage was equally sympathetic, but far more 'folksy'. Beginning with 'Asian visitor is welcome' (2. 9. 57), it captioned a picture of Diem eating cheese with 'There's nothing like this in my country' (5. 9. 57). Finally 'Terry meets a president from Asia' described Diem's visit to a Housing Commission estate ('How many rooms do you have?') and the 'Botanic Gardens, where the flower-loving President drove around the footpath in his car' (6. 9. 57).

The transformation of Diem's image was mainly the result of reporting by the Saigon press corps in 1962–63. The process by which this group became increasingly critical of Diem, the responses of the American and South Vietnamese governments and their own journalistic colleagues, and the political machinations resulting from US disillusion with Diem, constitute a celebrated and important case of interplay between news media, and political policy and outcomes.

The American and South Vietnamese governments had a common information policy of minimising the degree of American involvement, stressing the success of the war effort, and maintaining a positive image of the Diem government. Conflict arose because reporters sceptically probed official claims. Increasingly they punctured the optimistic accounts of senior officials by direct observation, by reporting the pessimism of middle-rank and field officers, and by some contact with Vietnamese bureaucractic and opposition groups, especially the Buddhists. A steady stream of stories exposed official lies and the deteriorating security situation.[9] Most importantly, the Buddhist crisis of May 1963, stimulated by the irrational repressiveness of the Diem government, was prominently and tenaciously covered by the press corps. The most spectacular and important single incident was the self-immolation of a Buddhist monk, the focal point of a large Buddhist rally at a central Saigon intersection. The photograph and Malcolm Browne's story captured wide international attention and effectively dramatised the depth of Buddhist grievances against Diem.

The responses of the South Vietnamese and American governments were consistently heavy-handed. In August 1962 Francois Sully of *Newsweek* was expelled, followed shortly after by NBC 'stringer' Jim Robertson. The regime also wished to expel Homer Bigart of the *New York Times*, but was finally dissuaded by the American Embassy. An American government press 'specialist' was brought to Saigon to 'straighten out' the correspondents. He wanted to 'keep them happy in Saigon' and 'take their minds off the war'. Part of his strategy was to issue a list of 'available' girls.[10] US government officials publicly criticised coverage as emotional and unbalanced. Private criticisms were even sharper. When Browne asked a question at a press conference, the visiting Admiral Felt replied 'So you're Browne. Why don't you get on the team!' In October the newly appointed publisher of the *New York Times*, Arthur Ochs Sulzberger, paid a courtesy visit to President Kennedy, who suggested that David Halberstam was too close to the story in Vietnam and asked if there were any plans to transfer him.[11]

During the Buddhist crisis, Madame Nhu's brother 'let it be known that a list of foreign correspondents slated for assassination had been prepared by the government. No attempts were ever made on any of us, and the presumption was that this rumor had been put forth to rattle us'. In July 1963, Browne and Peter Arnett of the AP (Associated Press) were beaten up by plainclothed secret police while observing a demonstration, then charged with assaulting the police, and interrogated for eight hours—despite the offers of eight other correspondents who witnessed the scene to testify to their innocence. After the monk's self-immolation, members of the Diem government publicly and privately charged that Browne had bribed the monks, and Madame Nhu labelled the event a barbecue.[12]

Under increasing pressure, the Saigon press corps became more united, but solidarity from visiting correspondents and their own home offices was often conspicuously absent. Senior journalists like Joseph Alsop and Marguerite Higgins denounced the Saigon corps. Higgins wrote: 'Reporters here would like to see us lose the war to prove they are right'. The most celebrated attack appeared in *Time* (September 1963), which accused the Saigon correspondents of confusing what they should be clarifying, and of never venturing into the field but sitting around in Saigon and reinforcing each other's cynicism. After this article *Time* correspondents Charles Mohr and Mert Perry both resigned.

Ironically, the leading correspondents in the Saigon press corps considered themselves supporters of the American involvement. Their adversary relationship, despite its intensity, had developed not from ideological opposition but from a desire to report accurately, and to replace ineffective policies with effective ones. Mohr, for example, was embarrassed that the martyrdom forced on him by *Time* led to accolades from the peace movement.

The dramatic developments of 1962-3 appeared in the Australian press, but in somewhat muted form. Correspondents like Bruce Grant and Denis Warner were fully aware of Diem's failings. The Australian government, however, contained the critical fallout, partly by Olympian aloofness in dismissing external criticism. Perhaps the most sweeping example of this came earlier, when Dr Evatt criticised the South Vietnamese elections as unfair to Diem's opponents. External Affairs Minister Casey replied: 'I do not think anyone ... should cast doubt on the conduct of affairs in a country with which Australia has friendly relations'.[13]

In addition, the Australian government (unlike the American) was never internally divided or doubtful in this period. The only occasion when official statements wavered from uncritical support for Diem was in mid-June 1963 when an official note was sent expressing repugnance at religious persecution. Even after Diem's overthrow, External Affairs Minister Barwick simply said he 'had been a sincere patriot, although some of his internal policies in recent times appeared to have lost him the popular support that was necessary to the continuance of his government'.[14]

Following the coup which deposed and killed Diem on 1 November 1963 there was a new 'honeymoon period' in press reporting, although the subsequent instability of South Vietnamese governments soon strained this relationship.

Tonkin Gulf
The Tonkin Gulf incident of August 1964, and the reprisal air strikes against North Vietnam, 'marked the crossing of an important threshold in the war, and it was accomplished with virtually no domestic criticism,

indeed with an evident increase in public support for the Administration'.[15]

Both Hanoi and Washington 'agreed that North Vietnamese PT boats had deliberately engaged the USS Maddox on August 2, though they differed as to where the engagement took place, the reason for the attack, and its outcome'.[16] The destroyer suffered no damage. Washington announced it did not consider the incident a 'major crisis'. It ordered reinforcement for the Maddox and the continuation of normal patrols. On August 4, the US charged that another attack had occurred much further from the coast. The US response was immediate and devastating. Heavy air-raids hit three major North Vietnamese bases which, according to Defense Secretary McNamara, destroyed 25 boats and almost all the local fuel depots.

President Johnson's political blitz was equally dramatic. He made a nationwide TV address, secured endorsement of his actions from rival presidental candidate Goldwater, and obtained overwhelming Congressional support for a resolution affirming the national determination to meet all such attacks and approving all necessary action to do so. The resolution, according to one of its sponsors, Senator Fulbright, was passed in an atmosphere which 'seemed to preclude debate'. The immediate effects were all beneficial to Johnson. The bombing was a tangible demonstration of US power and resolve, and so bolstered the political strength of the shaky Khanh regime in Saigon. 'The first public opinion poll [afterwards] ... boosted the 'approve' rating of the President's handling of the war from 42 per cent to 72 per cent.' Growing international pressure for 'premature' negotiations was defused.[17] Moreover Johnson had successfully defined and occupied the middle ground with a 'strong but restrained' response. A more hawkish opponent could be stigmatised as dangerous and sabre-rattling, a more dovish opponent as weak or soft. He had neutralised Vietnam as a potential problem in the coming president election. In Australia both the government and the ALP strongly endorsed the president's actions.

The episode demonstrated the vulnerability of the news media. In a situation of officially-defined crisis and bipartisan support, with little opportunity for independent gathering of evidence, the news media were reduced to passive conveyors of officials views. To the limited extent that they departed from this passive stance, it was to add 'colour', such as highlighting the supposed heroism and drama on the American ships. There was some analysis of the significance of the North Vietnamese actions, some musing on the communist motives but with a tendency, in the absence of firm evidence, to picture these in ways most supportive of a general threat schema (Chinese prompting, test of US will, etc).

All such analyses assumed that the American government's portrayal of the incident was reliable.[18] The explosive situation following the US response overshadowed the original events, and inhibited further probing into seemingly trivial details such as why US ships should be so close to the North Vietnamese coast, the appropriateness of the US bombing response, or the open-ended nature of the Congressional resolution. Nor was any curiosity shown about why Hanoi called the second incident a complete fabrication, in contrast to its propaganda claims about the first.

The Tonkin Gulf episode eventually came to be seen by some journalists and congressmen as the epitome of government manipulation and deceit, and their anger helped fuel anti-war sentiment. But in the short term it was a complete political success for President Johnson; perhaps the single most important incident in legitimising escalation of the war.

Escalation

The political management of escalation was far more successful in Australia than in America. The American government handled each step tortuously, taking great pains to publicly minimise its significance with claims that this 'did not represent a departure from existing policy', that it presaged 'no wider war'. Geyelin has argued that the government could not afford to confront the public with its open-ended, unpredictable commitment, and so adopted a course of concealment and manipulation. Charlton, a commentator consistently supporting American involvement, reached a similar conclusion.[19]

Part of the US Administration's manipulative strategy was to announce decisions taken for general political and military reasons as if they were responses to particular communist attacks. After Tonkin, the next occasion for escalation was a Viet Cong attack on an American establishment at Pleiku in February 1965. It was followed by renewed bombing of North Vietnam. Senior adviser McGeorge Bundy described the great scope the US had in deciding whether or not to respond to such incidents with the comment 'Pleikus are like street-cars'.[20] The Administration had allowed two comparable earlier attacks—at Bien Hoa shortly before the presidential election, and against American billets in Saigon—pass with little response.

Shortly after, in March, the first overtly combat troops landed at Da Nang. In July came the single biggest escalation, raising the number of US troops to 175,000, with further regular increases until the peak of over 500,000 in early 1968. In Australia, the Menzies government committed combat troops in April 1965. Prime Minister Holt increased the number to 4500 in March 1966, to 6300 the following December, and finally to 8000 in October 1967.

The politics of escalation proceeded more smoothly in Australia for three principal reasons.[21] First, official justifications continually stressed the cementing of the American alliance. Announcement of the initial combat commitment coincided with a SEATO conference. The decision received almost unanimous newspaper editorial support,[22] with a striking coincidence between editorial views and the public statements of ministers.

Harold Holt used his first major speech to Parliament as Prime Minister to announce the increase to 4500. A period of highly effective government dramatisation followed, with Holt conveying himself as the embodiment of the American alliance. He visited the United States in July 1966 ('All the way with LBJ'). Johnson visited Australia in October 1966, six weeks before the Australian election. Both leaders then attended an international conference on Vietnam in Manila. Holt visited the US again in June 1967.

Each of these events produced dazzling press coverage. The presidential visit exceeded a royal tour in the volume of news, and gave the Liberal government an inestimable electoral boost. Every visit emphasised the closeness and cooperation between the two leaders. A headline story on Holt's arrival in Washington, for example, had LBJ saying 'I welcome you as a brave leader, as a longtime and very loyal friend and as a wise statesman', and throughout Mr Holt's reply 'Mr Johnson listened attentively' (*The Herald* 2. 6. 67). Later the same paper printed a long feature on Holt 'At Home with Rancher LBJ'. The visits provided an ideal platform for the leaders to promote their views on Vietnam with a minimum of critical scrutiny. The press felt no need to provide 'balancing' critical statements.

The second factor helping to secure public acquiescence in escalation was our role as junior ally. The US faced major risks—would war with China result? Would the South Vietnamese government be stable or effective? And would military involvement become an expensive, endless commitment? Australia could deftly deflect such practical criticisms by taking its lead from American positions and re-affirming symbolic certainties—the US alliance, the threat of Asian communism, the danger of appearing aggression, the perfidy and disunity of the ALP.

A third difference was that Vietnam was more readily perceived as a direct security threat in Australia than in the USA. For two decades Liberal and Country Party ministers, prominently reported and editorially supported by most of the press, promoted the sense of threat with stunning simplicity:

> Should the forces of communism prevail, and Vietnam come under the heel of Communist China, Malaya is in danger of being outflanked and it, together with Thailand and Indonesia, will become the next target for further Communist activities. (Spender 1950)
>
> (The conflict in Indo-China is) part of a world struggle ... The French are defending liberty. (Hasluck 1954)
>
> Casey revealed that the pressing menace of Communism's southward advance was keeping him awake at night. (Casey 1954)
>
> ... the courageous people of Vietnam [are] in [the] front-line struggle against communist aggression ... Recruits are obtained by kidnapping and other coercive measures, and sent to North Vietnam for training and indoctrination. Later they come back to form new Viet Cong units. (Barwick 1962)
>
> There is not the slightest doubt that the North Vietnamese are puppets of the Chinese ... What is happening in South Vietnam today is perhaps only the first round of an attack by the Communist Chinese

to dominate the world. (Fairhall 1966)

Once troops had been sent, there flowed a steady supply of 'human interest' stories about their activities, their feelings and bravery. A high point occurred in June 1966 when the first Australian battle contingent returned home, their replacements having just landed in Vietnam. The soldiers paraded through Sydney in front of 'cheering lunchtime crowds'. Other stories told of 'A Kiss for Australia' (soldiers kissing the ground on their return), and 'Sister remembers' her fallen brother. (*The Herald*, 3, 8, 9 June 66).

The *Sun* (Sydney) correspondent Pat Burgess accompanied the new battalion to Vietnam. His story 'Diggers—Ten Times Better than Reds' said 'Australia's 1st Battalion proved it was ten times better than the Viet Cong—on the Communists' terms and on their terrain' (8 June). 'They Didn't Cheer Diggers—At First' told how quickly the Australians won over the villagers at Vung Tau, and received a popular reception (10 June).

In sum, the politics of escalation in Vietnam was a major success for the Australian government, and generated largely supportive press coverage. There was no change in this situation until American thinking about the war decisively changed.

Tet 1968

Many analysts, and not only hawks, argue that while the Tet offensive was a military failure, it was a 'psychological' success which broke American resolve by shattering official optimism. The role of the news media is seen as a major cause of this outcome.

Tet was certainly an important catalyst in domestic American politics. In the second half of 1967, the Johnson administration had mounted a sustained public relations campaign claiming that the war was being won, but this only heightened the shock that the Tet offensive caused. Tet provided the opportunity for many politicians and commentators with silent misgivings about the war to voice their doubts. Most importantly, for a crucial period near the beginning of the Democratic primaries, the event crystallised the issues of administration failure, the credibility gap, and public war-weariness. This gave impetus to Eugene McCarthy's surprisingly successful campaign in the New Hampshire primary (42 per cent against the incumbent president), which in turn emboldened Robert Kennedy. The increasing discord among the Democrats momentarily climaxed with Johnson's announcement that he would not run again. The longer term effect in that election year was a public consensus to end the war, but the consensus was couched in the vaguest terms, and controversy surrounded all specifics about the methods and implications of withdrawal.

Peter Braestrup's well-documented *Big Story* argues the case against US news media coverage of Tet, which he covered in Vietnam for the *Washington Post*.

> Rarely has contemporary crisis-journalism turned out, in retrospect, to have veered so widely from reality. Essentially, the dominant themes of the words and film from Vietnam ... added up to a portrait of defeat for the allies. Historians, on the contrary, have concluded that the Tet offensive resulted in a severe military-political setback for Hanoi in the South ... The special circumstances of Tet impacted to a rare degree on modern American journalism's special susceptibilities and limitations. (p 705)

He points out that there were several early difficulties in reporting: the number of attacks, their geographic dispersion, the surprise achieved, and uncertainties about Viet Cong strength and success. There were two main journalistic responses to the uncertainty, each producing its own pathologies. The news agencies and TV tended to emphasise specifics, to catch particular dramatic actions with the appearance of first-hand reporting. This produced serious sins of omission. 'It was "news", but not information. It did not tell us how the war, overall, was going', Braestrup says (p 717). He particularly criticises the focus on attacks against the US Embassy, which gave the impression of the last bastion in the country under siege, and concentration on the attacks on Khe Sanh, which suggested dubious parallels with the 1954 siege of Dien Bien Phu. On the other hand, news magazines and quality newspapers tried to interpret the overall scene, but so much ambiguity about specific details often led to undisciplined analysis and instant judgements.

A guiding frame of disaster and pervasive destruction quickly permeated coverage, after developing into a sense of futility symbolised by the American officer at Ben Tre who pleaded that it was necessary to destroy the town in order to save it. The journalists were genuinely shocked; the war had directly disrupted life in Saigon for the first time; the attacks were intense and persistent, in contrast to the previous experience of localised skirmishing; and American official responses were an incompatible mixture of anxious bewilderment and bland optimism. Braestrup rejects the idea that the correspondents were motivated by anti-war ideology, but he does see them as suspicious and resentful, seeking retribution for prior manipulation by officials.

In consequence, the amount of devastation and despair was overdrawn, and the subjective shock and disarray of the journalists were wrongly transformed into a picture of objective defeat and chaos. Moreover, the short attention span of the media turned immediate impressions into abiding ones. The gradual recovery by the US and South Vietnamese in the weeks following Tet never clearly emerged.

Two of Braestrup's criticisms of news content are questionable. Was the amount of physical damage and destruction really over-drawn? Tet brought a marked change in sensibility to this aspect of the war, which beforehand had been relatively neglected. Braestrup has admitted his own limited interest in the question:

As a former infantryman in Korea I was perhaps less shocked by war's waste and destruction than were my colleagues experiencing these for the first time. I was probably more interested in such matters as logistics, 'foxhole strength', enemy tactics and allied deployments than they were.

Peter Arnett (AP reporter in Vietnam, 1962–70), later criticised this attitude:

> It is the pre-occupation with the military level of the war that I believe is *Big Story's* basic flaw ... Braestrup's tables of 'negative' and 'positive' trends in news stories ... neutralizes the real flavor of our reporting of Tet, and that was the sense that a historical change had taken place in the war. It seemed to me then, and seems to me even more so now that Saigon has fallen, that Westmoreland had little understanding of the need to build a nation in Vietnam, and had faith in his own forces but little use for the Vietnamese army. Only at Tet, when it was too late and the price too high, did the errors of his strategy become apparent, statistical military victory or not.[23]

And was the Tet offensive a complete political loss for the communists in Vietnam? Arnett, for example, quotes a 1969 article by Henry Kissinger which points out that in a guerilla war, psychological and political factors can outweigh the strict military assessments, and concluded:

> On that level the Tet offensive was a political defeat in the countryside for Saigon and the United States.

In the Australian press, coverage of military developments was similar to the American cases cited by Braestrup. Great prominence was given to the activities of Australian troops, but the Tet offensive prompted little questioning among Australian editorialists. *The Australian* was reinforced in its opposition to our involvement and its pessimism about the course of the war (eg 'Where Are We Winning?' 1. 2. 68). *The West Australian*, under the heading 'Warning in Vietnam' actually catalogued, the reasons for allied optimism about the war, and would have astonished General Giap with its conclusion that 'Time is on the side of the West ... ' (2. 2. 68). *The Daily Telegraph* though it was 'A Time for America to Get Tough', and that the 'one lesson is that more bombs are needed on North Vietnam' (2. 2. 68). The *Sydney Morning Herald* was concerned ('Outgeneralled'), and *The Age* agonised ('The Pain of War'), but neither changed its policy prescriptions.

In retrospect, Tet also marked a turning-point in Australian political rhetoric about the war, although this was barely discernible at the time. John Gorton had become prime minister only two weeks before. In an apparently off-the-cuff remark, made without prior cabinet consultation, he said no more Australian troops would be sent to Vietnam, and that as far as he was concerned this was a permanent decision (all papers, 3. 2. 68). Although this style of comment later caused Gorton great political trouble, he was then still in a honeymoon period with both his party and the press. Still, a limit had been placed on Australian commitment, and after this remark the government's public position began to lack its previous coherence and assurance.

In contrast, the ALP's statements began to attain greater, but still fragile and limited, coherence. Vietnam policy had been a pawn and symbol in the ALP's factional struggles, especially the Calwell-Whitlam antagonisms, as Kim Beazley shows elsewhere in this book. The statements of ALP spokesmen from 1964 to 1967 were a morass of ambiguity and inconsistency. After Tet, there were continuing differences of style and internal party clashes, but also greater public consistency, emphasising the war's futility.

Vietnamisation

Post-mortems emphasising the centrality of Tet tend to forget that the war lasted another seven years. The number of combat deaths remained on the same scale as before, while US bombing tonnages were much greater. The wars in Laos and especially Cambodia were enormously escalated. One central difference in the new period was that public rhetoric and (to a very ambiguous degree) policy aims were oriented toward western withdrawal, although still clinging to the original goal of a non-communist South Vietnam.

Phillip Knightley's admirable *The First Casualty* harshly judges western news coverage during this period:

> At a time when the most damage of the war was being inflicted on Indo-China, the news coverage was at its worst, because editors and producers had decided that the ground war was virtually over and that with the steady withdrawal of United States troops under way, public interest had declined.[24]

There is much evidence to support this contention. Many news editors and decision-makers thought 'the Vietnam story' had grown stale, that the public was weary of the war. And following the opening of negotiations with North Vietnam, editors decided that the focus of interest had moved away from events within Vietnam, a decision quite unrelated to what was happening in Vietnam. As one example, the executive producer of (American) ABC news sent the following telex to its Saigon bureau in March 1969: 'I think the time has come to shift our focus from the battlefield, or more specifically American military involvement with the enemy, to themes and stories under the general heading: We Are On Our Way Out of Vietnam ... '. A similar decision had been reached at NBC in November 1968. Combat footage was sent to New York from Saigon virtually every day for the next two months, but it was used only three times in the *Evening News*, whereas, in the preceding year combat film was shown three to four times per week. 'The "focus" in the content of the news coverage was thus changed, not by the amount of combat footage available (which remained about the same)', nor by actual developments in Vietnam, 'but by the producer's perception of what *type* of story was called for'.[25]

Changing fashions in demand for news can be further illustrated by the attention to massacre stories during this period. My Lai, the most infamous massacre, occurred in March 1968, and finally became public in November 1969.[26] After this there was a rush of massacre stories, with many correspondents relating atrocities which they had witnessed earlier but were only now reporting, because of changes in the definition of news.[27] But this fashion also faded. Kevin Buckley and Alec Shimkin of *Newsweek's* Saigon bureau spent three months researching civilian casualties of Operation Speedy Express in the Mekong Delta between December 1968 and May 1969. They documented that civilian casualties totalled up to 5000, as a direct and deliberate result of military policy. They sent the story to *Newsweek* in January 1972, but the magazine seemed uninterested. Finally, *Newsweek* ran the story 'savagely cut' in June 1972. Although it lacked some of the ghoulish irrationality of My Lai, it was in many ways the most substantial and damning massacre story of the war, but it remains virtually unknown.[28]

The major western tactical change from ground combat to an air war greatly affected news coverage. It was no longer possible to accompany western combat troops and witness their battles and casualties. Human interest stories about the troops declined. The heaviest bombing in the history of warfare, causing immense and indiscriminate suffering, and of dubious military value, remained a largely invisible and unpublicised part of the war.

There are also grounds for qualifying Knightley's judgement. First, until after the Peace Accords of January 1973, the number of journalists in Vietnam remained relatively high (although below its Tet peak). By 1973, some reporters had developed considerable expertise in Vietnamese affairs, and a growing number of reportorial initiatives increased public knowledge in important ways. Several are mentioned later in this chapter.

Secondly, while it seems true that the 'normal' level of coverage declined, every escalation in the American military effort or the intensity of fighting attracted heavy coverage: the invasion of Cambodia in May 1970, the incursion into Laos in March 1971, the 1972 North Vietnamese offensive and the Christmas 1972 bombing of Hanoi.

Thirdly, the range of debate and comment in editorials, columns and news was much broader and more informed. But this time, too, critics of the war were more thoroughly reported. In Australia, there was more extensive coverage of the ALP, whose political fortunes were rapidly improving, and of congressional opposition to presidential policies in the US. Anti-war protests received greater, although not always sympathetic, attention.

Just as escalation posed different political problems for the Australian and American governments, so did Vietnamisation, but in many ways the problems were now reversed. After 1968, a ceiling had been placed on the American involvement. The Nixon Administration was not initially perceived as trying to justify fresh involvements, but as managing a massive and unwelcome inheritance. Within the broad guidelines of Vietnamisation, gradual US troop withdrawal, and negotiation, it had enormous scope. An announcement of a troop increase is a more tangible target for criticism than a delay in withdrawal. This scope was exploited in the timing of initiatives. Most obviously, Kissinger's announcement that 'Peace is at hand' came immediately before the 1972 presidential election, and the heaviest bombing of the war coincided with the Christmas holidays, when public attention is always at its lowest.

Leadership differences were also important. Johnson was a politician of the centre, overwhelmingly concerned with consensus, perceiving political danger from both right and left, and so threatened by all opposition. Because he was expanding involvement, he required more active policy support. Nixon, operating from the certainties of secure conservative support and liberal opposition, never sought consensus, but rather exploited polarisation in ways that left his political base untouched. Between 1969 and 1973, Nixon's political management of the war was largely succeeding domestically—until Watergate intervened.

In Australia the Vietnam issue was clearly not the electoral advantage for the Liberals that it had been before 1968. International developments increasingly challenged the central Liberal emphasis on the US alliance and Asian communist aggression. Simple reiteration of unqualified anticommunism was not well attuned to the more calculating ethos of the Nixon doctrine. The domino theory was losing its potency as the US government turned to *detente* and *realpolitik,* and as the Sino-Soviet split intensified. Whitlam portrayed the Liberal government as rigid and out of step with both US policy and the changing international environment. He scored a great success when his mid-1971 visit to China was followed by Nixon's announcement of his own intention to visit. The Gorton and McMahon governments were thus facing increasing problems, including a more active and critical Canberra press gallery.[29] Perhaps the manipulative public relations skills of the American government had improved while the Australian government seemed increasingly inept and defensive about its Vietnam commitment.

The final takeover

In the period of the fall of Saigon (30 April 1975), developments in Vietnam received saturation press coverage. Between 1 April and 9 May *The Age,* for example, ran 211 items on Indo-China. More than one in four focussed on refugees and orphans; about one in seven described military developments; one in six and one in eight described Australian and US politics respectively. The remainder, about one in 12 each, was divided between South Vietnamese politics and the North Vietnamese and Viet Cong.

Heavy emphasis by the Australian press on the plight of refugees and orphans contrasted strangely with their almost total neglect earlier in the war. The news coverage was stark and simple, often portraying the refugees' plight as a choice between life and death: 'Safe from the Jaws of War', 'Save a Million Viets—US plan', 'Australian planes in a lifeline for 60,000', 'Viet refugees rely on aid flights for survival', etc.

The imagery of life and death sometimes became totally divorced from any actual physical death, and extended to the communist victory—for instance in Bruce Wilson's retrospective piece 'Diary of a Dying City' on Saigon's 'last days' (*The Herald* 6. 5. 75). The focus also emphasised the earnest goodwill of the west in its efforts to rescue the refugees.

President Ford and the US government received very sympathetic treatment. Ford was seen 'blaming Hanoi', ruling out bombs, urging Congress for more aid, ordering a huge evacuation of refugees, pleading for unity and no recriminiations—although if there were any they should be directed at Congress. He was also seen as strongly concerned: 'It makes me sick' (*Herald* 17. 4. 75); and when Saigon fell, the Fords spent an 'agonising night at the White House' (*The Age* 30. 4. 75).

In contrast, coverage of this episode involved a disadvantage for the Whitlam Labor government. First, a political storm followed the publishing of leaked cables in *The Age* (30. 4. 75), showing that Whitlam had communicated in quite different ways to the Saigon and Hanoi regimes, allegedly condoning the North's aggression. The *Sydney Morning Herald* called this 'the gravest scandal since Federation' (30. 4. 75). Secondly, the government's tardiness in allowing South Vietnamese refugees to come to Australia was the subject of stinging criticism: 'I have never felt ashamed of my government before. But I felt profoundly ashamed of it in Saigon on Friday ... [its actions were] a miserable and mean-hearted betrayal', wrote Michael Richardson (*The Age* 28. 4. 75). It was probably the first time any Australian journalist had expressed any shame about Vietnam.

The defeat of the Saigon regime was an occasion for the revivial of domino theories. The Whitlam view that Australia was not in any immediate danger was strongly overshadowed by contrary assertions. *The Herald* chose to make a front-page headline of Anthony's statement, 'We're so alone/Anthony warns on red threat' (3. 5. 75). He was quoted at length on how instability in the region gave many Australians a sense of uncertainty and loneliness. No other views were included in the story. The *Sydney Morning Herald* editorialised that 'We are witnessing a cataclysm that is already driving Thailand into the arms of Peking' (26. 4. 75).

No paper was at all complimentary to the war's critics. Indeed, they were condemned for alleged indifference to the refugees. This was a prominent theme in cartoons, the strongest of which showed peace marchers including Whitlam and Cairns happy and smiling, turning their backs on pleading and miserable Vietnamese (Collette, *The Herald* 1. 4. 75).

Only minor attention was given to the last-minute reshuffling of government in Saigon. The Thieu government's views were still reported without immediate comment on their credibility. Coverage of the victorious enemy was also a low priority in all papers, although they varied greatly in coverage of alleged and predicted atrocities. The *Age* gave little credence to bloodbath stories, but the *Herald* was less circumspect: 'New Regime Starts with a Vengeance' (11. 4. 75); 'Colonel's Friends face Death' (14. 4. 75), a reference to a Country Party MP, former Colonel Sullivan, visiting old friends in Vietnam, whom he expected to be executed); 'Suicide on the lawns' (Denis Warner, 16. 4. 75), writing about a South Vietnamese who committed suicide rather than live under the communists, said that his attitude was 'widely held', and that captured documents indicated a bloodbath after victory; and 'One million death list' (16. 4. 75), etc.

The military stories were generally physical descriptions of the progress of the final rout. Remarkably little space was devoted to analysis of reasons for the defeat. Denis Warner blamed the US Congress, and ascribed the precipitate retreat of the ARVN to miscalculation and disorganisation: 'The shattering loss of Central Vietnam ... was not caused by enemy action but by blunders'. Until these blunders, he said, 'the South Vietnamese regional and popular forces were doing well and the situation was fully under control' (*The Herald* 5. 4. 75). Not all correspondents presented the communist victory as if it were some sort of fluke. But the most striking feature of coverage of the war's end was its failure to examine why twenty years of massive western involvement had resulted in total failure.

Evaluations

There can be no taken-for-granted or consensual criteria for evaluating news coverage of the Vietnam War. Adequacy is very much in the eye of the beholder. Moreover, the war and its reporting defy easy comparison with other wars. Vietnam was a 'limited war' in that the western nations were neither directly endangered nor totally mobilised. The American government in particular was concerned to minimise the domestic impact of the war, both politically and economically. It was largely a 'guerilla war', where no very reliable or meaningful military scoreboard was available to chart its progress. The line between military and socio-political elements was extremely blurred. The war was portrayed as part of a global struggle between east and west, posing complex problems of geo-politics, and the relation between these and local conditions in Vietnam was extremely controversial.

The logistics of international communication were enormously superior to those of any previous war, and it was the 'first television war'. Western correspondents did not face official censorship, and there were relatively few cases of expulsion. There was perhaps less secrecy, and greater freedom of movement for journalists, than in previous wars. But there was also a mammoth public relations effort by the US government, to create images and disseminate often suspect information which would build support for the war.

As is common with news coverage, the bulk of the material was remarkably ephemeral, contributing little to understanding or perspective. Military developments and western policy received the heaviest attention. Reporting battles is inherently dangerous (especially for cameramen) and verification is difficult in chaotic situations. Military coverage relied heavily on official battle statistics, but such 'scoreboard' coverage was neither accurate nor meaningful, and it tended to bury all moral dimensions. The frustrations were well caught by one correspondent who said to a briefing officer: 'Yes, General, but aren't your victories getting closer to Saigon?'

Most journalists saw their task as covering the war, not Vietnamese society. Very few spoke Vietnamese, although many compensated partly by having some working relations with Vietnamese interpreters for assistants. Some, notably Robert Shaplen of *The New Yorker,* gave close attention to South Vietnamese politics. But very few analysed broader social forces such as the relations of villagers to the government and military, and how the village had been affected by war. On those rare occasions when social structure was examined, it was usually in highly stereotyped form; for example, in Denis Warner's account of the Buddhist crisis in June 1966, the variety of views was squeezed into pro- and anti-US positions giving no insight into their sentiments. (*The Herald,* 1, 2, 4. 6. 66). But the war could not be understood without reference to the society in which it was fought. Corruption, oppression, and atrocities against civilians not only raised moral questions, but also affected in complex and intangible ways the alignments of the people.

The least reliable reporting in any war deals with the enemy. Lack of access, working from only one side in a conflict, editorial and audience attitudes, official propaganda, and usually the correspondent's own views, mitigate against accuracy, balance and detailed knowledge. Information about the enemy comes from three sources: (1) its own usually unreliable and selective propaganda; (2) the problematic testimony of defectors, prisoners, and captured documents, all typically available to journalists only after filtering and processing by officials; (3) reports from visitors to the enemy country, although these are usually sympathetic and so considered suspect.[30]

In this unpromising situation, negative caricaturing is the most likely distortion. One interesting exception was a strong image of the North Vietnamese and Viet Cong as competent and efficient, a view which may have been qualified by closer observation. Most news media were strangely uninterested in probing even the imperfect sources of information available. Little insight was provided into North Vietnamese morale, or strategic thinking; or into developments in Vietnamese-Chinese-Soviet relations.

The coverage of anti-war dissent in Australia was consistently negative, with rarely any suggestion that it deserved serious consideration.[31] The most prominent parliamentary critic of government policy, Dr Cairns, had by the normal standards of political discourse accumulated considerable expertise on Vietnam. Yet his views were neglected and constantly disparaged. Apart from *The Australian,* the overwhelming media support for the Liberal government severely restricted the range of comment and debate presented, and coloured news coverage of dissent.

Perhaps the greatest indictment of the Australian press is how little it improved, and how little the news organisations grew in their understanding of Vietnam. *The Australian* performed best. Within its limited resources, it took the coverage of international news seriously, and used a wide range of syndicated material from overseas newspapers. But in 1971 its proprietor, Rupert Murdoch, fired his editor Adrian Deamer, and reoriented the paper away from long feature articles and towards shorter news items and a more restricted range of views. By war's end in 1975, *The Australian* was locked in combat with the Labor government it had supported in 1972. Although still receiving a similar range of syndicated material, it seemed less able or inclined to make fruitful use of it.

The period of Australia's involvement in the Vietnam War coincided almost exactly with Graham Perkin's editorship of *The Age*. This was a time of enormous change at *The Age:* from a declining circulation to a steadily increasing one; from a largely moribund paper to the best quality paper in Australia. *The Age* sent three distinguished correspondents to Vietnam—Bruce Grant, Creighton Burns, and Michael Richardson.[32] However its coverage of American developments was consistently coloured by the strongly hawkish views of its Washington correspondent, Roy Macartney. Its editorials expressed increasing qualms, but the only coherent policy position one can trace is a general support for the war. *The Age's* coverage of Vietnam was superior to most other Australian newspapers, but compared to other dramatic improvements during the Perkin decade, its treatment of Vietnam lagged badly.

The Herald in Melbourne emphasises the priorities of a popular paper—crime, accidents, human interest, sports—but has always devoted considerable resources to international news. Its editorial support for the war was constant, and its principal correspondent on Vietnam, Denis Warner, was one of the most vociferous partisans of the American effort.[33] The *Sydney Morning Herald,* Australia's other quality newspaper, moved against the general tide of opinion. In the period from the late sixties to the mid-seventies, 'Granny' performed relatively badly—seemingly unable to appreciate either the sentiments for reform within Australian society, or the more penetrating and lively possibilities in serious journalism. Its views on foreign policy had become profoundly pessimistic, more conservative, and this general distaste for the changing world influenced its responses to Vietnam.[34]

Effects

Since the war ended, many have claimed that the news media heavily contributed to American failure. Perhaps the most vociferous and prominent of these critics has been General Maxwell Taylor, who on different occasions[35] has said the following:
When questioned about the people's right to know during the Pentagon Papers releases:

> I don't believe in this as a general principle. You have to talk about cases. What is a citizen going to do after reading these documents that he wouldn't have done otherwise? A citizen should know the things he needs to know to be a good citizen and discharge his functions, but not to get into secrets that damage his government and indirectly damage himself.

During the Paris negotiations:

> Recognising that in a democracy, leaders are necessarily responsive to the will of the people, [the communists] bombarded our domestic opinion with continuing propaganda from Paris and Hanoi, often using for that purpose the "free world" media ... The conclusion is inescapable that our adherence to traditional democratic practices appropriate for times of peace made it very difficult for our side to compete on an equal footing with our totalitarian adversaries 'in the settlement of an undeclared limited war'.
>
> The press—not all, but the vast majority—was opposed to our Vietnam policy and very vocal. The television also. Allowing television on the battlefield after our troops got there created an impossible situation at home. Even in World War II I think we would probably have left Britain, or France, or Germany to come home if the bloody pictures which were available on those battlefields had been flashed into the American living-room as was the case in Vietnam.

Some anti-war critics have charged the opposite: that the news media acted as an arm of American imperialism, that its orientations showed ideological support for the war's rationale.[36] Precise delineation of the effects of mass media is always elusive. The dominant research tradition has been concerned with effects on public attitudes and perceptions. A more recent research approach looks at how the operations and practices of the news media affect the relations between political actors and institutions, and how the role of news as an independent source of public disclosure of significant information affects political processes and outcomes.[37] The various discussions of the media and the Vietnam War seem to highlight two particular problems, one stemming from each research tradition. The first is the special role of television, its huge audience and visual immediacy. The second is the active, initiating role of the press in publicising information which governments may wish to screen or delay or suppress.

Vietnam was the first TV war. Most commentators have suggested that TV fuelled anti-war revulsion, although some have argued the opposite view—that TV de-sensitised the public to the war's brutality.[38] Both arguments tend to proceed with a minimum of evidence.

Epstein has convincingly demonstrated that the overwhelming bulk of US TV news from Vietnam was neither violent nor 'negative'. The conventional wisdom to the contrary has grown up partly because of political vested interests and selective perception. But there were also spectacular exceptions to these normal patterns, whose significance far exceeded their frequency. Examples include:

1   The self-immolation of Buddhist monks in 1963;
2   Morley Safer's report for CBS[39] of US troops setting fire to village huts at Cam Ne in 1965;
3   South Vietnamese General Loan summarily shooting a captured Viet Cong in the head in a Saigon street during Tet 1968;[40]
4   ARVN troops in disarray and clinging to overloaded helicopters during their retreat from Laos in March 1971.

What of the news media's role in independent disclosure? The press was neither consistently probing and sceptical nor always docile. As indicated earlier, governments had considerable initiative in their public relations strategies. From a governmental view there were temporary crises when many correspondents would strongly dissent. These crises seem to have prompted an ethos inducing important policy shifts, most notably during the downfall of Diem and the Tet offensive. On such occasions, however, the sense of challenge and confrontation dissipated into a fresh accommodation. The following examples of investigative reporting stand out:

1   The revelations by the Saigon press corps of the corruption and deficiencies of the Diem regime, and the fallacies of American official rhetoric about Diem;
2   The visit to Hanoi by Harrison Salisbury of the *New York Times* Christmas 1966, which helped focus attention on the civilian casualties caused by US bombing;[41]
3   The disclosure of the My Lai massacre, both important in itself, and as a stimulus to greater sensitivity to the question of war atrocities;[42]
4   The momentous release of the Pentagon Papers in 1971[43] and the growing effort to re-explore earlier incidents and decisions;[44] and
5   Disclosure of the secret bombing of Cambodia and North Vietnam during the Nixon administration.

General Taylor's claims are wildly exaggerated. TV news was hardly the searing experience alleged. Significant disclosures indeed challenged official claims, but these stemmed less from ideological opposition in the press, than from the mendacity and ineptitude of government. Commentary and analysis at times ran strongly counter to the government's wishes. On balance, however, more newsfilm, reporting and editorial commentary supported the governments rather than challenged them. The dramatic anti-war effects claimed for the American news media are clearly over-drawn, although genuine complexity and ambiguity did attend their role.

By contrast, the performance of the Australian media was overwhelmingly timid, and there was less independent probing, less willingness to devote adequate resources to reporting the war, and a far more restricted range of opinion and analysis. Even bearing in mind the enormous disparities in population, and their vastly different roles in the war, on any comparison the Australian news media were deplorably inferior to their American counterparts.

9 Conclusion
PETER KING

This book has explored the west's and, more especially, Australia's role in the suffering and triumphs of Vietnam since the fateful American decision to support and later supplant French imperialism in Indo-China. It has also explored the impact of 'Vietnam' on Australian politics—from party policies on the war itself to the role of our expeditionary force; from the impact of the war on the conscripts who fought in Vietnam to its impact on the potential conscripts who refused to go; from the performance of the press to the performance of the public. One conclusion must be that the Vietnam experience exposed much that was faulty or flawed in official Australian strategic perceptions, in Australian military policy-making and practice, and above all in Australian political processes. The unwisdom and injustice of Australia's combat intervention in Vietnam was founded on an unnecessary and unjust revival of conscription. It was four years before the electorate saw fit to give even a check (in 1969) to the government responsible for these policies—policies on which an election was fought in 1966, and whose only fruit was military failure and a unilateral change at Australia's expense in the terms of the American alliance.

No doubt the Vietnam issue marginally helped the Whitlam government to power in 1972 and led to a new, more flexible approach to relations with Indo-China, Southeast Asia and the American presence in the western Pacific. But the flexibility of Australian policy towards Indo-China during the Whitlam years which persisted under the Liberal Foreign Affairs Minister, Andrew Peacock, the striving for what Carlyle Thayer has called coexistence with Vietnam,[1] finally gave way to a policy of diplomatic if not military confrontation with the communist states of Indo-China, when the Fraser government suspended aid and cultural exchanges to Hanoi in January 1979. There was a particular occasion for this shift—growing Sino-American rapprochement in Indo-China, continuing Chinese support for the Pol Pot regime, and the Vietnamese invasion of Kampuchea with Soviet support. However, it was only under extreme pressure from China and the *Khmers Rouges* that Vietnam turned towards the Soviet Union and

CONCLUSION

away from a policy of limited domestic conciliation accompanied by an active search for western involvement in its own economic reconstruction.

The invasion of Kampuchea was meant to put an end to disruptive attacks on southern Vietnam, and was more justifiable in purely economic and human terms than the war on petty capitalism in the South which preceded it and led quite rapidly to a mass exodus of boat people without apparently solving economic problems.

Moreover, if Hanoi's policy after the crackdown on private trade in March 1978 was in some ways a return to form, so also was the Australian response to the occupation of Kampuchea. In this context it is worth noting some fresh evidence that has recently come to light on diehard attitudes among senior officials which continue to shape Australian government policy-making as it affects war, peace and revolution in Indo-China and Southeast Asia generally. Particularly instructive was the performance of senior diplomatic advisers when faced with the post-Vietnam War situation. Some of the views expressed within the bureaucracy at that time are an object lesson in the resilience and persistence of an inappropriate professional mind-set. In 1975, after the fall of Saigon, and under prodding from Prime Minister Whitlam's own choice for permanent head of the Foreign Affairs Department, Alan Renouf, a circular letter was sent out from Foreign Affairs under the signature of Nicholas Parkinson, Deputy Secretary, to Australia Ambassadors and High Commissioners abroad. It was prefaced thus: 'We have it in mind to examine many of our existing assumptions about the region and Australia's interests in it'. Parkinson invited relevant 'posts' to make a response. The invitation itself showed a remarkable openness to subversive thought, including as it did the suggestion that exaggerated emphasis on such notions as 'threat', 'security', 'stability' and 'subversion' had led the department astray in the past; the further suggestion that Australia might consider 'trying to encourage social, political and agrarian reforms' in Southeast Asia; that North Vietnam (*sic*) might be encouraged 'to develop as a Southeast Asian Yugoslavia'; and that future communist governments in the rest of Southeast Asia, excepting Indonesia, might not necessarily threaten Australia's interests and popular tranquility.[2]

The response to this rather remarkable invitation seems to have been less than overwhelmingly enthusiastic, at least on the available evidence. We have, for instance, Sir James Plimsoll's cable from the Moscow Embassy, which must have given Parkinson and Renouf a serious case of *déjà vù*. Plimsoll, a former permanent head of the department himself and the doyen of the Australian diplomatic corps, responded to the questions cautiously raised by the department with some rhetorical questions of his own which, *inter alia*, showed that he thought the victory of the NLF in Indo-China had opened the way for communism to spread by 'domino' effects to Burma(!) immediately, and 'soon perhaps' Thailand, and then the rest of the Southeast Asia.[3] He also declared that new communist regimes would mean mainly more communist or anti-communist wars of intervention; that Australians would need to demonstrate a capacity to multiply themselves demographically in a communist Southeast Asia; and that our political fate, with or without accelerated procreation, might be to become 'a sort of Finland ... or Bulgaria'. Finally, Sir James had a question-answer for those who might seek to encourage Asian Yugoslavias: 'Does Vietnam want to develop intimacy or genuine cooperation with a group except when that group has a form of communism or the conditions for it'?[4] Sir James must have felt thoroughly vindicated in November 1978 when Vietnam, rebuffed by the major western powers and the World Bank in its bid to liberalise and diversify its international economic dealings, at long last joined COMECON, the Soviet bloc economic organisation which includes Mongolia and Cuba as well as most of the countries of East Europe, as a full member.

In this connection one wonders how much self-fulfilling prophecy as well as *schadenfreude* went into the American decisions to deny unified Vietnam any chance to operate an outward-looking economic and diplomatic strategy, as well as into the Australian government's eventual decision to cut off aid to Vietnam in 1979. Certainly it was a rich if rather distasteful irony that the United States sacrificed the chance of drawing Vietnam into a neutral or cooperative role in Southeast Asia on the altar of rapprochement with China, the nation whose putative expansionism had been the cause or pretext for America's massive entry into the Vietnam War in the first place. Even though some self-fulfilling prophets found themselves comfortably back at square one in relations with socialist Vietnam by 1978, nobody at all in east or west seems to have predicted the precise sequence of extraordinary events in Indo-China after 1975. Who would have thought that a communist Kampuchea which owed its very existence to the Democratic Republic would break with Vietnam over irredentist questions and thus attract the support of China, despite pursuing a policy which amounted to revolutionary genocide? Or that this regime in turn would be overthrown in Phnom Penh by its own dissidents in collaboration with Vietnam, and still find international succor and a kind of respectability in its last strongholds along the Thai border, while the Khmer population must accept with reluctant relief Vietnamese protection against a revival of the nightmare of 1975-79?

In this situation Australia does not possess much leverage, but then, apparently, neither do the policies of other powers for the time being. In any case it is important for Kampuchea, Vietnam and the future of the whole region to get policy right (at last), since the Kampuchean nation is in some danger of extinction, and the whole Kampuchean issue stands in the way of normalising Vietnam's internal order and her relations with China, the region and the world. Australia has certainly retained a measure of independence in policy. Diplomatic relations with socialist Vietnam have been continuous since December 1972. The Australian government finally

CONCLUSION 191

responded to overwhelming public pressure at the beginning of 1981 and withdrew its anomalous recognition of the Pol Pot regime, China and ASEAN notwithstanding. The *Khmers Rouges* were and are a government without a capital or any political viability apart from Chinese and Thai/US support; and they were and are loathed throughout Kampuchea. But derecognition of the *Khmers Rouges* is only a beginning in Indo-China, a beginning which is evidently in danger from the Chinese determination to preserve a dominant political role for Pol Pot in the resistance to the Vietnamese client regime of Heng Samrin in Phnom Penh. China is manoeuvering to force a coalition of Sihanoukist and other non-communist nationalist forces with a reconstituted but fundamentally unchanged *Khmers Rouges*. But only a definitive break with the Stalins and Berias of Kampuchea affords any hope of Vietnamese withdrawal from Phnom Penh, since while there is a prospect of Pol Pot and Khieu Samphan returning to power there will be a popular basis for the Vietnamese occupation and hence for the legitimacy of Heng Samrin.

By the crudest kind of attrition, the Chinese are pursuing the dialectial chimera of one, two, more Kampucheas (or Afghanistans) to tie down and wear out the Soviet social-imperialists, the new tsars. But Kampuchea is only attrition at second hand for the Soviets, and rather cheap to boot, since there is no effective national resistance to their client's occupation policy. Besides, it was Chinese material and moral support for the intransigent and bloody border confrontation of Vietnam in 1977-8 which led to Kampuchea's loss of independence in the first place. Vietnam could scarcely have been expected to tolerate the border raids, the shellings, the mayhem and the refugees issuing from Democratic Kampuchea indefinitely; and now the world must perforce be greatful that Vietnam has rid Asia of the worst regime in its recorded history, even if this was not the motive of Vietnam's intervention.

To persuade Vietnam to leave Kampuchea eventually should remain a goal of policy, but it must be admitted that the indigenous Khmer forces capable of achieving this have been greatly weakened by the cumulative disasters which have befallen the country since 1970. Yet it may still be possible, if the stick of a non-communist resistance, such as that embodied in the Khmer People's National Liberation Front of Son Sann, is combined with the carrot of offering Vietnam alternatives to its pro-Soviet strategic and economic orientation. It remains true if paradoxical that this policy would serve the cause of anti-Sovietism better than the present policy of ASEAN, China and the United States. Vietnam's obligation to collaborate strategically with the Soviet Union would be at an end if it could escape the need to solicit large subsidies to face the Chinese threat in both the north and the west. Despite Soviet and east European aid and trade, the Vietnamese economy seems to be facing indefinite stagnation, and this reinforces the risk of becoming strategically over-extended which Vietnam has been running since early 1979. (Also subject to Chinese challenge is the 60,000 strong Vietnamese army of semi-occupation in Laos.) The 1945 generation of leaders in Hanoi has begun to give way to leaders who may make different choices; but even the generation of 1945 has on at least two occasions (1945–46 and 1976–77) made overtures for a fundamental *rapprochement* with the United States.

While the prospects for settling the affairs of Kampuchea and Indo-China generally can scarcely have been enhanced by the election of a Reagan administration in Washington, there must nevertheless be a glimmer of tortuous hope that Reagan's inclination to Taipei will free American policy from undue indulgence of China's peculiarly inflexible and unprincipled anti-Sovietism. As for the ASEAN powers, they are divided between a group led by Indonesia whose inclination is to fear China more than Vietnam or the Soviet Union and a group which, whether for reasons of strategic geography or national susceptibility, has chosen to treat Vietnam and its exportable Chinese minority as a dangerous pariah in the region (Thailand, but also Singapore above all). A basis for ASEAN flexibility therefore exists, primarily through Indonesian influence, and it could be the Australian role to exploit this; to emphasise that the Chinese strategy is a dead-end which brings about and sustains what it is ostensibly designed to eradicate, namely Soviet influence and a Soviet presence in Indo-China.

Looking again at Australia's Indo-China policy involves looking again at the American connection and Australia's general approach to pro-Western regimes in Southeast Asia in the light of the values expressed in the Parkinson Letter quoted earlier—stability, justice and the search for a true definition of Australian interest. If the de-recognition of the *Khmers Rouges* was a step in the right direction, there are several others that need taking nearer to home. Australian policy in the region generally suffers from mutually reinforcing inhibitions concerning Australia's two major foreign relationships—with the United States and with Indonesia. The Vietnam involvement showed a promiscuous determination on Australia's part to keep America engaged and occupied wherever possible in mainland Southeast Asia. But Australia has also consistently supported America's leading clients in offshore Southeast Asia—Indonesia since 1965, and the Philippines throughout the post-war period—on the understanding that what was good for America's clients in a strategic and economic sense was good for Australia. Australia is far more deeply involved in strategic military collaboration with the US than is Indonesia, or even (perhaps) the Philippines, both through ANZUS and through the American strategic facilities sited on Australian soil. Moreover the American intelligence services have played a dubious role in Australian politics in the post-war period, especially during the constitutional crisis of 1975 which led to the dismissal of the Whitlam government; and enormous pressures to conform to American policy in Southeast Asia arise from the strategic relationship. These pressures can only increase now that the Fraser government has

CONCLUSION

actively sought and gained an American strategic military presence in the form of overflights and refuelling facilities at Darwin for B—52 intercontinental bombers based in Guam.

A superior course of action for Australia would be to distance itself from American policy in Southeast Asia, especially in a period of right-wing Republicanism, and deliberately politicise some of its relationships with the right-wing regimes of the region in order to gain at least a little leverage over their domestic and foreign policies. Australia is a considerable supplier of both military and economic aid to Indonesia, yet has signally failed to exploit the aid relationship in the Australian or the general interest. Among the consequences of Australia's impotence *vis a vis* Indonesia is the widespread assumption in Papua New Guinea that Australia would not stir to protect the country from Indonesian aggression or subversion beyond evacuating its own nationals in an emergency. Yet from 1974 to the present Australian relations with Indonesia have deteriorated over the issue of East Timor and, lately, the right of Australian journalists to report Indonesia at first hand. Throughout this period—through Labor and Liberal-National regimes—Australian governments have found themselves opposed to public opinion and caught up in deceit and prevarication. For over 15 years, since the abortive left-wing army coup of 1965 and the bloody suppression of Indonesian communism which followed, a fixed principle of Australian foreign policy has been that good relations with Djakarta were a priority second only to good relations with Washington, and in fact a crucial ingredient of them. How is this to be accounted for?

Apart from the pervasive influence of this fixed principle among those with a strategic and conservative cast of mind, there is in Australia a group (perhaps, at times, even a cabal) of senior diplomats with Djakarta experience who are prominent both within and beyond the Foreign Affairs Department, and who cheerfully advocate paying the heavy price that seems to be needed on Australia's part to preserve the Djakarta axis. A retired ambassador to Djakarta returned to Australia recently bearing the message that Australians need to exert themselves much more to understand official Indonesia's allergy to criticism and its harsh ways with domestic opponents and foreign journalists. There is also an influential academic lobby among Indonesianists who favour the fixed principle, and there are certain fully unrepentant politicians, amongst whom it would be pointless not to mention Gough Whitlam.

Public opinion, however, has on the whole shown a different tendency. Unimpressed or ignorant of the strategic imperative of not offending General Suharto, their attention has been focussed on Indonesian policies rather than the intractable geo-strategic fact which so impresses Australian governments: that Indonesia is a numerous, regionally influential, resource-rich and potentially powerful country straddling Australia's main lines of communications with Europe and most of Asia. The readers of newspapers observed the anti-leftist pogrom of 1965–66, the indefinite detention, mostly without trial, of tens of thousands of residual victims of these pogroms, the forcible annexation of East Timor, the pursuit of policies in West Papua which threaten the cultural and political extinction of the indigenous people, and the muzzling of Australian journalists. And then there are the close students of Indonesia's New Order economy who have drawn attention to the creeping immiseration of Java's urban and peasant masses, as the Indonesian elite collaborates corruptly in enclave investment with Japanese and western multinational corporations, selling off irreplaceable natural resources at an extraordinary rate. The corruption of the regime is typified by the multi-billion dollar bankruptcy of the state oil corporation, Pertamina, in 1977.[5]

The Australian public and officialdom have marched out of step on the question of Indonesia for years, although not for lack of some disingenuous re-writing of Indonesia's recent history. One Australian Army colonel-publicist (retired) has even come up with a version of the Army-Muslim massacres of 1965–67 in which 'savage fighting' takes place between two formidable opponents; the Communist Party of Indonesia forms a Peoples' Liberation Army in 1966; and 300–500,000 lives are found to have been lost after 'overt resistance' comes to an end.[6] This is rather like treating the Holocaust as a sort of civil war between Jews and Germans in Europe. (The same writer has Fretilin aiming for Timorese independence in 1974 'with a form of African sociology'.[7]) The question to be asked is whether appeasing Indonesia has worked at all, or whether a healthier relationship would have developed from simply criticising what deserved criticism, and making clear that Indonesia's social and political order leaves so much to be desired that the forcible incorporation of new territories has become intolerable since the more or less legitimate irredenta of West Irian was, however tragically, satisfied in 1963–69. The decision for intervention in East Timor in 1975 may have been so finely balanced that a bipartisan Australian stand could have tipped the argument in favour of the more hesitant leaders in Djakarta. Fretilin and the Timorese might have been saved from the same kind of immolation as the PKI a decade earlier.

The Australian Defence Department, by contrast with Foreign Affairs, had some misgivings about Indonesian annexation of East Timor, a non-Dutch territory which is after all closer to Western Australia than Djakarta. In the event that serious conflict develops between Indonesia and Papua New Guinea or Australia in the future, the passing of East Timor into Indonesian hands may be deeply regretted. In any case it has proven embarrassing, demeaning and largely futile to conduct a policy towards Indonesia which flies in the face of Australian popular sentiment and scholarly concern. There is something finally unworthy about the combination of the two dominant imperatives of Australian diplomacy—double deference to the United States and Indonesia. But there are still official advisers who place an enormous value not so much on the friendship as the mere existence of regimes like the Indonesia of Suharto and the

CONCLUSION

Philippines of Marcos. Indeed the prime minister's foremost mentor and speech writer, Owen Harries, has built an edifice of theory for the conduct of Australia's relations with the Third World generally in which the Salvation of the Suhartos of this world is central. In the dialectic of the Harries Report 'radical' and 'moderate' elements contend for the soul of individual Third World countries where 'radicalism' is a function of propensity to socialism, susceptibility to communist influence, or a pro-Soviet alignment in foreign relations, and 'moderation' is the obverse.[8] It is unequivocally in the interest of Australia and the west for 'moderates' to prevail, and this can be achieved by manipulating the benefits of aid, trade and investment —which are even capable of transforming the attitudes of 'radicals'.

Without attempting a detailed critique of Harries here,[9] one must first of all question the characterisation of the regimes responsible for the massacres of Java and the slums of Manila as 'moderate'. (The Marcos regime has deliberately held down urban worker incomes to attract foreign investment, and per capita food consumption seems to have declined in both Indonesia and the Philippines during the 1970s.) In Thailand as well as Indonesia and the Philippines the style of moderation being practised may have the same kind of political and social effects as the 'moderate' and very pro-western rule of the Shah of Iran. The true moderate in such social situations—the leader who sets about containing social conflict constructively—would surely be a radical reformer.

As to the requirement of anti-Sovietism, it is of great importance to the Australian prime minister as well as his leading advisers. The Harries Report makes this abundantly clear in its treatment of the foreign policy of socialist Vietnam, which it characterises as aggressive and expansionist without considering the dilemmas posed for Vietnam by Chinese support of Khmer irredentism.[10] The Chinese attack on Vietnam in early 1979 is noted in a spirit which sounds like suppressed applause.[11] Particularly since Andrew Peacock ceased to be Foreign Affairs Minister, it has been clear that the Australian government still believes that Australia's interest lies in playing second or third (behind ASEAN) fiddle to the United States in the new Great Game of the post-détente Cold War. Yet Australia has to live alongside Southeast Asia and the United States does not.

Why should not Australia, in the terms of the Parkinson Letter, work for better social and political regimes in Southeast Asia? Is not a diplomacy of human rights and meliorism possible for a small to middling developed power on the fringes of Asia? Cannot the national interest be defined in a way which avoids a completely binding and potentially suicidal choice between the two sides in the superpower Cold War? If Australia does come into collision with one or other of its authoritarian regional neighbours in taking a principled stand, can it not manage the power politics of such a conflict without American backing?

Australia's location and regional interactions give us some ability to demonstrate directly in a Third World milieu the virtues of parliamentary forms, media freedoms, social egalitarianism, welfare politics, free trade unionism, and (at times) socially responsible capitalism. Asian and African visitors to Papua New Guinea are sometimes astounded at the local practice of some of these Australian virtues, which have taken root in at least one very un-Australian environment. Australian diplomacy should stand at least for the values which have been imperfectly translated into her own social reality, and not instinctively make excuses for corrupt or reactionary or oppressive or otherwise overbearing Southeast Asian elites. Australia's American alliance can be preserved as a precondition of popular and official confidence, but it should be given a purely Australian-continental content. (The case for nuclear disengagement in the ANZUS alliance is overwhelming.[12]) Australia should approach regional neighbours without a fixation on the possibility of antagonising regimes locked deeply into economic or strategic relationships with the United States or her major Asian ally, Japan. Tackling these issues on their merits would have had a salutary effect on Australia's relations with Southeast Asia over the past decade, or at least would not have left Australian governments looking hypocritical as well as ineffectual.

In the last analysis Australia has the naval and air power and the industrial infrastructure to match any of her regional neighbours in a strategic context; a sound relationship with Indonesia and the other ASEAN states may have to be built on Australian military power. But, in the meantime, the economic and diplomatic levers for influencing the tragic course of events in Indo-China, and the increasingly embittered drift in Australian-Indonesian relations, have not yet been properly grasped.

Endnotes

1 Introduction *Peter King*

1. Michael Sexton *War For the Asking: Australia's Vietnam Secrets* Melbourne: Penguin, 1981; G J Munster and J R Walsh (eds and publishers) *Documents on Australian Defence and Foreign Policy, 1968-75* Sydney, 1980. An outline and chronology of Australia's involvement can be found in Frank Frost and Carlyle A Thayer 'Australia and Vietnam, 1950-1980' *Dyason House Papers* Vol. 6, No. 3, March 1980. A pathbreaking analysis of the first phase of the domestic politics of the Vietnam War is Henry S Albinski *Politics and Foreign Policy in Australia: the impact of Vietnam and conscription* Durham, North Carolina: Duke University Press, 1970. G Clark *In Fear of China* Melbourne: Lansdowne, 1967, and J F Cairns *The Eagle and The Lotus* Melbourne: Lansdowne, 1969, sounded the tocsin against the war for the left in Australia. The first book-length journalistic account of Australia's war was G L Stone, *War Without Honour* Brisbane: Jacaranda, 1966. See also Alan Renouf *The Frightened Country* Melbourne: Macmillan, 1979, and Graham Freudenberg *A Certain Grandeur: Gough Whitlam in Politics* Melbourne: Macmillan, 1977
2. *In Fear of China*
3. Peter King 'Australian Foreign Policy: A Paranoid Posture?', in H Mayer (ed.) *Australian Politics: A Second Reader* Melbourne: Cheshire, 1971
4. T B Millar 'Indo-China: The Implications for Australian Security' *Quadrant* Vol. XIX, No. 4, July 1975

2 Vietnam, China and the foreign affairs debate in Australia *Gregory Clark*

1. *In Fear of China* Melbourne: Lansdowne Press, 1967
2. ibid.; see also my articles in *Meanjin Quarterly* No. 2, 1973, and *Nation* (Sydney) January 1966.
3. Alan Renouf was a prominent member of this group. I should add that he too managed quite well at the time to conceal the dismay he has since claimed to have felt over the government's China and Vietnam policies.
4. See their booklet *Vietnam and Australia*
5. Bruce Grant's 1972 book *The Crisis of Loyalty: A Study of Australian Foreign Policy* is typical of this brand of timid progressive thought. It contains only one page on Vietnam, and whole chapters on how we could help the 'security' of friendly Asian states such as Indonesia, Malaysia, and Singapore.
6. See my debate with Owen Harries in *Communism in Asia: A Threat to Australia?* Australian Institute of Political Science Summer School, January 1967, Sydney: Angus and Robertson, 1967.
7. See my article 'What's wrong with Our Diplomats?' *Australian Quarterly* Vol. 47, No. 2, June 1975.

8   Information was a powerful aphrodisiac, and the US agencies used it to good advantage. A small group of hawks in Canberra had consistent advance information on US bombing and other strategics against North Vietnam, and used that information to bolster their bureaucratic positions.
9   The record of ASIO/ASIS penetration of the universities, particularly the ANU International Relations Department, is already partly known. A similar and successful effort was made to influence media commentators on foreign affairs. Material from bogus news services such as Forum World Features found ready access to Australian newspapers. As a desk officer in 1962, I was surprised by the way we would be asked to file intelligence requests in advance of Asian visits by 'friendly' foreign affairs commentators. Most of such cases were journalists from the Fairfax group, I might add.

3 Federal Labor and the Vietnam commitment   Kim C Beazley

1   Official Report of the Special Federal Conference on Foreign Affairs and Defence, March 1963, p. 21
2   The Conference is discussed at length by the writer in 'Federal Labor and The American Installations; Prelude to Government' *Australian Outlook* Vol. 33, No. 2 pp. 166–181
3   Official Report of the Special Federal Conference on Foreign Affairs and Defence, March 1963, p. 10
4   A B Bishop 'The interaction of ALP policy on Indonesia and on Australian Armed Forces in Malaya 1960–1963' (unpublished M A thesis, Flinders University, 1977) p. 122
5   Official Report of the Twenty-fifth Commonwealth Conference, July–August 1963, pp. 23–24
6   *Sydney Morning Herald* 10 February 1962.
7   *Commonwealth Parliamentary Debates* (CPD) Vol. 40, 25 September 1963, p. 1379
8   *CPD* Vol. 35, 13 April 1962, p. 881
9   *CPD* (House of Representatives) (H of R), Vol. 45, 25 March 1965, pp. 384–385
10 A B Bishop *op. cit.*, pp. 139–141.
11 A B Bishop *op. cit.*, p. 145.
12 ibid., p. 117
13 *The Age* 15 November 1963.
14 Official Report of the Special Federal Conference on Foreign Policy, p. 6
15 E G Whitlam 'Australian Foreign Policy and our Asian Neighbours', *The West Australian* 21 August 1964
16 J Wilkes (ed.) *Australia's Defence and Foreign Policy* Melbourne: Angus and Robertson, 1964 p. 154
17 A B Bishop *op. cit.*, p. 159
18 *Fact* 2 April 1965
19 J F Cairns, *Vietnam, Is it the Truth We want?* Melbourne: Victorian Branch ALP, 1965
20 *Fact* 10 December 1965
21 *Sydney Morning Herald* 25 September 1963
22 *CPD* (H of R) Vol. 35, 5 April 1962, p. 1459
23 *CPD* (H of R) Vol. 39, 22 August 1963, p. 428
24 *The Age* 27 July 1964
25 *The Age* 15 June 1964
26 *Federal Executive Minutes* 4 August 1964
27 *The Age* 10 August 1964
28 *The Australian* 25 August 1964
29 *The Age* 13 August 1964
30 *The West Australian* 21 August 1964
31 *FPLP Minutes* 18 February 1965
32 *The Age* 10 August 1964

ENDNOTES

33 *CPD* (H of R) Vol. 44, 21 October 1964, p. 2165
34 This was based on conversations with the late A D Fraser in February 1973 and K E Beazley in August 1979.
35 *Sydney Morning Herald* 26 March 1965
36 *FPLP Minutes* 25 March 1965
37 *CPD* (H of R) Vol. 45, 8 April 1965, p. 836
38 *CPD* (H of R) Vol. 45, 25 March 1965, p. 384
39 Interview with K E Beazley, February 1973
40 *The Age* 30 April 1965
41 *FPLP Minutes* 4 May 1965
42 *CPD* (H of R) Vol. 46, May 1965, p. 1104
43 ibid., 6 May 1965, p. 1286
44 ibid., 4 May 1965, p. 1115
45 ibid., 6 May 1965, pp. 1238-1239
46 ibid., 4 May 1965, p. 1105
47 ibid., 6 May 1965, p. 1252
48 ibid., p. 1253
49 ibid, 4 May 1965, p. 1107
50 ibid., p. 1251
51 *The Daily Telegraph* 11 March 1965
52 *The Australian* 15 March 1965
53 Official Report of the Proceedings of the 26th Commonwealth Conference, August 1965, p. 104
54 Interviews with Mr Freudenberg and Mr C R T Matthews, February 1973
55 Official Report of the Proceedings of the 26th Commonwealth Conference, August 1965, pp 251-258
56 ibid., p. 79
57 ibid., p. 182
58 Federal Executive Minutes, 9 February 1966, p. 32. Voting for the Foreign Affairs Committee was as follows: Cairns 10, Uren 9, S H Cohen 9, J M Wheeldon 8, J Cavanagh, A Mulvihill 6, elected. Dunstan 5, W G Hayden 4, S Benson 4, A Fraser 3, R Holt 3, G Gray 3, defeated.
59 *The Age* 12 February 1966
60 *FPLP Minutes*, 27 April 1966
61 *FPLP Minutes*, 12 May 1966
62 *The Age* 8 October 1966
63 *The Age* 21 February 1966
64 K E Beazley 'Labor and Foreign Policy' *Australian Outlook* Vol. 20, No. 2, p. 132
65 *CPD* (H of R) Vol. 57, 8 March 1966, p. 240
66 *FPLP Minutes* 19 October 1966
67 *The Age* 25 November 1966
68 *ALP News* 28 August 1966
69 *FPLP Minutes* 17 August 1966
70 ibid.
71 *The Age* 25 August 1966
72 *The Age* 10 September 1966
73 *The Age* 25 November 1966
74 *The Daily Mirror* 17 November 1966
75 *The Age* 18 November 1966
76 *The Age* 23 November 1966
77 Transcript of interview with Tony Charlton, TCN 9, 18 February 1968
78 *FPLP Minutes* 8-9 February 1967
79 *FPLP Minutes* 6 April 1967. Those identified with Whitlam were Beazley, Barnard, Davies, Cross, Willesee, Drury and Mullvihill. Only Cairns and Bryant were successful from the left.

80 *FPLP Minutes* 1 March 1967
81 Letter from Whitlam to the WA State Executive, 18 December 1969
82 EG Whitlam *Beyond Vietnam* Melbourne: Victorial Fabian Society, 1968
83 *The West Australian* 8 June 1967
84 From a copy of a letter circulated in Perth Trades Hall
85 *The Daily News* 8 June 1967
86 'The Labor Party is opposed to continuance of the war in Vietnam and Australia's participation in it. The Party will work to end the war and Australia's participation in it'. Official Report of the 27th Commonwealth Conference, August 1967, p. 72.
87 ibid. p. 18
88 Interview with Mr C Lloyd, February 1973
89 *The Age* 19 February 1968
90 For example, see Whitlam's and Barnard's speeches on foreign policy in *CPD* (H of R) Vol. 56, 14 August 1967 and *CPD* (H of R) Vol. 57, 26 October 1967
91 CPD (H of R) Vol. 56, 17 August 1967, p. 222
92 These opinions are based on interview with persons close to Whitlam at the time who did not want their views attributed.
93 CPD (H or R) Vol. 58, 28 March 1968, p. 476.
94 *The Age* 2 October 1969.
95 See for example, Whitlam's speech in *CPD* (H of R) Vol. 78, 9 May 1972, p. 2266 and Barnard's speech *CPD* (H of R) Vol. 71, 24 February 1971, pp. 564–566.

4 Australia's war in Vietnam   *Frank Frost*

1 Department of Defence *Brief History—Australian Force in Vietnam 1962-1972* February 1972 p. 15. *Commonwealth Parliamentary Debates* (CPD) House of Representatives Vol. 75, 9 December 1971, p. 4538f; *CPD* The Senate Vol. 51, 22 February 1972, p. 22
2 *Current Notes on International Affairs* Vol. 40, 9 September 1969, p. 550; *CPD* (H of R) Vol. 78, 31 May 1972, p. 3409; R J O'Neill 'Australia and Vietnam' in D Pettit ed. *Selected Readings in Australian Foreign Policy* Melbourne: Sorrett, 1973, pp. 175–185, p. 18
3 See H S Albinski *Politics and Foreign Policy in Australia* Durham: Duke University Press, 1970, pp. 31–56, 101–162; G Greenwood 'The Political Debate in Australia' in G Greenwood and N Harper eds *Australia in World Affairs 1966-1970*, Melbourne: Cheshire, 1974, pp. 30–102; D Altman 'Australia and Vietnam, Some Preliminary Speculations' *Australian Quarterly* Vol. 42, No. 2, June 1970, pp. 61–69.
4 See John Dux and P J Young, *Agent Orange: The Bitter Harvest* Sydney: Hodder and Stoughton, 1980
5 *Australia's Military Commitment to Vietnam, Paper tabled in accordance with the Prime Minister's statement to the House of Representatives 13 May 1975*, pp. 2–3
6 ibid, p. 5
7 *Army Press Release* No. 4981, Canberra, 13 July 1967, p. 3
8 F P Serong 'Australia in Vietnam', in K Grenville *The Saving of South Vietnam* Sydney: Alpha Books, 1972, pp. 213–224
9 *The Canberra Times* 17 August 1971
10 *Australia's Military Commitment to Vietnam* pp. 14–19
11 Gerald Stone *War Without Honour* Brisbane: Jacaranda Press, 1966, p. 56; P G Bourne *Men, Stress and Vietnam* Boston: Little, Brown & Co, 1970, pp. 175–176
12 *The Bulletin* 12 November 1966, p. 15
13 *The Age* 2 November 1966
14 Alan Stretton, *Soldier in a Storm* Sydney: Collins, 1978, pp. 182–183
15 *Australian Financial Review* 27 May 1970
16 R J O'Neill *Vietnam Task* Melbourne: Cassell, 1967, pp. 9–13
17 Cf speech by the Minister for External Affairs (Mr Barwick), 21 August 1962, in *Cur-*

ENDNOTES

rent Notes on International Affairs, Vol. 33, No. 8, August 1962, pp. 54–5; Alan Watt, *Vietnam: An Australian Analysis* Melbourne: Cheshire, 1968, pp. 130–1
18 *CPD* (H of R) 23 March 1965, p. 232
19 *The Long Hai Mountains* (Nui Dat, mimeograph 1970) pp. 3–5
20 Captain M R Battle, ed. *The Year of the Tigers: The Second Tour of 5th Battalion, the Royal Australian Regiment in South Vietnam* Sydney: published by the Battalion, 1970, p. 108
21 O'Neill *op. cit.*, p. 14
22 ibid., pp. 16–17
23 Douglas Pike *Viet Cong* Cambridge, Mass: MIT, 1966, pp. 210–231
24 Major L D Johnson, ed. *The History of 6 RAR-NZ (ANZAC) Battalion: Volume Two, 1967 to 1970* Townsville: Published by the Battalion, 1972, p. 40
25 Major A Clunies Ross, ed. *The Grey Eight in Vietnam, The History of the Eighth Battalion, the Royal Australian Regiment, November 1969–November 1970* Brisbane: Published by the Battalion, 1971, p. 127
26 Cf Jeffrey Race, *War Comes to Long An* Berkeley: University of California Press, 1972; Carlyle A Thayer *The Origins of the National Front for the Liberation of Viet-Nam* PhD thesis, Australian National University, 1978.
27 Major Ian G McNeill 'An Outline of the Australian Military Involvement in Vietnam, July 1962–December 1972' *Defence Force Journal* No. 24 September–October 1980, pp. 42–53, p. 48
28 Major-General C M I Pearson, Interview, Canberra, 9 November 1972
29 The PAVN—regular army of the DRV
30 CORDS—Civil Operations and Rural Development Support. A division of the US Military Assistance Command, Vietnam, responsible for the 'pacification' programe in the RVN
31 McNeill, *loc. cit.* p. 48
32 *Sydney Morning Herald* 5 January 1971
33 O'Neill *op. cit.* p. 230
34 *CPD* (H of R) Vol. 64, 29 August 1969, p. 912
35 Battle *op. cit.*, p. 59
36 *Australian Army Monthly Summary* Canberra, May 1970, p. 3
37 O'Neill *op. cit.*, pp. 217–221, in Clunies-Ross *op. cit.*, p. 55
38 Clunies-Ross *op. cit.*, pp. 103–109
39 McNeill *loc. cit.*, p. 50
40 ibid., p. 48
41 ibid., p. 53
42 Lieutenant-Colonel Nguyen Van Tu, Interview, Baria, 10 March 1972
43 *The Australian* 29 May 1971
44 Race *op. cit.*, pp.267–276; Allan E Goodman 'South Vietnam and the New Security' *Asian Survey* Vol. XII, No. 2, February 1972, pp. 121–137
45 *The Australian* 29 May 1971; *Sydney Morning Herald* 29 October 1970
46 McNeill *loc. cit.*, p. 50

5 Australian soldiers in Vietnam   *Jane Ross*

1 Thomas S Gates *The Report of the President's Commission into an All-Volunteer Armed Force* US Government Printer, 1970 p. 44
2 *Army Manning Review (AMR)* 1969–70. The figures are for 30 June 1970.
3 These figures are from the *1971 CGS Exercise* which gives details of unit strengths and location. See Vol. 2, 'Exercise Papers'
4 These figures are from the Defence Department
5 *AMRs*, 1966–72. One could argue that 'training' is the main activity of all soldiers—see below on the way 7RAR spent the years 1965–70.
6 ibid., 1969–70

7   One example: the author was being shown over the Recruit Training Battalion area at Kapooka, NSW. The officer escort, keen to impress with the fairness of it all, said: 'We don't even know who the nashos are. Now take my driver, you're a nasho, aren't you, and you like it, don't you? ...'
8   For a rosy view of NS training, see T B Millar 'The Man of the Year', *The Bulletin* 7 January 1967
9   See 'Tropical Warfare Training before Operational Service in South East Asia' *Army Routine Order 106/70*, 24 July 1970
10 *Seven in Seventy, a Pictorial Record of Seventh Battalion the Royal Australian Regiment, 1970-1971* Sydney: published by the Battalion, Printcraft Press 1971, p. 12
11 See, for instance, the Peers Commission report: *The My Lai Massacre and its Cover-up: Beyond the Reach of Law*, Introduction by J Goldstein, B Marshall and J Schwartz New York: The Free Press, 1971
12 The title of an article in the *Catholic Worker* No. 407, May 1970
13 Revised June 1967, No. 7610-66-023-3281/1
14 See my 'The Conscript Experience in Vietnam' *Australian Outlook* Vol. 29, No. 3, December 1975, pp. 315-322
15 See my 'The Australian Army: some views from the bottom', *Australian Quarterly* Vol. 46, No. 3, September 1974, pp. 35-47 (which reports changes only in army-related attitudes between recruits and dischargees).
16 D R and M I. Segal 'The Impact of Military Service and Trust in Government, International Attitudes and Social Status', in N L Goldman and Segal *The Social Psychology of Military Service* Beverly Hills: Sage, 1976, p. 211
17 There was some disagreement over whether NS men could refuse service in Vietnam: see *The Australian* 29 October 1970, 27 September 1971, 7 November 1971
18 *AMRs* 1967-1972
19 *AMR* 1972
20 Barry Wain *The Australian* 8 May 1971
21 Hospitalisation rates are found in the *AMRs*
22 And see his PhD thesis: *The Operations of the Australian Army in South Vietnam 1966-71: Political and Military Problems* Department of Government, Sydney University, 1976.
23 R O'Neill has also criticised the 'battle orientation' of 'most commentators, observers, soldiers and members of the public at large', in 'Australian Military Problems in Vietnam', *Australian Outlook* Vol. 23, No. 1, April 1969, p. 46.
24 Martin Russ *Happy Hunting Ground* New York: Atheneum, 1968, was told by an officer that 'The Task Force has pacified ... 90 per cent of Phuoc Tuy' (p. 149)
25 D Warner *Sydney Morning Herald* 31 December 1969
26 Major K E Newman *The ANZAC Battalion: a Record of the Tour of 2nd Battalion, The Royal Australian Regiment, 1st Battalion, The RNZIR. In South Vietnam 1967-68* Sydney, 1969, pp. 72-3.
27 A R Roberts *The Anzac Battalion, 1970-71* Sydney: Printcraft Press, 1972, p. 51
28 R L Sayce and M D O'Neill *The Fighting Fourth, 4RAR/NZ 1970-72* Sydney: Printcraft Press, 1972, p. 82
29 I McL Williams *VIETNAM: a Pictorial History of the 6th Battalion, The Royal Australian Regiment* Sydney: Printcraft Press, 1967, p. 32
30 *The Bulletin* 20 January 1968
31 *SMH* 30 December 1969. See also praise from a British counterinsurgency expert, *The Australian* 26 May 1969
32 Martin Russ 'How Aussies Behave in Vietnam' *Life* (Australia), 1 April 1968, pp. 52-4
33 R S Garland *Australian Army Journal*, No. 206, July 1966, pp. 3-11.
34 See battalion histories cited above.
35 Frost *op. cit.*, p. 136
36 Personal communication to the author at 1ATF, January 1971.
37 Frost *op. cit.*, p. 249

38 *Bleeding Earth* Sydney: Alpha Books, 1967, p. 109
39 *Sunday Australian* 28 March 1971.
40 See T Stapleton 'A New Role for the Australian Army?' *Australian Outlook* Vol. 25, No. 1, April 1971, pp. 3-12
41 One officer at the Task Force in 1971 actually said he had never heard of it.
42 Psyops was considered an American fad. Its gadgetry, Buddhist ghost music broadcast from spotter planes, leaflet drops, etc., was considered amusing, but a waste of time. The Psyops officers publicly lamented the lack of understanding of their task on the part of some infantry commanders. One described an incident after a contact when Psyops planned to send a team to encourage ralliers. But the infantry unit's commander responded, 'Hell, we don't want people like that, we want bloody kills to chalk up on the board'. *The Australian* 26 March 1971. See also K Kellen 'War on the Mind' *Armed Forces and Society* 6(2), 1980, pp. 313-25
43 Forst *op. cit.*, p. 229. Ian Mackay claims that Vietnamese also liked the Australians because they were hardworking, well-behaved, good fighters, and had realistic civic action projects. *Australians in Vietnam* Adelaide: Rigby, 1968, p. 161
44 These comments apply primarily to the other ranks.
45 Peter G Bourne *Men, Stress, and Vietnam* Boston: Little, Brown, 1970, pp. 167-186 on 'the Australians'
46 ibid., p. 170. The reviewer of a recent Australian novel set in Vietnam commented: 'The author displays a considerable xenophobia, but that ... is part of the Australian make-up and probably taken to its extreme among our serving men. There is grudging respect for the Communist troops, contempt for the South Vietnamese and derision for the Americans.' *The National Times* 12-18 October 1980
47 Bourne *op. cit.*, p. 185
48 ibid., p. 171
49 ibid., p. 175-7. Some Australians originally made rather patronising overtures to black US soldiers, but these were rebuffed and relations deteriorated, partly because of a confusion between the terms 'digger' and 'nigger'.
50 Lieutenant, CMF.
51 *Happy Hunting Ground, op. cit.*, pp. 185 and 194
52 On 'morale' as an unsatisfactory concept, see A L George 'Primary Groups, Organization, and Military Performance', in Roger W Little (ed.) *Handbook of Military Institutions* Beverly Hills: Sage, 1971.
53 John Keegan *The Face of Battle* Harmondsworth: Penguin, 1978, p. 276
54 Taken overall: some units suffered heavy casualties in particular short engagements.
55 A summary of the literature is in George, *loc. cit.*
56 V Madej 'Effectiveness and Cohesion of the German Ground Forces in World War II', *Journal of Political and Military Sociology*, 6, Fall 1978, pp. 233-48, argues that cohesion may be the *result* of combat success.
57 James G March (ed.) *Handbook of Organizations* Chicago: Rand McNally, 1965, p. 839
58 My emphasis. F J Kviz 'Survival in Combat as a Collective Exchange Process', *Journal of Political and Military Sociology* 6, Fall 1978, p. 219
59 Paul Savage and Richard Gabriel, 'Cohesion and Disintegration in the American Army: An Alternative Perspective' *AFS*, Vol. 2 No. 3, May 1976, p. 344
60 ibid., p. 371
61 ibid., pp. 340-1, 364
62 Keegan *op. cit.*, p. 333; See also Murray Polner, *No Victory Parades* London: Orbach and Chambers, 1971
63 *Loc. cit.*, pp. 354-5
64 Reported in more detail in my 'The Australian Army: some views from the bottom' *loc. cit*
65 A E Hippler 'Some Psychological Aspects of Army Life', *Journal of Human Relations* Vol. 19, No. 1, 1971, pp. 97-114
66 Communication to the author from Directorate of Co-ordination, Department of

Defence, 18 December 1979
67 While not all officers share his attitude, at least one captain's view of the processes of law was 'we know he's guilty, so why waste time with a court martial'.
68 Report from the *Senate Select Committee on Drug Trafficking and Drug Abuse* 1971. At p. 4351 of the evidence submitted by the Army Office there is some detail on the types of penalty imposed for drug use.
69 Charles R Figley (ed.) *Stress Disorders among Vietnam Veterans* New York: Brunner/Mazel, 1978, p. xvi; see also Bourne, *op. cit.*, p. 180.
70 Keegan *op. cit.*, p. 335
71 ibid., p. 351, from evidence to Congressional Hearings, 1972.
72 Harry R Kormos 'The Nature of Combat Stress', pp. 3-22 in Figley *op. cit.*
73 I believe, however, that there was some *attitudinal* distancing: see 'The Conscript Experience in Vietnam' *loc. cit.*
74 *Op. cit.*, p. 180. He states there were 25 psychiatric cases in 1966 out of a force of about 1500-1.7 per cent
75 Warner: 'I understand that some isolated and minor cases of war fatigue have involved disciplinary action'. *Sydney Morning Herald*, 4 February 1971; see also *The Australian* 31 October 1971, for an article by a conscript who claimed 'In my unit, one third of the members suffered some sort of emotional breakdown. Several had to have their weapons locked away for the night.'
76 Communication from Directorate of Co-ordination, Department of Defence, 18 December 1979. See also evidence by Army Office to *Senate Select Committee, loc. cit.*
77 Lee Patterson 'Drink and Drugs in Australia's Armed Forces', *Australian Playboy* December 1979, pp. 71-6. (His figures are for 1975)
78 *The Australian* 27 July 1971
79 *New Nation* (Singapore) 1 March 1971
80 *Senate Select Committee, op. cit.*, p. 4347. See also pp. 4342-6
81 Personal communication from the then Operations Officer, 1ATF, January 1971.
82 D Warner *Sydney Morning Herald* 4 January 1971
83 Mackay, *op. cit.*, p. 105. See also the account by Martin Russ.
84 The words of Peter Robinson, *Australian Financial Review* 26 May 1970
85 Opinion polls always showed a majority of all age groups in favour of compulsory military training: see for instance M Goot 'Beyond the Generation Gap' pp. 153-175 in H Mayer (ed) *Australian Politics: a second reader* Melbourne: Cheshire, 1969, esp. pp. 157-8.
86 Army studies usually found over 85 per cent of NS men 'unfavourable' to the idea of making a career in the army — see A G Owens, 'Attitudes of NS men to Enlistment in the Regular Army'. *Australian Army Psychology Research Report 3/67*. And see my 'The Australian Army — some views from the bottom', *loc. cit.*, pp. 43-44
87 ibid., p. 38
88 See 'Pogo', in C J Clarke (ed.) *Yours Faithfully, 3RAR, 1969-71* Brookvale: Printcraft Press, 1972, p. 46
89 An example is in the poem 'Mates in Vietnam', in Newman, *op. cit.*, p. 41. This meant that the FIGMO syndrome ('fuck it I've got my orders') was probably found only in support units. See Charles C Moskos, 'Why Men Fight: American Combat Soldiers in Vietnam', *Trans-Action* Vol. 7, No. 1, November 1969, pp. 13-23.
90 Cf Moskos *loc. cit.*, on the 'Americanism' ideology of the GI. He also discusses 'The fighting man's peace demonstrator', whom the GI similarly perceived as being directed against himself personally and not against the war.
91 Barry Wain in *The Australian* 29 May 1971
92 *The Bulletin* 7 January 1967
93 Mackay, *op. cit.*, p. 199
94 For a general discussion of 'authoritative sanctions for killing' see Chaim F Shaton, 'Stress Disorders among Vietnam Veterans: the Emotional Content of Combat Continues', in Figley *op. cit.*, pp. 43-5

95 Alex Carey *Australian Atrocities in Vietnam* Sydney: Vietnam Action Committee, 1968. The practice may have continued with Australian consent and involvement: a Psyops officer in 1971 told me 'of course we still use water torture, and lots of other methods too; you've got to, if you want information quickly'. Was there some bravado in this claim?
96 M D Feld *The Structure of Violence* Beverly Hills: Sage, 1977, p. 16.
97 Quoted in Carey *op. cit.*, p. 10
98 See Joseph A Blake 'The Organization as Instrument of Violence' *The Sociological Quarterly* Vol. 11, No. 3, Summer 1970, p. 344, on the sort of situation likely to lead to, for example, unauthorised killing of prisoners. Australians sometimes shot the wounded: see Carey *op. cit.*, p. 16 on the aftermath of Long Tan.
99 See for instance, J Helmer *Bringing the War Home* New York: Free Press, 1974 (reviewed by J Bramson in *AFS* Vol. 21, No. 1, Fall 1975, pp. 140–5); review article by J Ladinsky, 'Vietnam, the Veterans, and the Veterans' Administration' *AFS* Vol. 2, No. 3, Spring 1976, pp. 435–67; and reference below.
100 Ladinsky *loc. cit.*, p. 438
101 For discussion of the evidence see Charles R Figley 'Psychosocial Adjustment among Vietnam Veterans: an overview of the Research', in Figley *op. cit.*, pp. 57–70; and Jonathan F Borus 'The Re-entry Transition of the Vietnam Veteran' *AFS*, Vol. 2, No. 1, Fall 1975, pp. 97–114.
102 See reference above. The RSL accused a 'noisy minority' of 'making servicemen scapegoats for the war' *Sun-Herald* 18 July 1971.
103 David R Segal and John D Blair 'Public Confidence in the US Military' *AFS* 3(1), Fall 1976, pp. 3–12; and Ronald Inglehart, 'Changing Values and Attitudes toward Military Service among the American Public', in Goldman and Segal *op. cit.*, pp. 255–78.
104 *Sydney Morning Herald* 8 July 1980; and John Dux and P J Young *Agent Orange: the Bitter Harvest* Sydney: Hodder and Stoughton, 1980.
105 I refer particularly to the Dat Do minefield which was responsible for many Australian deaths and injuries. The Agent Orange claims differ from ordinary veteran demands in that the VVAA is seeking compensation, not merely recognition of disability and concomitant pension rights.
106 *Sunday Australian* 28 May 1972. See also *National Times* 2–7 August 1971. Repatriation benefits were outlined in pamphlets from the Repatriation Department entitled 'Repatriation Benefits for Special Overseas Service'.
107 'Soldiers' Rehabilitation Board, Republic of Vietnam', n.d.
108 Robert J Lifton 'Vietnam: Betrayal and Self-Betrayal', *Trans-Action* October 1969, pp. 6–7
109 See Figley *op. cit.*
110 *Australian Financial Review* 13 August 1971; *The Australian* 20 August 1971; *The Australian* 28 May 1972, which quotes a regular soldier who will 'miss the action. "After all, why dirty our own backyard when we can dirty theirs?" '
111 See my *The Myth of the Diggers: the Australian Soldier in Two World Wars* Sydney: Hale and Iremonger, forthcoming

6 The resisters   Michael E Hamel-Green

1 See L C Jauncey *The Story of Conscription in Australia* Macmillan, 1968; J M Main, *Conscription: The Australian Debate, 1901-1970*; and K S Inglis in R Forward & R Reece (eds) *Conscription in Australia* St Lucia: Queensland University Press, 1967, p. 27 ff
2 Inglis, ibid
3 Forward & Reece *op. cit.*
4 20 year olds were required to register in two fortnightly periods during January–February and July–August of each year.
5 H S Albinski *Politics and Foreign Policy in Australia, The Impact of Vietnam and Con-*

scription Durham, North Carolina: Duke University Press, 1970, p. 32

6 The odds of being chosen in the ballot declined from approximately 1-in-10 in the early years to less than 1-in-15 in the later years.
7 Automatic exemption was granted to theology students and those who were married or members of the CMF at the time of registration. Under conscientious objection provisions, applicants were required to prove their sincerity before a magistrate; if the magistrate were not convinced, he might deny the application or order the applicant to perform non-combatant duties in the army.
8 In the case of failure to register, a consideration which probably weighed more heavily than either fines or short gaol terms was the fact that it was supposed to result in being automatically called up—but bluff rather than actual legal coercion was the secret to the scheme's early success.
9 See Jauncey, *op. cit.*, and L L Robson *The First AIF: A Study of its Recruitment, 1914-1918* Melbourne: Melbourne University Press, 1970.
10 See Dean Rusk's candid remarks recorded in *SEATO Record* Vol. III, No. 5, October, 1964, pp. 20-23, and N Chomsky *At War With Asia* Fontana, 1971, pp. 7-64
11 Inglis *op. cit.*, p. 27
12 From 1965-67, I participated in the Vietnam Coordinating Committee and YCAC activities in Melbourne, and carried out research for the Vietnam Study Group at Melbourne University. During 1968-69 I was involved in the Draft Resistance Movement (DRM), Melbourne University SDS anti-conscription, anti-war campaigns, and in the succession of national actions and conferences on conscription and the Vietnam war. From 1970 to 1972 I participated in the campaigns of the Draft Resisters' Union and Vietnam Moratorium; for the last 18 months of this period I was a member of the draft resistance underground. The account is based on the following sources: (a) my own collection of pamphlets, handbills, newsletters, circulars, minutes and press clippings (which Frances Newell and I made a practice of keeping from 1968 onwards); (b) a file of press-clippings on conscription from newspapers all over Australia which Vivienne Abrahams, the editor of *Peacemaker*, kindly loaned me; (c) interviews with, and documents loaned to me by, Trevor Ashton, Charles Smith, and Barry Robinson, relating to the 1964-67 YCAC period; (d) my personal recollection of meetings, people and groups in the anti-conscription movement; (e) a survey of material relating to conscription in *The Age, Hansard, SEATO Record, Tribune, Guardian, Peacemaker*, and Gallup Polls, during the period 1960-72.
13 *The Pentagon Papers* The New York Times edn, Bantam Books, 1971, p. 88, p. 108
14 CPD (H of R) 15 March 1962, p. 847
15 *SEATO Record* Vol. II, No. 3, June 1963, p. 38
16 *New York Times* 2 October 1964.
17 Cited in C L Pettit, *The Experts* N J: Lyle Stuart, 1975, p. 184
18 *Pentagon Papers*, pp. 240-1
19 *SEATO Record* Vol. III, No. 2, April 1964, p. 44
20 *The Bulletin* 22 February 1964.
21 *The Bulletin* 22 August 1964
22 ibid.
23 CPD (H of R) 4 March 1964, p. 267 & p. 265
24 ibid. 21 April 1964, p. 1262 ff
25 ibid.
26 ibid., 13 May 1964, p. 1810
27 I Moffat *The Australian* 19 June 1971.
28 *The Age* 25 June 1964
29 *The Age* 10 July 1964, 3 August 1964 (RSL) and 15 July 1964 (DLP).
30 *The Pentagon Papers op. cit.*, pp. 264-265
31 CPD (H of R) 11 August 1964, p. 22
32 ibid. 13 August 1964, p. 185 ff
33 *The Age* 15 January 1964; 10 July 1964; 1 August 1964; 20 August 1964; and *The*

ENDNOTES

    Herald 26 October 1964
34 *The Herald* 26 October 1964
35 A home-defence only scheme might have been forced on it if it had permitted lengthy public debate before the measure was submitted to Parliament.
36 *The Bulletin* 22 August 1964
37 *Pentagon Papers op. cit.*, pp. 322–323
38 ibid., pp. 363–364
39 ibid., pp. 332–334.
40 ibid., pp. 334–335
41 CDP (H of R) 10 November 1964, p. 2715 ff
42 ibid., p. 2718
43 ibid., 12 November 1964, p. 2923 ff.
44 ibid., p. 2934
45 ibid., p. 2984 (Johnson), and p. 3021 (Beazley)
46 At least, none reported in either the mainstream or radical press.
47 See V G Childe *How Labor Governs*, 2nd edn, Melbourne University Press, 1964, pp. 145–6
48 I cannot personally recall any such appeals, nor are any references found to such appeals in the press.
49 Department of Labour and National Service *News Release* 28 June, 1965, p. 1
50 There is no evidence in either the daily newspapers or peace movement publications of any of the 'hundred odd' defaulters referred to by Mr McMahon.
51 The government certainly had little trouble in gaining the cooperation of employers, the medical profession, and college and university administrators.
52 T Christiansen 'Conscientious Objection is Not Enough' *Peacemaker* January– February 1966, p. 6. Also see Sydney University Labor Club *Wednesday Commentary* 24 June 1966
53 Convened by Rev. Alan Walker.
54 Convenor: the Youth Conference Committee of the Australian Congress for International Cooperation and Disarmament (AICD).
55 YCAC handbill, December 1964. The first Australian street demonstration against conscription did not take place in Australia at all but in London, where members of a newly-formed London anti-conscription committee picketed Australia House on 26 February 1965. They delivered a letter to the Australian High Commissioner, Mr Downer. See *The Australian* 27 February 1965. The first anti-conscription street demonstration in Australia itself did not take place until 10 March 1965 when 12 members of a newly-formed Melbourne anti-conscription group, the Youth Against Conscription Committee, picketed outside the Department of Labour and National Service in Melbourne at the drawing of the first ballot: *The Australian* 11 March 1965.
56 Interview with Barry Robinson (6 February 1970), secretary of YCAC Sydney from 1964–66. Also see *The Guardian* 18 March 1965.
57 *The Age* 17 March 1965
58 ibid., 7 May 1965
59 ibid., 7 May 1965
60 Interview with Trevor Ashton, Ian Carroll and Charles Smith, 15 February 1970. Ashton was Secretary of YCAC Melbourne from 1965–66; Carroll and Smith were committee members over the same period.
61 Interview with Barry Robinson, 6 February 1970. The Melbourne YCAC was formed 22 August 1965 at a meeting of 40 people at the Young Labor Association coffee lounge. 'The Whip', in Lygon Street, Carlton. The Brisbane branch of YCAC was established in late 1965 by Jim Beatson, Kit Guyatt, and Brian Laver. The West Australian YCAC branch began in early 1966. The Canberra branch was formed in late 1965. An account of YCAC's history and aims is given in Guyatt's 'The Anti-Conscription Movement, 1964–66' in Forward & Reece *op. cit.*, pp. 178–181.
62 *YCAC Newsletter* No. 1, August 1965

63 See *The Age* 13 September 1965, letter by Mrs Mary Stricklan.
64 Barry Robinson letter to Trevor Ashton, 13 November 1965.
65 The first draft card burnings took place in Sydney in Belmore Park on the occasion of the third intake of conscripts 2 February 1966: three burnt their registration cards and two were subsequently prosecuted 7 April.
66 No YCAC activities I interviewed could not recall any of the draft card burners going on to further stages of non-compliance.
67 For a powerful statement by a CO who won his case but later had second thoughts, see T Christiansen 'Conscientious Objection is Not Enough' *Peacemaker* Jan–Feb 1966, p. 6
68 *YCAC Newsletter* September 1966
69 *The Three Objectives of the Bill White Defence Committee* roneo circular, 1966
70 *Vote No Conscription Campaign* printed leaflet authorised by Glen Tomasetti, Melbourne, 1966
71 See Table 4–11 in Forward & Reece *op. cit.*, p. 129
72 The only exceptions were some small SOS demonstrations at conscript intakes in Melbourne.
73 See Geoff Mullen's letter to the National Service Department in December 1967, reprinted in *Peacemaker* January 1968. Details of the stands taken by other early non-compliers may be found in *Peacemaker* over the period 1967–68.
74 Brian Ross 'Statement to Orbost Court', 6 March 1968, *Peacemaker* April 1968
75 See Denis O'Donnell letter from Puckapunyal Military Camp, 28 March 1968 *National U* Vol. 4, No. 5, 10 June, 1968, p. 1. The treatment of Simon Townsend in Holsworthy Military Prison received nationwide publicity when it became known that he was being woken up at half-hourly intervals throughout the night, allegedly as a precaution against his committing 'suicide'.
76 *Peacemaker* February-March 1968
77 See J Larkin and G Barker in *The Age* 19 June 1968, and Mike Jones' article in *Arena* (Macquarie University), 21 October 1968.
78 Estimate based on the number of separate signatories to the 'Don't Register' leaflet, together with the number of participants in the major 'Don't Register' leafleting drives.
79 *The Daily Mercury* Wollongong, 23 April 1969
80 *The Australian* 18 June 1969
81 ibid. 30 June 1969.
82 Statement signed by Gordon Barton, Lesley Haylen, Tom Uren, George Petersen, Jack Ferguson, Dal Stivens, Alex Carey, Cecil Steady, Robin Gollan, Rev. Malcolm Black, Les Waddington and others. Neither the *Sydney Morning Herald* nor *The Australian* would print the statement as an advertisement, the former explaining that it would not be party to 'breaking the law': *Fact* 25 July 1969.
83 Ken McLeod *The Defiance Campaign* typewritten manuscript, August 1969, p. 2
84 Lawyers acting on behalf of the committee succeeded in securing a magistrate's ruling that the Statement of Defiance was in violation of the incitement clauses of the Crimes Act; the committee then began prosecuting its own members in batches. The intention of many members was to go to gaol for non-payment of fines, but, for the most part, magistrates reacted by waiving or simply not enforcing gaol penalties in lieu of fine payment.
85 *The Advertiser* 20 November 1969
86 See Department of Labour and National Service *Press Releases* 30 April 1966 & 10 August 1969 on statistics of breaches in the Act.
87 The 18–19 May Conference at Friends' House, Sydney, is described in *Peacemaker* July–August 1969, p. 5; the 23–24 August Conference is described in *Resist* (SDS Anti-Conscription Committee Newspaper) No. 4, 3 September 1969.
88 *Resist* as above
89 The full text is given in *Downdraft*, Melbourne Draft Resisters' Union handbook, 1st

ENDNOTES

edn, 1971.
90 *The Age* 16 December 1969
91 *The Australian* 17 December 1969
92 Gallup Poll 205, 15 August 1969, *APOP Printout*
93 *APOP 1916-1931* July/October 1966; *APOP 2087-2104*, November 1968/February 1969, and for all other polls: *APOP Printouts*.
94 See Table 4-11 in Forward & Reece *op. cit.*, p. 129
95 *APOP Printouts*
96 The moratorium concept was first developed within the American anti-war movement in late 1969, having been advanced by David Hawk and others in the Youth for McCarthy campaign. The first American Vietnam Moratorium demonstrations took place 15 October 1969 when demonstrations of unprecedented size took place in almost every American city. For a full account of the Vietnam Moratorium actions see Fred Halstead *Out Now* New York: Monad Press, 1978.
97 See V G Abraham *'Conscientious Non-Compliers with Conscription for Military Service in Australia'* roneo document, Sydney, 1970
98 Brian Ross was sentenced to two years' gaol at Orbost Court on 26 October 1969.
99 *The Age* 25 October 1970
100 Two left for overseas after a year of waiting, and four others eventually accepted conscientious objection status after more than three years of waiting.
101 See *Peacemaker* 1969 issues; also *Resistance Notes*, the newspaper of the SDS anti-conscription committee at Melbourne University.
102 *Resist* (formerly *Resistance Notes*), Melbourne University, Vol. 2, No. 4, 18 September 1970
103 Unionists and draft resisters quickly rejected such an 'alternative'. See Harry van Moorst's letter, *The Age* 27 May 1970; and the articles, 'Unions Bitter on NS Civilian Plan' and 'NS Triplets Reject Alternative' in ibid., 29 May 1970.
104 *The Australian* 8 June 1970
105 ibid., 11 June 1970.
106 *The Age* 13 June 1970
107 For a full account of one such episode, see *Peacemaker*, October-November 1970, p. 6. The other unrecorded case was that of Joe Eftermeyer in 1972.
108 *National Service—1965-1972* typewritten document, supplied to the author by Mr K C MacKenzie, Commonwealth Department of Labour, 21 June 1973
109 Based on reports of reception of call-up notices in *Peacemaker* and *Resist* during 1970
110 ibid. 1971
111 *Resist* Vol. 2, No. 1, 3 July 1970
112 ibid.
113 T Dalton & T Harding in *Downdraft*, Melbourne DRU handbook, 2nd Edn, July 1972
114 See 'DRU Goes National' *Resist* Vol. 3, No. 1, 10 February 1971, p. 2. The New South Wales DRU was later to publish its own newspaper, also called *Resist*.
115 See for example the lead article, '11,500 Defy Draft—NS Files Show 10% Prosecuted', in *Resist* Vol. 3, No. 1, 10 February 1971, p. 1
116 *Press Release* 3 September 1972, Minister for Labour and National Service, Mr Lynch.
117 Figures compiled from reports of reception of call-up summons or warrants as published in *Peacemaker* and *Resist* during 1968-72.
118 See my article, 'Underground Resistance' in *Downdraft*, handbook of the Melbourne DRU, 2nd edn, 1972, pp. 12-13.
119 A group of lay Catholics associated with the Melbourne magazine, *Catholic Worker*
120 Tony Dalton and myself
121 Gary Cook, Tony Dalton, Paul Fox, and myself. The resisters' action was announced at a press conference 28 June 1971
122 *Channel 7* interview with Senator Greenwood, 3 October 1971
123 Radical Action Movement, formerly Melbourne University SDS
124 Mike Matteson, John Scott, Tony Dalton, Paul Fox and myself

125 Mike Matteson and myself
126 *Channel 7* interview with Senator Greenwood, 3 October 1971
127 For the Sydney University action, see *Honi Soit* 3 August 1972, pp. 8-9. For another 'resistance commune' see *Lot's Wife*, 24 July 1972 and the following issue
128 Notably *Downdraft*, First and Second Eds of the DRU handbook; and *Conscience and the Law*, Heinemann Educational Books, 1974.
129 *The Age* 15 June 1970
130 *Sydney Morning Herald* 16 June 1970
131 See *The Australian* 10 July 1970, and *Sydney Morning Herald* 16 September 1970
132 *Outreach* July/August 1972
133 *Sunday Australian* 4 June 1972
134 *Catholic Worker* June 1972
135 *The Age* 9 August 1972
136 *The Age* 3 April 1972
137 Gallup Poll 230, 29 April 1972, *APOP Printout*
138 Gallup Poll 235, 21-28 October 1972, *APOP Printout*
139 Gallup Poll 227, 12 February 1972, *APOP Printout*
140 *The Australian* 21 March 1973
141 A J Forbes 'National Security and Defence', in R Aitchison (ed.) *Looking at the Liberals* Melbourne: Cheshire, p. 130

7 Public opinion and the politics of the polls Murray Goot and Rodney Tiffen

Thanks are due to Elizabeth Fletcher, Peggy Ridley and Dennis Rose for research assistance; Gary Morgan and Roy Morgan for access to their records; Don Aitkin for permission to reanalyse data from his surveys; Dr George Gallup; Gordon Tubbs and Leo Crespi of the USICA; officers of the Australian Labor Party, Liberal Party of Australia and National Country Party; Joan Elder for typing; Macquarie University for study leave; and the Australian Research Grants Committee for funding under the project title 'Opinion Polls in Political Decision Making'. Don Aitkin and Elizabeth Reid commented in detail on an earlier draft. We also acknowledge, with thanks, the comments of Alan Cameron, Stewart Firth and Michael Sexton.

1 See R Cooksey 'Australian Public Opinion and Vietnam Policy' *Dissent* Autumn 1968, pp. 5-6; Murray Goot 'Red, White and Brown: Australian attitudes to the world since the Thirties' *Australian Outlook* Vol. 24, No. 2, August 1970, pp. 197-200; H S Albinski *Politics and Foreign Policy in Australia: The Impact of Vietnam and Conscription* Durham: Duke University Press, 1970, Ch. 9, which concentrates on the impact of the issues on party choice; and Murray Goot 'Party Dominance and Partisan Division 1941-1972' in Cameron Hazelhurst, ed. *Australian Conservatism: Essays in Twentieth Century Political History* Canberra: ANU Press, 1979, pp. 267-269 which stresses Liberal/Labor differences.
2 See Terence W Beed, Murray Goot, Stephen Hodgson and Peggy Ridley *Australian Opinion Polls 1941-1977* Sydney: Hale & Iremonger, 1978, esp. pp. 137-140 (conscription), pp. 322-324 (Vietnam),
3 Roy Morgan interviewed by Murray Goot, 5 May 1977. Craig McGregor argues that Holt's support for banning the Communist Party in 1951 was based 'on the Holt-like ground that the Gallup polls of the time showed 80% of people supported it!', *Profile of Australia* Sydney: Hodder and Stoughton, 1966, p. 193.
4 See for example, the polls conducted by two Queensland MHRs, R Patterson (Dawson) and G Gray (Capricornia) prior to the 1966 election: Rex Patterson: 'Vietnam Survey 1966', ML MSS 2083 Box 119 Item 271; Albinski *op. cit.*, 226 n. 22; D Stephens, 'The Politics of a Permeable Coalition: The Australian Labor Party 1955-1972', ANU PhD 1979, p. 298.
5 The Liberal Party of Australia 'Tasmanian Survey' 4 Dec. 1965, ML, MSS

ENDNOTES

2385/K53632 Item 15; 'Summary of Survey findings conducted August 16, 1969', ML MSS 2385 Y 4706 Item 7; 'Report from The Survey Committee Young Voters Survey, March 1964', 'Survey in Selected areas of South Australia', 30–31 July, 1966; 'Report on survey conducted on August 4, 1967 on the Corio by-election'; and 'Bendigo By-Election-Survey Report', 20 June, 1969—these last four surveys from The Melbourne University Archives Liberal Party (Victoria Division) Second Accession, State Elections General Information. The most sophisticated of these Young Liberal surveys is reported in M Stockdale, 'Marketing a Candidate: The 1966 Hawkins Liberal Campaign in Yarra, *Politics* Vol. 2, No. 2, Nov. 1967, pp. 229–244; and Leo Hawkins 'For whom the opinion polls' *Australian Journal of Marketing Research* Vol. 1, No. 1, March 1968, pp. 3–6.

6 Lloyd A Free 'Press Reports on World Opinion' Institute for International Social Research, Princeton [1967?] mimeo. *Polls* (1965–1968) also carried results from the Morgan poll.
7 Roy Morgan to Goldman, 15 May 1964; 1 June 1964
8 Roy Morgan to Lloyd Free, 18 May 1964; 3 July 1967. Morgan had organised the Australian end of things when Cantril had directed a UNESCO project in 1948 on 'Tensions Affecting International Understanding'. See W Buchanan and H Cantril et al. *How Nations See Each other* Urbana: University of Illinois Press, 1953.
9 The relevant reports are: 'Some Indications of World wide Public Opinion Toward the US and the USSR', R-141-63 (R) July 1963 (survey conducted March-April 1963; N=830); 'Attitudes Toward Elements of the Nixon Doctrine: Japan, Australia, Philippines' R-13-17 September 1971 (survey conducted by International Research Associates? March-April 1971; N=644 with at least a secondary education); 'Public Opinion in Australia on US Standing and President Nixon's USSR visit' M-43-72 May 1972; 'Foreign Evaluation of US Policies Following the President's Visit to China', R-39-72, September 1972; 'US Standing in Foreign Public Opinion Following the President's visit to China' R-27-72 May 1972; 'Foreign Image of External Threat and Expectations of US Defense Assistance' R-51-72, October 1972, N=1094, (the last four reporting a survey conducted March 1972; M-43-72 includes data from a survey conducted June 1970, N=1000); 'US Standing in Foreign Public Opinion Following Recent Indochina Developments' USA/IOR/R, July 1975 (May 1975, N=1108), 'Australian Public Opinion on Regional Alignment and U.S.-Australian Relations', R-14-76, June 1976 (September 1975, N=933); and 'Australian Attitudes Toward Security and Economic Relations with the U.S.', R-28-78, October 1978 (March-April 1978, N=1055; includes data from surveys conducted January 1972, N=1093 and February 1974, N=1878).
10 Throughout this chapter reference to Morgan's reports are to the subscribers' reports.
11 See also R Tiffen *Communications and Politics: The Press, The Public and the Third World* Canberra: Australian Council for Overseas Aid, 1974, p. 10. For a critique of the American polls, which overlaps ours, see Michael Wheeler *Lies, Damn Lies and Statistics: The Manipulation of Public Opinion in America* N Y: Bell, 1976, Ch. 7.
12 Roy Morgan to the Assistant Editor of the Gallup Poll in America, [1964?]
13 Asked, in November 1964, what 'the United Sates should do next in Vietnam' 30 per cent of Americans had 'no opinion', the next largest group, 15 per cent, said that the US should make some 'definite move', get out *or* fight. G Gallup, ed. *The Gallup Poll: Public Opinion 1935–1971* N Y: Random House, 1972, Vol. 3, p. 1909. All subsequent references to the findings of the American Gallup Poll are to this work.
14 In 1966–67, when a sample of the South Vietnamese were asked 'who, or which countries, have tried to bring peace to Vientam?', only 7 per cent named Australia; 27 per cent named the US. *Polls* Vol. 3 No. 1, 1967 p. 91.
15 Morgan to George Gallup, Jnr, 6 July 1970
16 Morgan to Gallup, 8 September 1966
17 '6-Nation Survey on Vietnam War' Gallup International, Princeton. Press release. Morgan dropped the words 'Just ... read'.

18 J E Mueller 'Trends in popular support for the wars in Korea and Vietnam' *American Political Science Review* Vol. 65 No. 2, June 1971, p. 364; H Schandler *The Unmaking of the President* Princeton: Princeton University Press, 1977, ch. 9
19 Emphasis, here as elsewhere, in the original.
20 The complexity of opinion following widespread disenchantment but not consistent opposition to the war is best illustrated by American data. See J E Mueller *War, Presidents and Public Opinion* N Y: John Wiley, 1973, pp. 97–8.
21 Whether public opinion would have acquiesced in response to a government initiative is another matter. In America, on the eve of the Cambodian invasion only 7 per cent favoured sending troops. Immediately after the invasion 50 per cent agreed with Nixon's decision. M J Rosenberg, S Verba and P E Converse *Vietnam and the Silent Majority* N Y: Harper & Row, 1970, pp. 26–27.
22 A postal ballot organised in Canberra by the local Labor MHR Kep Enderby, showed that 'of those who are sufficiently concerned about these issues to vote' (4282 out of the 40,000 who received ballots), 'National Service in its present form' was supported by ony 25 per cent; 'the commitment of Australian troops to Vietnam', by 35 per cent. 'Canberra Postal Referendum on Vietnam and Conscription'. Press release, 20 November 1970.
23 None the less, some commentators were raising doubts about the economics of the scheme and arguing the practicability of an all volunteer army. See P D Groenewegen 'The public finance of Australia's participation in the Vietnam War' *Australian Quarterly* Vol. 52, No. 4, Dec. 1970, pp. 63–73; G Withers *Conscription: Necessity and Justice* Sydney: Angus and Robertson, 1972
24 D A Aitkin *Stability and Change in Australian Politics* Canberra: ANU Press, 1977, p. 289.
25 J S Western and P R Wilson 'Attitudes to conscription', in R Forward and Bob Reece, eds *Conscription in Australia* St. Lucia: University of Queensland Press, 1968, p. 227; also, abridged, in *Politics* Vol. 2 No. 1, May 1967, p. 49
26 R E Tiffen 'Symbolic processes of out-group politics: The press, the public and the Third World', PhD Thesis, Monash University, 1976, p. 232.
27 This and the preceding evidence casts considerable doubt on the claim that disenchantment with the war was 'to a considerable extent, catalysed by the increasingly militant anti-Vietnam War anti-conscription movement that developed after 1968'. M Hamel-Green 'Conscription and legitimacy, 1964–1972' *Melbourne Journal of Politics* No. 7 1974–75, pp. 11–12. A more cautious view is M J Saunders 'The Vietnam Moratorium Movement in Australia: 1969–73' Department of History, James Cook University, n.d., pp. 127–130, pp.156–157. On the impact of demonstrations in America and Australia, see E M Schreiber 'American politics and the Vietnam issue: demonstrators, votes and public opinion' *Politics* Vol. 10 No. 2, Nov. 1975, pp. 207–209; C A Rootes 'On "Demonstrations, votes and public opinion" ' *Politics* Vol. 13, No. 2, Nov. 1978, pp. 329–331; 'E M Schreiber 'Reply to Rootes' ibid. pp. 331–333.
28 Dennis Altman 'Australia and Vietnam: Some preliminary speculations' *Australian Quarterly* Vol. 42, No. 2, June 1970, p. 62; reprinted, as 'A more general and considered view of The Vietnam War' in *Coming out in the Seventies* Ringwood: Penguin, 1980, p. 179
29 Murray Goot *Policies and Partisans* University of Sydney, Department of Government and Public Administration, Occasional Monograph No. 1, 1969, pp. 67 and 75
30 Murray Goot and R W Connell *Social Patterns in Public Opinion* (forthcoming)
31 See M Useem *Conscription Protest and Social Conflict* N.Y:, John Wiley, 1973, pp. 109–110, for the *US*.
32 Compare the claim that there were 'no clear sex differences' and that 'young people generally were far more likely to oppose all aspects of conscription than older people'. Hamel-Green *loc. cit.*
33 See Murray Goot, 'Beyond the generation gap' in H Mayer, ed *Australian Politics: A*

ENDNOTES

Second Reader Melbourne: Cheshire, 1969, pp. 166-172
34 For the high proportion of professionals (students and fully-fledged) in the moratorium marches, see J W Berry 'Who are the marchers?' *Politics* Vol. 3 No. 2, Nov. 1968, pp. 163-175; 'The Vietnam marchers', in H Mayer, ed. *op. cit.*, pp. 205-207.
35 See the interesting discussion of 'domain legitimacy', Hamel-Green *Op. cit.*, p. 12-15
36 A Hughes *Psychology and the Political Experience* London: Cambridge University Press, 1975, pp. 132-134
37 L Mann 'Attitudes towards My Lai and obedience to orders: an Australian survey' *Australian Journal of Psychology*, Vol. 25, No. 1, April 1973, pp. 17-21
38 Hughes *op. cit.*, pp. 198-200; Aitkin *op. cit.*, pp. 276-288; Tiffen *op. cit.*
39 R W Connell *The Child's Construction of Politics* Melbourne: Melbourne University Press, 1971, Ch. 5
40 Tiffen *op. cit.*, pp. 349-354
41 Aitkin *op. cit.*, pp. 235
42 D W Rawson 'The Vietnam war and the Australian party system' *Australian Outlook* Vol. 23, No. 1, April 1969, p. 67
43 C A Hughes and B D Graham *A Handbook of Australian Government and Politics 1890-1964* Canberra: ANU Press, 1968, pp. 374-419; C A Hughes *A Handbook of Australian Government and Politics 1965-1974* Canberra: ANU Press, 1977, pp. 79-94. On professional support for the Australia Party, see D. Kemp 'Social Change and the future of the political parties: the Australian case', in L Maisel and P M Sacks, eds. *The Future of Political Parties* Beverly Hills: Sage, 1975, pp. 153-159.
44 R W Connell and Murray Goot 'The end of class, re-run' *Meanjin* Vol. 38, No. 1, Autumn, 1979, p. 15
45 Denis P Altman 'Foreign policy and the elections' *Politics* Vol. 2, No.1, May 1967, p. 57
46 Hamel-Green *op. cit.*, p. 15
47 See C A Hughes 'The rational voter and Australian foreign policy' *Australian Outlook* Vol. 24, No. 1, April 1970, pp. 5-6; N Harper 'Australia and the United States' in G Greenwood and N Harper, eds *Australia in World Affairs* Melbourne: Cheshire, 1974, p. 294; A. Hughes 'Psychological disposition and political attitudes' PhD thesis, ANU, 1970, ch. 8, for three different accounts of the 'importance' of Vietnam and conscription in 1966.
48 For an earlier critique of this question, see D W Rawson 'Foreign Policy and the Political Parties' in Max Teichmann, ed. *New Directions in Australian Foreign Policy* Ringwood: Penguin, 1969, pp. 22-25
49 Aitkin, *op. cit.*, p. 228
50 *Ibid*, pp. 231-232, 234-235. Unfortunately Aitkin does not address himself to the differences between his own data and the findings of the public opinion polls.
51 Susan Read 'How electors confound the pundits: The Vietnam War, 1969' *Politics* Vol. 10, No. 2, Nov. 1975, pp. 200-206
52 Spectrum International Marketing Services 'Political parties, leaders and issues: a pilot study of voters' attitudes conducted for the Australian Labor Party', Sydney, 1971, p. 53
53 McNair Surveys 'Reasons for the swing to Labor: the Federal election, December 2, 1971' Australian Broadcasting Commission, n.d., pp. 5-6
54 Both surveys, specially commissioned, are reported in Arthur Huck 'A note on the Volatility of Threats' *Australian Outlook* Vol. 35, No. 1, April 1981, pp. 88-91. The survey is wrongly attributed to the APOP (McNair).
55 ibid.
56 *Perspectives on Productivity: Australia* Sydney: Sentry Holdings Ltd, 1981, pp. 37-8
57 For Aitkin's 1979 data, see 'Macquarie University Australia Political Attitudes Survey 1979', n.d., p. 24
58 Kenneth Rivett 'Towards a policy on refugees' *Australian Outlook* Vol. 33, No. 2, August 1979, p. 149. Refugee arrivals from Asian countries amounted to 40,000 by

September 1980, with 8478 in 1977-78 and 14,000 expected in 1980-81. See also 'Australia's Policy on Refugees' Department of Immigration and Ethnic Affairs, 1980.
59 Morgan has claimed that people's knowledge of issues makes no difference to their responses. (Roy Morgan interviewed by Murray Goot). Since the Morgan poll rarely fathoms these depths the basis of his statement remains obscure. Certainly one finding on Vietnamese refugees contradicts his claim. Less than a quarter knew Mr Mackellar was the minister responsible for refugees. However, of those who knew this a majority approved his handling of the job, while only 30 per cent of the uninformed did so. In a sample of 100 Melbournians, c. 1969, the threat of China was stronger among the less knowledgeable. Jonathan King ' "A big ogre, an illiterate giant" ' *Australian Outlook* Vol. 24, No. 3, December 1970, pp. 320-327.

8 News coverage of Vietnam   Rodney Tiffen

1 Elaborations of newsmaking perspectives can be found in L Sigal, *Reporters and Officials* Lexington, Mass: Heath, 1973; G Tuchman, *Making News: A Study in the Construction of Reality* New York: Free Press, 1978; H Gans *Deciding What's News* New York: Pantheon Books, 1979; R Tiffen, *The News from Southeast Asia, The Sociology of Newsmaking* Singapore: Institute of Southeast Asian Studies, 1978.
2 More data on the news agencies can be found in Tiffen *op. cit.* A summary of the structure of the Australian press can be found in H Mayer, 'Media' in H Mayer and H Nelson (eds) *Australian Politics: 5* Melbourne: Longman Cheshire, 1980. In this chapter most attention is given to *The Age*, *The Herald*, and *Sydney Morning Herald* and *The Australian*.
3 B Cohen *The Press and Foreign Policy* Princeton, NJ: Princeton University Press, 1963, p. 13
4 Few are completely immune either, to the private displeasure of government leaders. As is well-known, Dean Rusk chastised journalists for lack of patriotism during the Tet offensive: 'There gets to be a point, when the question is whose side are you on. I'm Secretary of State and I'm on our side.' D Wise *The Politics of Lying, Government Deception, Secrecy and Power* New York: Random House, 1978, p. 311; W Small, *To Kill a Messenger: TV News and the Real World* New York: Hastings House, 1970, p. 124.

A much less well-known example followed Morley Safer's report of the Americans burning the village of Cam Ne. CBS Vice President Frank Stanton received a call from his close friend Lyndon Johnson:

' "Frank," said the early morning wake-up call, "are you trying to fuck me?" "Who is this?" said the still sleepy Stanton.
"Frank, this is your President, and yesterday your boys shat on the American flag," Lyndon Johnson said, and then administered a tongue lashing: how could CBS employ a Communist like Safer, how could they be so unpatriotic as to put on enemy film like this? ... '
CBS executives, talking to Stanton in the days following the incident, knew that Stanton had it in for Safer, that he would have dearly liked to dump him ... And there was at CBS in the next couple of weeks a constant effort to get more positive things on the air to balance the Safer report: D Halberstram *The Powers that Be* New York: Alfred A Knopf, 1979, pp. 490-1.

5 P Knightley *The First Casualty* London: Harcourt Brace Jovanovich, 1975 pp. 377, 379
6 E J Epstein *News From Nowhere* New York: Random House, 1973, p. 250; Tiffen *op. cit.*, p. 113
7 See eg T Crouse *The Boys on the Bus* New York: Ballantine Books, 1973
8 Knightley *op. cit.*, p. 423. Michael Herr has claimed that 'Conventional journalism

ENDNOTES

could no more reveal this war than conventional firepower could win it' (*ibid.*). There were few examples of 'new journalism' from Vietnam. The most notable were Herr's own *Dispatches* London: Picador, 1977 and Tomalin's 'The General Goes Zapping Charlie Cong' in T Wolfe and E W Johnson (eds) *The New Journalism* London: Picador, 1975. More within the journalistic mainstream, there was some inspired feature writing, which helped to make the human realities of Vietnam more real for a western audience. Dan Southerland of the *Christian Science Monitor* went into a village which was government-controlled by day and Viet Cong controlled by night, and described the changes between day and night, such as the meek coffee shop owner becoming the steely-eyed cadre. This vignette, full of interest itself, also gave insight into the nature of the war.

9 Further information on the Saigon press corps in the Diem period can be found in Knightley *op. cit.*, pp. 374–381; J Aronson 'The Media and the Message' in N Chomsky and H Zinn (eds) *The Pentagon Papers: Volume V. Critical Essays* Boston: Beacon Press, 1972; J Hohenberg *Between Two Worlds* New York: Praeger, 1967; D Halberstam *The Making of a Quagmire* London: Bodley Head, 1965; D Halberstam *The Powers That Be* New York: Alfred A Knopf, 1979, pp. 459–467; M Browne, 'Vietnam Reporting: Three Years of Crisis' in A Balk and J Boylan (eds) *Our Troubled Press* Boston: Little Brown, 1971; S Karnow 'The Newsmen's War in Vietnam' in L Lyons (ed.) *Reporting the News* Cambridge, Mass: Harvard University Press, 1965; D Warner *Not With Guns Alone* Melbourne: Hutchinson, 1977, pp. 117–29.
10 Hohenberg *op. cit.*, p. 38
11 D Halberstam *The Powers That Be*, pp. 445–6
12 M Browne, *op. cit.*, p. 102
13 The Australian government upheld an almost unlimited right to censorship at that time in its decision to ban a BBC film that might cause offence to France. Deputy Prime Minister McEwen said:

> The truth of the matter is that the the government of the country, whatever party forms it, should have the right and should exercise the right to control anything which in its judgement will impair friendly relations with any ally: *Commonwealth Parliamentary Debates* Vol. 38, 23 March 1963, p. 151

14 D Marr *Barwick* Sydney: George Allen and Unwin, 1980, p. 183
15 *The Pentagon Papers* New York: New York Times edn, 1971, pp. 269–70
16 G Kahin and J Lewis *The United States in Vietnam* New York: Delta, 1969, p. 157
17 Aronson *op. cit.*, p. 219; Shurmann *et al. The Politics of Escalation in Vietnam* New York: Fawcett, 1966, p. 36.
18 Within these limits there was some good analysis, notably by Bruce Grant: *The Age* 6 August 1964. More generally on the Tonkin Gulf incident, see J Goulden *Truth is the First Casualty* Chicago: Rand, 1969; D Stillman 'Tonkin: What Should Have Been Asked?' *Columbia Journalism Review* Winter, 1970; W Lutz ed. *The Age of Communication* Pacific Palisades, Calif: Goodyear Publishing Co. Inc., 1974.
19 P Geyelin 'The Press', in A Lake *The Vietnam Legacy* New York: New York University Press, 1976, pp. 166–69; M Charlton and A Moncrieff *Many Reasons Why* Harmondsworth, England: Penguin, 1977
20 Geyelin *op. cit.*, pp. 182–3
21 More information on Australian escalation can be found in H Albinski *Politics and Foreign Policy in Australia: The Impact of Vietnam and Conscription* Durham, North Carolina: Duke University Press, 1970; A Watt, *The Evolution of Australian Foreign Policy* London: Cambridge University Press, 1967; A Watt *Vietnam* Melbourne: Cheshire, 1968; A Renouf *The Frightened Country* Melbourne: Macmillan, 1979; T E Millar *Australia in Peace and War* Canberra: ANU Press, 1978; E Whitton *The National Times* 28 April 1975, 5 May 1975, 11 May 1975.
22 *The Australian* editorial was headed 'The War That Can't Be Won', and asserted: 'The

Menzies Government has made a reckless decision on Vietnam ...', concluding 'It could be that our historians will recall this day with tears' 30 April 1965.

23 P Braestrup *Big Story: How the American Press and Television Reported and Interpreted the Crisis of Tet 1968 in Vietnam and Washington* (2 Vols.) New York: Anchor Books, 1979; P Arnett 'Tet coverage; a debate renewed' *Columbia Journalism Review* January/February 1978, p. 46.
24 Knightley *op. cit.*, p. 399
25 Epstein *op. cit.*, p. 17-8
26 S Hersh 'The Story Everyone Ignored' *Columbia Journalism Review*, Winter, 1969/70; L Downie *The New Muckrakers* Washington; New Republic Books, 1976
27 Knightley *op. cit.*, pp. 390-98; Sigal *op. cit.*, p. 41
28 Knightley *op. cit.*, pp. 399-400; N Chomsky and E S Herman *The Washington Connection and Third World Fascism: The Political Economy of Human Rights Vol. 1*, Boston: South End Press, 1979, p. 313ff.
29 See eg C Lloyd 'The Parliamentary Press Gallery', MA thesis, ANU, 1980
30 The prime example was Wilfred Burchett, an Australian communist journalist who had excellent access and wide experience in North Vietnam. No Australian daily paper was interested in Burchett's writings, presumably on the grounds that he was not a *bona fide* journalist. In addition, there was almost no use of the French material emanating from *Le Monde*, Agence France Presse and other sources in North Vietnam.
31 J O'Hara 'Press coverage of the First Vietnam Moratorium Demonstration' *Melbourne Journal of Politics*, No. 6, 1973
32 *The Age* actually closed its Singapore bureau for about six months in 1971. The previous correspondent had been John Bennetts, who later went to work for the Joint Intelligence Organization. It is widely believed among journalists that he was working for Australian intelligence while still employed by *The Age*.
33 Warner first visited Vietnam in 1949, and was a frequent visitor until 1975. His work appeared in Herald and Weekly Times publications, the *Sydney Morning Herald*, as a commentator on Melbourne's Channel Seven, and in various overseas publications. He was the most influential Australian correspondent, and was never shy about mixing advocacy and journalism. Interesting insights into his work and attitudes can be found in his *Not With Guns Alone*. The flavour of his views can be gained from this statement, made after Australia's first commitment of troops: 'But for the power of the Seventh Fleet and American economic aid, I'm sure all of Asia would have collapsed into communism long ago': *Sydney Morning Herald* 1 May 1965.
34 For the internal debates in John Fairfax & Sons Ltd, see Gavin Souter *Company of Heralds: A Century and half of Australian publishing by John Fairfax Limited and its predecessors 1831-1981* Melbourne: Melbourne University Press, 1981, especially pp. 429-34 and pp. 478-80.
35 These quotations can be found in: Aronson *op. cit.*, p. 56; M Taylor 'Waging Negotiations' in A Lake ed. *op. cit.*; Charlton and Moncrieff *op. cit.*, pp. 150-1
36 See eg Chomsky and Herman *op. cit.*, and N Chomsky and E S Herman *After the Cataclysm. Post-war Indochina and the Reconstruction of Imperial Ideology. The Political Economy of Human Rights Vol. 2* Boston: South End Press, 1980
37 See eg D McQuail 'Mass Media Effects' in J Curran *et al.* eds, *Mass Communication and Society* London: Edward Arnold, 1977.
38 F Wertham 'Is TV hardening us to the war in Vietnam?' in O Larsen ed. *Violence and the Mass Media* New York: Harper and Row, 1966
39 Accounts of Safer's story on Cam Ne can be found in Halberstam *op. cit.*, pp. 486-92; Small *op. cit.*, pp. 99-101; G P Gates *Air Time: The Inside Story of CBS News* New York: Berkeley Publishing Co., 1978, pp. 166-70; Charlton and Moncrieff *op. cit.*, pp. 152-3
40 More information on the execution by General Loan can be found in G Bailey and L Lichty 'Rough Justice on a Saigon Street: A gatekeeper study of NBC's Tet execution film' *Journalism Quarterly* Vol. 49, Summer 1972, and D Culbert 'Historians and the

Visual Analysis of Television News' in W Adams and F Schreibman eds *Television Network News* Washington: George Washington University, 1978. The effects of TV coverage is the most interesting question for media theory to emerge from the war, but unfortunately it is largely irrelevant to Australia. Only the ABC attempted regular coverage. Compared to American audiences, we saw much less, and much less graphic, TV news.

41 H Salisbury *Behind The Lines—Hanoi* New York: New York Times, 1967
42 News of the My Lai massacre was revealed by Seymour Hersh through the shoe-string Despatch News Agency in late 1969, 18 months after it occurred. The trial of Lt Calley was held in early 1971—keeping the question of atrocities before the public eye.

The relation between mainstream media and fringe media is very different in the US and Australia, partly due to the wider spectrum of political publications in the US which helps support something like Despatch. Editors on the *New York Times* were more likely to take seriously stories appearing in *New Republic, Nation* or *Ramparts*, than were *Sydney Morning Herald* editors to seek out stories appearing in *Tribune* or *National U*. The American fringe media were responsible for uncovering several stories that the mainstream media later took up, such as My Lai, and the Con Son tiger cages.

43 Geyelin described the publication of the Pentagon Papers as the most monumental security breach in American history: *op. cit.*, p. 192. More detail on the Pentagon Papers can be found in J Witcover 'Two Weeks That Shook The Press' *Columbia Journalism Review* Winter 1971, Charlton and Moncrieff *op. cit.*; Aronson *op. cit.*; Halberstam, *op. cit.*, and E J Epstein *Between Fact and Fiction* New York: Vintage Books, 1975.

Brian Toohey has revealed secret testimony from the court case where the US government tried to prevent publication of the Papers. One argument used was that the disclosures would weaken the McMahon government, and that this would be a serious blow to US security interests. The most revealing information about Australia to emerge from the Papers is just how little we counted in US thinking and decision-making: *National Times* 26 October 1980.

44 The two most notable reconstructions were J Goulden *op. cit.*, and W Shawcross *Sideshow: Kissinger, Nixon and the Destruction of Cambodia* London: Fontana, 1980. The most important Australian effort was Evan Whitton's series in the *National Times*: 28 April 1975, 5 May 1975, 12 May 1975, which remains an important source for anyone examining Australian policy. This series was also notable for the heavy-handed attempts by the Fairfax management to intervene in the publication of the second and third articles. The alterations made were fairly peripheral. For a full list of the excisions see 'Sir Warwick Re-writes the Truth about Vietnam' *New Journalist* No. 18, May 1975. See also G Souter *op. cit.*, pp. 489–494.

9 Conclusion   Peter King

1 'Australia and Vietnam, 1950–1980' Part II, *Dyason House Papers* Vol. 6 No. 2, March 1980, p.11
2 *Documents on Australian Defence and Foreign Policy 1968-1975* J R Walsh and G J Munster ed. and pub.), Sydney, 1980, pp. 151–2
3 ibid., p. 153
4 ibid., p. 154
5 See Hamish McDonald *Suharto's Indonesia* Melbourne: Fontana, 1980.
6 C H A East 'TNI—the Indonesian National Army', *Pacific Defence Reporter*, Vol. VII, No. 8, February 1981
7 ibid
8 *Australia and the Third World* Canberra: Australian Government Publishing Service, 1979
9 See Peter King and Martin Indyk 'Australia's Relations with the Third World: A

Critique of the Harries Report' *Current Affairs Bulletin*, Vol. 56, No. 12, May 1980
10 *Australia and the Third World* pp. 111 and 154
11 ibid., p. 81
12 Peter King 'Beyond the National Interest: Australian Foreign Policy in the 1980s,' in Henry Mayer and Helen Nelson (ed), *Australian Politics: a Fifth Reader* Sydney: Longman Cheshire, 1980.

Index

'Abolish Conscription Now' 111; *see also* draft resistance
Aboriginal poverty 150
Adelaide 108, 116
Afghanistan 30, 191
Africa 32, 162
Age 130, 157, 166, 169, 177, 180-2, 184; poll 157-9, 161-3; *see also* news coverage, opinion polls
agent orange 15, 96, 98-9
Aitkin, Don 131, 144, 149-50, 153-5, 158-9; *see also* opinion polls
Alsop, Joseph 171
Altman, Dennis 131, 146, 151; *see also* opinion polls
Amalgamated Engineering Union (AEU) 113, 116
American alliance 15, 26, 36-7, 40-2, 46, 49, 52, 56, 156, 164, 173-4, 180, 196
American Broadcasting Corporation 178
American lackey 30; *see also* American alliance
American strategic facilities 39, 192; *see also* North West Cape
Anderson, R 126
Anthony MP, Douglas 18; *see also* Liberal Country Party coalition
anti-communism 9-11, 18, 32-3, 100, 169, 195
ANZUS 37, 58, 159, 192, 196
Armstrong, Karl 112
Arnett, Peter 170, 177
ASEAN 11, 191-2, 195-6
Ashcroft, Ms Pat 108; *see also* draft resistance
Asian Yugoslavia 190
Australia Party 151
Australian 28, 130, 177, 184 *see also* news coverage

Australian Air Force 58, 158
Australian Army in Vietnam 56-99; Army Task Force 13, 15, 58, 60-72; Army Training Team 12, 58-9, 68, 70, 72, 82; casualties 56; Civic Action 15, 66, 81; COMAFV 63; Logistics Support Group 72; military instructors 41, 59; Mobile Advisory Training Team 68; Special Air Service 72, 80, 91, 96; *1RAR* 59, 72; *2RAR* 80; *4RAR* 80; *5RAR* 63, 66
Australian Broadcasting Commission 166
Australian defence policy 37-8, 42, 58, 102, 157-8, 164; *see also* Australian Labor Party, conscription, Liberal Party
Australian foreign policy 12, 18, 21-2, 24-5, 27-8, 30-2, 34, 37, 58-9, 193; lack of professionalism 31
Australian government 18, 21-3, 25-32, 34, 46, 59, 114, 120, 131, 171; *see also* Australian Labor Party, Liberal Party of Australia
Australian Institute of Political Science 103
Australian Labor Party 10, 13, 16, 28-9, 34, 36-44, 45, 47-9, 91, 102, 104, 106-9, 111, 125, 127, 136, 142, 146-7, 150-2, 154-5, 157, 161, 164, 172, 174, 178-9; Federal Conferences *1963*, 37, 38, 40, *1965* 47, 49, *1967* 52, *1971* 125; Foreign Affairs & Defence Committee 13, 37-8, 40, 42, 44-5, 47-9,.51-2; Labor government 12, 31, 35, 70, 141-3, 158, 161, 169, 181, 184, 188, 193; NSW Branch 28, 42; Victorian Branch 29, 46-7, 125; Western Australian Branch 38
Australian National University 34, 147-8
Australian Nationwide Opinion Polls 127, 130-31, 141-2, 144, 148, 156-7, 159; *see*

also opinion polls
Australian Navy, 58, 158
Australian No-Conscription Fellowship 109
Australian press 16, 165–87; *see also* news coverage
Australian Sales Research Bureau 126, 130–31, 144–5, 147; *see also* opinion polls

Barnard MP, Lance 13, 51–4; *see also* Australian Labour Party
Barwick MP, Sir Garfield 20, 104, 171, 174; *see also* Liberal Party
Batt MP, Neil 52; *see also* Australian Labor Party
'Battle of Sydney' 114; *see also* draft resistance
Beazley MP, Kim 39, 45, 48, 50–1, 53, 105, 178; *see also* Australian Labor Party
Ben Tue 176
Berry, J.W. 131
B-52 bombers 159, 193
Bien Hoa 59, 72, 83, 173
Bigart, Homer 170
Bill White Conscientious Objectors' Defence Committee 110; *see also* draft resistance
Binh Gia 81
Birch, Charles 115; *see also* draft resistance
Bissett, David 112
Bonnet MP, 'Duke' 120; *see also* Liberal Party
Bowen, Attorney-General Nigel 115; *see also* Liberal Party
Braestrup, Peter 175–7
Brisbane 108, 114
Browne, Malcolm 170
Bryant MP, Gordon 45; *see also* Australian Labor Party
Buckley, Kevin 179
Buddhism 170, 183, 186
Bulletin 130 *see also* news coverage, opinion polls
Bundy, McGeorge 173
Bundy, William 105
Burchett, Wilfred, 21–2
Burgess, Pat 82, 175
Burns, Creighton 184

Cairns MP, J.F. 13, 29–30, 40–1, 43–5, 50–1, 53, 105–6, 114, 182, 184; *see also* Australian Labor Party
Calder MP, Sam 120; *see also* Liberal

Country Party coalition
Calwell MP, Arthur 13, 28–9, 37, 39, 41–2, 44–52, 104–5, 111, 131, 178; *see also* Australian Labor Party
Cambodia 11, 31, 42, 54, 60, 123, 132, 140–1, 148, 156, 161, 178–9, 186; *see also* Kampuchea
Cameron MP, Clyde 39, 44, 105–6; *see also* Australian Labor Party
Cam Ne 186
Campbell, Chris 111
Canada 21, 105
Cantril, Hadley 132
Canungra 77
Carlton (Melb) 114, 120
Carmichael Jr, Laurie 112, 116, 122
Casey, Lord 169, 171, 174; *see also* Liberal Party
Catholics 61, 81, 169
Catholic Worker group 123
Chamberlain, F.E. 38, 52; *see also* Australian Labor Party
China, People's Republic of, 9, 11–13, 17, 31, 33–4, 39–40, 45–6, 53, 133–4, 138, 147, 150, 156–7, 161, 172, 174, 180–1, 184, 188, 190–2, 195; 'aggression' 30, 191–2; cultural revolution 26, 34; and India 24, 29, 46; and USA 188; and USSR 20, 21, 25, 180
Chou En-lai 23, 25–7; *see also* China
Christofides, L. 115
Churchill, Sir Winston 169
civil disobedience 111, 121, 125
civil liberty 145, 164
Cohen, Senator Sam 47, 51, 166; *see also* Australian Labor Party
Cold War 38, 133, 195
COMECON 190
Committee in Defiance of the National Service Act 115, 117–8, 121; *see also* draft resistance
Commonwealth Crimes Act 113–4
Commonwealth Police 114, 123–5; *see also* police
communism 41, 47, 100–4, 133–4, 147, 156, 168–9, 172, 174–5, 180–2, 185, 188–90, 193, 195
Congress for Cultural Freedom 29
Congress for International Co-operation and Disarmament 113, 116
Connell, Robert 131, 149
conscientious objectors 16, 94, 101, 109–10, 112, 144–5, 164; absolute pacifism 110; *see also* draft resistance

INDEX

conscription 12, 17, 100-3, 132, 142, 146-8, 151-2, 155, 164, 188; conscripts 17, 42, 93, 143, 146-7; see also draft resistance, national service
Conscription Protest Meeting Committee 107
conscription referenda 1916-17 100
Cook, Gary 123
Cormack, Senator Sir Magnus 120; see also Liberal Party
'corpse-counting' 16
corruption 14, 169, 186, 194
Curtin, PM, John 131
Cutler, Sir Roden 116, 126

Da Nang 173
Daily Telegraph 177; see also news coverage
Dalton, Tony 112, 124
Dat Do 61-2, 66-7, 71
Deamer, Adrian 184
Democratic Labor Party 27, 102, 104
Democratic Republic of Vietnam (DRV) 10-13, 18-21, 25, 29-30, 32, 42-3, 45, 48, 52, 61, 63, 69, 139, 141, 149-50, 168, 172-3, 176, 179, 181, 185-6, 188-9, 192; Peoples's Army of Vietnam 64-6, 69
demonstrators 145-6, 148, 164, 170; see also draft resistance
Deng Xiaoping 26, 34; see also China
Diem, Ngo Dinh 21, 42, 46, 62, 100, 134, 167-71, 186
Dien Bien Phu 176
direct action 111, 118; see also draft resistance
Dissent 28
Djakarta see Indonesia
domino theory 10-12, 26, 30, 111, 189
'Don't Register!' 114, 121
draft card burnings 109; see also draft resistance
draft resistance 16, 100-128, 164; in America 11; see also conscription, national service
Draft Resistance Conference 114
Draft Resistance Movement (DRM) 113, 127
Draft Resisters' Union 120-23, 127
drugs 86, 89-90
Duke, John 107
Dunstan, Premier Don 125; see also Australian Labor Party

East Timor 30, 39, 193-4

Eastern Europe 26, 30, 190
editors 165-6, 173, 178; see also news coverage
Eisenhower, US President Dwight 11
elections 15, 37, 132; *1966* Reps 36, 54; *1967* Senate 36; *1969* Reps 36
Europe 32, 39; see also North Atlantic Treaty Organisation
Evatt MP, H. V. 27, 48, 52, 171; see also Australian Labor Party
Evening News 178; see also news coverage

Fairhall, MP, Alan 116, 175; see also Liberal Party
Felt, US Admiral 170
'fight them there rather than here' 146, 149; see also opinion polls
Finland 44, 190
First Indo-China War 10
Fitzgerald, Stephen 28; see also Australian foreign policy
'five o'clock follies' 166
Flinders University 116
Foley, Sean 112
Forbes, MP, A.J. 104, 127; see also Liberal Party
Ford, US President Gerald 181
Fox, Paul 123
France 10, 12, 14, 61, 133, 141, 168-9, 174, 185, 188
Fraser MP, Alan 43, 47, 49; see also Australian Labor Party
Fraser, Malcolm 14, 17, 21, 34, 59, 157, 195; Fraser government 158, 162, 188, 192; see also Liberal Party
Free, Lloyd 132
'Free Ross' 113
'Free Zarb' 113
'Freedom Ride' 116
French Indo-China 133, 168; see also France
Fretilin 194; see also East Timor
Fulbright, US Senator William 172

Gallup International 117, 126, 130, 132, 137; see also Morgan, Roy
Galvin MP, Patrick 44; see also Australian Labor Party
Geneva Conference *1954* 42, 48, 50, 100, 169
Germany 185, 194
Giap, Gen. Vo Nguyen 177
Gilling, Jeremy 112
Goldwater, US Senator Barry 42, 103, 136, 172

Golgerth, Joyce 108; *see also* draft resistance
Gorton PM, John 12, 26, 53, 113, 117, 123, 131, 135, 177–8, 180; *see also* Liberal Party
Grant, Bruce 171, 184
Greenwood, Senator Ivor 120–1, 123–4, 126; *see also* Liberal Party
Gromyko, Andrei 18–19; *see also* Soviet Union
guerrilla 14, 30, 32, 102, 182

Haiphong 139
Halberstam, David 16, 168, 170
Hamel-Green, Michael 149, 151; *see also* draft resistance
Hanoi *see* Democratic Republic of Vietnam
Hansen Rubensohn-McCann Erickson 131, 132; *see also* Australian Labor Party
Harries, Owen 195
Hartley, W.H. 41; *see also* Australian Labor Party
Hasluck MP, Sir Paul 18–21, 23, 26, 30, 34, 61, 174; *see also* Liberal Party
Hayden MP, Bill 30, 44: *see also* Australian Labor Party
Haylen MP, Les 40; *see also* Australian Labor Party
Heldzingen, Errol 111
Herald and Weekly Times group 130; *see also* news coverage
Herald, (Melbourne) 166; *see also* news coverage
Hicks, Jonathon 112
Higgins, Marguerite 171
Hilsman, Roger 103
Hitler, Adolph 26
Hoa Long 15, 66, 68, 82
Holsworthy 112
Holt PM, Harold 49–50, 108–9, 131, 134–5, 139, 173–4; *see also* Liberal Party
Hong Kong 22–3, 31
Hughes MP, Wilfred Kent 102–3, 121, 149; *see also* Liberal Party
Hughes PM, William 100, 105
Hull, Cordell 132
Humphrey, US Senator Hubert 47–8

ideology 36, 165, 176, 185
India 20, 24–5, 29, 40
Indian Ocean 17, 38
Indo-China 23–5, 118, 133, 147, 156, 161–2, 178, 188–91, 196; *see also*
Southeast Asia
Indonesia 26, 30–1, 39, 58, 105, 111, 159, 161, 174, 189, 192–6; Communist Party 194
intelligence agencies 33, 35
international news agencies 166

Japan 26, 30–1, 35, 159, 194, 196; NARA Treaty 35
Jensen, Graham 112
Jess MP, John 102, 120; *see also* Liberal Party
Johnson, Barry 124–5
Johnson, US President Lyndon 11, 16, 28–9, 41–4, 48, 54, 103–5, 109, 132, 136, 139, 146, 169, 172, 174–5, 180; administration 41–2, 54, 102, 104, 175
Johnson MP, Les 105; *see also* Australian Labor Party
Jones MP, Charles 49; *see also* Australian Labor Party
Jones, Mike 112

Kampuchea 161, 188–92; *see also* Cambodia
Kapooka 74
Kennedy administration 40, 41, 54, 102
Kennedy, US Senator Robert 46, 102, 170, 175
Kennelly, Senator Patrick 49; *see also* Australian Labor Party
Khanh, Nguyen 172
Khe Sanh 176
Khmers Rouges 11, 188, 190–2, 195; *see also* Cambodia, Kampuchea
Kissinger, Henry 177, 180
Knightley, Phillip 178–9
Korea 11, 33, 43, 89, 95, 156; war 12, 56, 101, 177
Kosygin, USSR Premier Alexei 18–20; *see also* Soviet Union
Ky, Premier Nguyen Cao 135; *see also* South Vietnam

Labor Club, Monash University 113
Laos 31, 42, 46, 54, 105, 118, 133, 166, 178–9 186, 192
Latrobe University 116
Lee Kwan Yew 28, 33, 38; *see also* Singapore
Liberal Party of Australia 106, 116, 152, 164; Liberal Country Party coalition 26–7, 54–5, 78, 103, 147, 150, 153, 155, 193; in government 36, 73, 100, 111,

INDEX

144, 146, 152, 157-8, 171-2, 174, 180, 184; voters 111, 152, 155
Liberal Reform Party 150
Lippmann, Walter 167
Liu Shao-chi 26; see also China
Loan, General 186
Lon Nol 11; see also Cambodia
Long Dien 61
Long Hai 61, 66-7
Long Son 82
Long Tan 66, 80, 82

Macartney, Roy 184
Malaya 37-8, 59, 174
Malaysia 38-9, 42, 46, 58, 111, 153, 156
manufacture of opinion 15; see also opinion polls
marijuana 86, 90
Martin, Charles 115
Matteson, Mike 111, 124-5
Melbourne 106, 108-14, 118, 120-3, 131, 149
Melbourne University 113, 123-4, 147; Union 124
Menadue, John 144; see also Australian Labor Party
Menzies, R.G. 10, 17, 31, 41, 49, 59, 104-5, 131, 134, 146; Menzies government 101-4, 173; see also Liberal Party;
Millar, T.B. 102-4; see also conscription
Mohr, Charles 171
Monash University 113
Morgan, Roy 130-2, 137-8, 152; Morgan Gallup Polls 130, 132-48, 151-2, 154-9, 162-4; Morgan Gallup Consumer Omnibus Survey 130; see also opinion polls
Mowbray, David, Robert & Graham 112
Mullens, Geoff 112
multinational corporations 194
Murdoch, Rupert 130, 184; see also news coverage
Murphy, Senator Lionel 51; see also Australian Labor Party
My Lai 77, 95, 131, 149, 179, 186
MacKay, Ian 15
McCarthy, US Senator Eugene 175
McLeod, Ken 115
McMahon PM, William 12, 115, 131; government 180; see also Liberal Party
McNair Anderson Associates 130, 148, 155-6, 158, 162-3; see also opinion polls
McNamara, Robert 172

McNeill, Major I.G. 63, 68, 70

napalm 44
National Civic Council 102; see also Democratic Labor Party
National Liberation Front of Vietnam 10, 13, 17, 21, 25, 30, 59-70, 81, 118, 189; see also Viet Cong
national service 73-7, 88, 91-2, 94, 125, 142, 144-5, 152-3; 'nashos' 74-7, 88, 91-2, 94, 143; Act 104, 110, 112, 116, 120, 125-6; Department 116, 124; see also conscription, draft resistance
National Union of Australian University Students (NUAUS) 116
NBC News 167, 178, see also news coverage
New South Wales 49, 120
New York Times 169-70, 186; see also news coverage
New Zealand 20, 35, 38, 105; Passive Resisters Union 109
Newington College 125
news coverage 165-87
News Ltd 144
newspaper proprietors 165; see also Murdoch, Rupert
Newsweek 167, 169-70, 179; see also news coverage
Nhu, Madame 170-1
Nixon, US President Richard 10, 12, 53-4, 118, 140, 161, 166, 180; Administration 180, 186; doctrine 10, 53, 180
'No Conscripts for Vietnam' 111
North Atlantic Treaty Organisation 40
North Vietnam see Democratic Republic of Vietnam
North West Cape 13, 38, 40; see also American strategic facilities
Nui Dat 60, 64, 66, 68, 72, 77

O'Donnell, Denis 112
official censorship 166, 183
Oliver, Charles 38; see also Australian Labor Party
O'Neill, Robert 62, 66
'Operation Rolling Thunder' 13, 46, 54
'Operation Speedy Express' 179
opinion polls 15, 129-64; see also *Age* poll, Australian Nationwide Opinion Polls; Australian Sales Research Bureau, McNair Anderson Associates, Morgan Gallup Spectrum International

Pacific Ocean 17, 38, 89, 101, 161, 188
pacifism 42, 101, 111, 120; Federal Pacifist Council 109
Papua New Guinea 18, 39, 79, 123, 193-4, 196
paranoia 83; see also Australian troops in South Vietnam
Parkinson, Nicholas 189, 192, 195; see also Australian foreign policy
Paull, John 112
Peace Accords *1973* 148, 179
Peacock MP, Andrew 67, 188, 195; see also Liberal Party
Peking see China
Pentagon Papers 102-3, 185-6
Pentridge prison 112-13
Perkin, Graham 184
Perry, Mert 171
Perth 108
Petrov, Vladimir 27
Phan Rang 15
Philippines 105, 174, 192, 195
Phillipson, D. 112
Phnom Penh 11, 190-1; see also Cambodia, Kampuchea
Phuoc Hai 66, 71
Phuoc Tuy 14-15, 17, 58-71, 80, 82-3
Pleiku 173
Plimsoll, Sir James 20, 28, 33, 189-90; see also Australian foreign policy
Pol Pot 11, 188, 191; see also Cambodia, Kampuchea
police 109, 124; see also Commonwealth police
Presbyterian Church of Victoria 126
press corps 169, 171; see also news coverage
propaganda 166, 183, 185
Provisional Revolutionary Government of South Vietnam 142
public opinion 15, 39, 129-164; see also opinion polls
public war-weariness 168, 175; see also opinion polls
Puckapunyal 74, 108

Quadrant 29
Quakers 28, 109
Queensland 109, 120
Queensland University 113

racism 149, 163
Read, Susan 155
Reagan administration 192

refugees 15, 161-3, 169, 181, 189
Renouf, Alan 189; see also Australian foreign policy
repatriation 15, 97
Republic of Vietnam 10-11, 14, 21-2, 26, 28-9, 31-4, 59-60, 63, 69, 72, 79, 81, 102, 132, 134, 139, 142-50, 161, 166, 168-73, 176-89; aggression from the north 32; Army 59, 60, 62, 64-71, 182, 186
Resist 123
Returned Servicemen's League 93, 102-4, 158
Reynolds MP, Len 49; see also Australian Labor Party
Richardson, Michael 181, 184
Rivett, Kenneth 162
Robertson, Jim 170
Ross, Brian 112-13, 116, 121
Rung Sat 61
Rusk, Dean 34, 40, 103

Saigon press corps 169, 171, 186
Sale prison 113, 116
Salisbury, Harrison 186
Save Our Sons 108-9, 113, 116, 121-2
Scheyville Officer Training School 74
SEATO 29, 40, 46, 58, 103-4, 173
self-fulfilling prophecy 190
self-immolation 170, 186
Senate, Australian 106-7, 152
Serong, Brig. Ted 82
Shaplan, Robert 183
Shimkin, Alec 179
Sihanouk, Prince Norodom 11, 140, 191; see also Cambodia
Singapore 24, 33, 38, 78-9, 166, 192
Sinkiang 19-21, see also China
sit-ins 114
Smith, Terry 115
Snedden MP, Bill 115, 119-20, 127; see also Liberal Party
socialism 111, 195
Solomon, David 119
South Australia 120-1, 124
South Vietnam see Republic of Vietnam
Southeast Asia 24, 102-3, 156-7, 161-2, 164, 167, 188-90, 192-3, 195; see also Indo-China
Spectrum International 155; see also opinion polls
Spender MP, Sir Percy 174; see also Liberal Party
Stalin, Josef 27, 191; see also USSR

INDEX

state aid for private schools 37
'Statement of Defiance' 115
Stewart MP, F.R. 44; *see also* Australian Labor Party
Students for Democratic Action (SDA) 113
Students for a Democratic Society (SDS) 113
subversion 102, 189
Suharto, Gen. 193-5; *see also* Indonesia
Sully, Francois 167, 170
Sulzberger, Arthur Ochs 170
Sun 175; *see also* news coverage
survey research 130-1; *see also* opinion polls
Sydney 106, 108-9, 111-4, 116, 124, 167, 175
Sydney Morning Herald 125, 130, 148, 166, 169, 175, 177, 181-4; *see also* news coverage
Sydney University 20, 113-14, 116, 125, 147; Regiment 116

Taiwan 22-3, 27, 29, 34, 39, 192
Tasmania University 113, 147
Taylor, US Gen. Maxwell 185-6
Tet offensive 16, 53, 66, 135, 168, 175-9, 186
Thailand 105, 111, 123, 133-4, 156, 174, 181, 189-92, 195
Thanat Khoman 40
Thayer, Carlyle 188
Thieu, Nguyen Van 182
'This Day Tonight' 124
threat 15, 102, 104, 174, 189; from the north 111
Tiffen, Rodney 131, 144, 149
Time Magazine 169, 171; *see also* news coverage
Tokyo *see* Japan
Ton San Nhut 22
Tonkin Gulf incident 16, 42-3, 104-6, 166, 168, 171, 173
Townsend, Simon 112
trade unions 121, 127
Trathen, Rev. D.A. 126
Truscott, Len, 112
Turner, Ian 123; *see also* draft resistance
TV war, first 167, 172, 186

UK 21-4, 32-3, 40, 105, 159, 166, 185
Underground Fund Committee 122
underground resistance 122, 125; *see also* draft resistance
unemployment 151, 163

United Nations 18-21, 23, 38, 47-8, 50, 147
universal call-up 143-4; *see also* conscription, draft resistance
Universal Declaration of Human Rights 38
University Study Group 28
university students 20, 34, 161; *see also* draft resistance Flinders University, La Trobe University, Melbourne University, Monash University, NSW University, Queensland University, Sydney University, University of Tasmania
Uren MP, Tom 49; *see also* Australian Labor Party
USA 9-13, 15, 19, 29-30, 32, 34-8, 41-50, 53, 58-60, 65, 70, 72, 77, 79, 80, 83, 85, 89-90, 118, 132-3, 135-40, 156, 158-61, 164-76, 182-4, 188, 190, 192-6; Congress 172-3, 181-2; Gallup 136-8; imperialism 185; Information Service 132-3, 156-62; International Communication Agency 132, 138; involvement in Vietnam 58-60, 65, 69, 84, 164-5, 170-72; State Department 22, 27, 32, 161
USSR 10-11, 13, 18-21, 25-7, 29-30, 33-4, 39, 43, 150, 157, 161, 184, 188-92, 195

Viet Cong 32, 53, 67, 69, 80-83, 142, 145, 150, 168, 173-6, 180, 183, 186; *see also* National Liberation Front
Viet Minh 61, 67
Vietnam *passim, see also* Democratic Republic of Vietnam, Republic of Vietnam
Vietnam Moratorium 16, 51, 114, 118-9, 121-4, 145, 147, 149; *see also* draft resistance, university students
Vietnam Veterans' Action Association 96
vietnamisation 12, 118, 140, 168, 178
Vote No Conscription Campaign 110
Vung Tau 60, 72, 175

Ward MP, Eddie 41, 106; *see also* Australian Labor Party
Warner, Denis 65, 166, 171, 182-4
Washington *see* USA
Washington Post 175; *see also* news coverage
Watergate 180
West Australian 177; *see also* news

225

coverage
West Irian 28, 39, 41, 194; see also Indonesia, Papua New Guinea
Western, John and Wilson, Paul 131, 144; see also opinion polls
Western Australia 120, 159, 194
Westmoreland, US Gen. William 177
Wheeldon, Senator John 30, 51; see also Australian Labor Party
White, Bill 50, 109-112, 121, 145
Whitington, Don 49
Whitlam, E.G. 13, 28-31, 34-5, 37, 39, 41-2, 44-7, 49-55, 105, 111, 127, 131, 135, 144, 157, 178, 180-2, 189, 193; see also Australian Labor Party, Labor government
Wighton, John 107
Willesee, Senator Don 51; see also Australian Labor Party
Wilton, Lt-Gen. 60
'Withdraw All Troops' 111
women's votes 146
Wootton, Rev. R. 126
World War I 84, 97, 100-1
World War II 9, 56, 84, 89, 97, 100, 102, 117, 185
Wyndham, Cyril 47; see also Australian Labor Party

Young Liberals 132; see also Liberal Party
Youth Campaign Against Conscription 107-11, 113; see also conscription, draft resistance
Yugoslavia 44, 189

Zarb, John 112-3, 119, 121

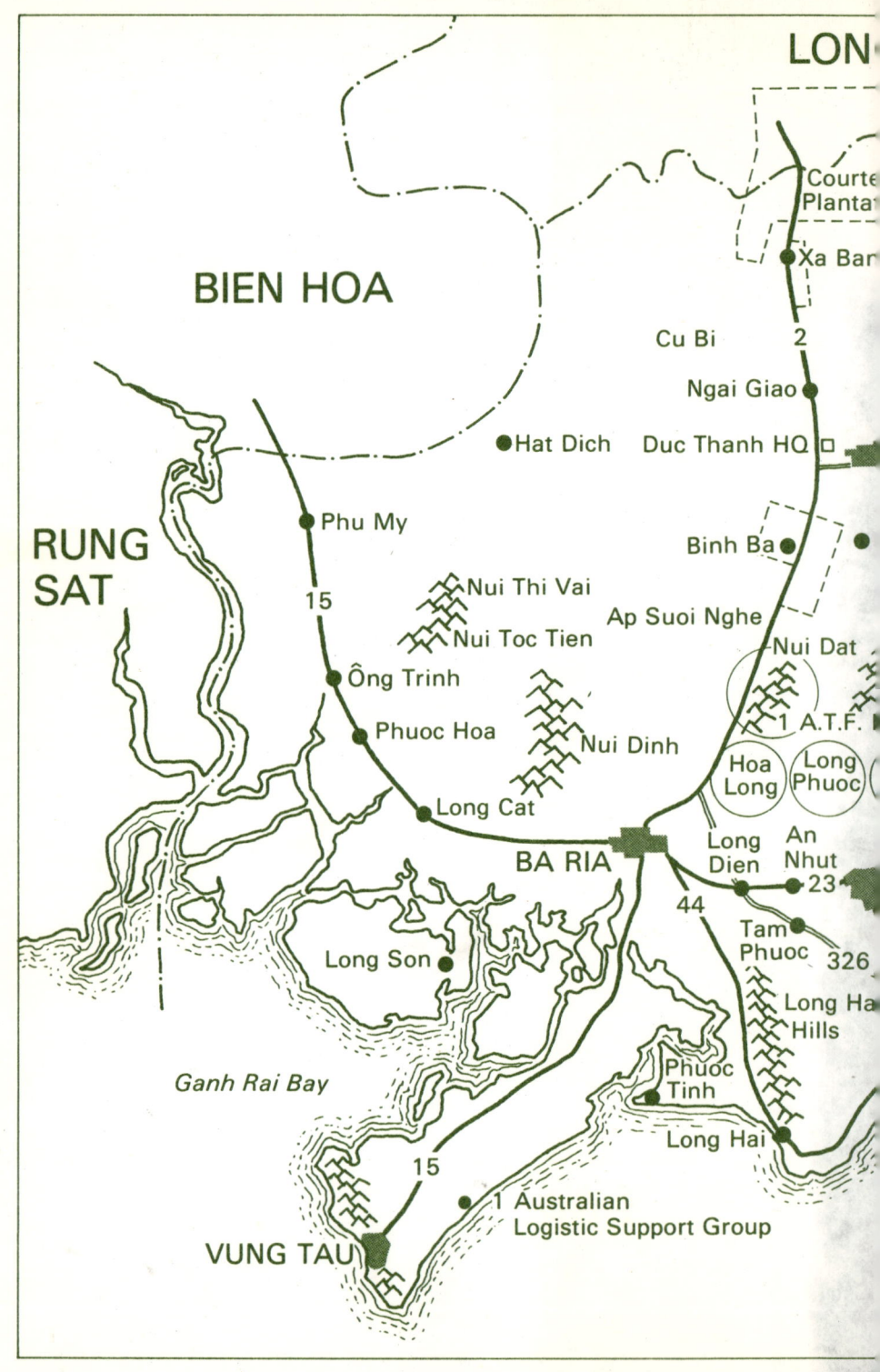